Beginning Ethereum Smart Contracts Programming

With Examples in Python, Solidity, and JavaScript

Second Edition

Wei-Meng Lee

apress®

Beginning Ethereum Smart Contracts Programming: With Examples in Python, Solidity, and JavaScript

Wei-Meng Lee
Ang Mo Kio, Singapore

ISBN-13 (pbk): 978-1-4842-9270-9   ISBN-13 (electronic): 978-1-4842-9271-6
https://doi.org/10.1007/978-1-4842-9271-6

Managing Director, Apress Media LLC: Welmoed Spahr
Acquisitions Editor: Joan Murray
Development Editor: Laura Berendson
Editorial Assistant: Gryffin Winkler
Copy Editor: Mary Behr

Cover image designed by eStudioCalamar

Distributed to the book trade worldwide by Springer Science+Business Media New York, 1 New York Plaza, Suite 4600, New York, NY 10004-1562, USA. Phone 1-800-SPRINGER, fax (201) 348-4505, e-mail orders-ny@ springer-sbm.com, or visit www.springeronline.com. Apress Media, LLC is a California LLC and the sole member (owner) is Springer Science + Business Media Finance Inc (SSBM Finance Inc). SSBM Finance Inc is a **Delaware** corporation.

For information on translations, please e-mail booktranslations@springernature.com; for reprint, paperback, or audio rights, please e-mail bookpermissions@springernature.com.

Apress titles may be purchased in bulk for academic, corporate, or promotional use. eBook versions and licenses are also available for most titles. For more information, reference our Print and eBook Bulk Sales web page at www.apress.com/bulk-sales.

Any source code or other supplementary material referenced by the author in this book is available to readers on GitHub (github.com/apress). For more detailed information, please visit www.apress.com/source-code.

Printed on acid-free paper

Table of Contents

About the Author xi

About the Technical Reviewer xiii

Acknowledgments xv

Introduction xvii

Chapter 1: Understanding the Science Behind Blockchain: Cryptography 1

What Is Cryptography? 1

　　Types of Cryptography 2

Hash Functions 3

　　Uses of Hashing 5

　　Implementing Hashing in Python 6

Symmetric Cryptography 7

　　Generating the Shared Key in Python 8

　　Performing Symmetric Encryption 9

　　Performing Symmetric Decryption 9

Asymmetric Cryptography 10

　　Generating and Saving the Public/Private Key Pairs 12

　　Encrypting Using the Public Key 14

　　Decrypting Using the Private Key 14

　　Digital Signature: Signing Using Private Key 15

　　Verifying the Digital Signature Using a Public Key 18

How Cryptography Is Used in Blockchain 18

　　Hashing 19

　　Symmetric and Asymmetric Cryptography 19

　　Digital Signature 20

Summary 21

Chapter 2: Understanding Blockchain 23

Motivations Behind Blockchain 24

    Placement of Trust 24

    Trust Issues 25

    Solving Trust Issues Using Decentralization 26

    Example of Decentralization 26

    Blockchain As a Distributed Ledger 29

How a Blockchain Works 30

    Chaining the Blocks 31

    Immutability of Blockchains 34

    Consensus Protocols 35

    Proof of Work 37

    Proof of Stake (PoS) 41

Blockchain in More Detail 43

    Types of Nodes 44

    Merkle Tree and Merkle Root 47

    Uses of Merkle Tree and the Merkle Root 48

Summary 49

Chapter 3: Implementing Your Own Blockchain Using Python 51

Your Conceptual Blockchain Implementation 51

    Obtaining the Nonce 53

    Installing Flask 55

    Importing the Various Modules and Libraries 56

    Declaring the Class in Python 56

    Finding the Nonce 57

    Appending the Block to the Blockchain 58

    Adding Transactions 59

    Exposing the Blockchain Class as a REST API 60

    Obtaining the Full Blockchain 60

    Performing Mining 60

    Adding Transactions 61

Testing Your Blockchain 62

Synchronizing Blockchains 67

    Testing the Blockchain with Multiple Nodes.. 72

Full Listing for the Python Blockchain Implementation... 78

Summary.. 85

Chapter 4: Creating Your Own Private Ethereum Test Network 87

Downloading and Installing Geth, the Ethereum Client... 87

    Installing Geth for macOS.. 88

    Installing Geth for Windows... 89

    Installing Geth for Linux.. 89

Creating the Private Ethereum Test Network 90

    Creating the Genesis Block.. 91

    Creating a Folder for Storing Node Data... 92

    Initiating a Blockchain Node.. 93

    Starting Up the Nodes 94

Managing Accounts.. 107

    Removing Accounts... 109

    Setting the Coinbase 109

Summary.. 110

Chapter 5: Using the MetaMask Crypto-Wallet.. 111

What Is MetaMask? 111

    How MetaMask Works Behind the Scenes 112

    Installing MetaMask.. 113

    Setting Up the Accounts 115

    Using the MetaMask Extension 119

Selecting Ethereum Networks 121

    Getting Test Ethers... 122

    Creating Additional Accounts... 126

    Transferring Ethers 129

    Recovering Accounts 135

Importing and Exporting Accounts 138

    Exporting Accounts 138

    Importing Accounts 142

Summary 144

Chapter 6: Getting Started with Smart Contracts 145

What Is a Smart Contract? 145

    How Smart Contracts Are Executed 146

Your First Smart Contract 148

    Using the Remix IDE 148

    Compiling the Contract 152

    Testing the Smart Contract Using the JavaScript VM 154

    Getting the ABI and Bytecode of the Contract 158

    Testing the Smart Contract Using the Goerli Testnet 162

Summary 166

Chapter 7: Storing Proofs Using Smart Contracts 167

A Smart Contract as a Store of Proofs 167

    Creating the Smart Contract 168

    Compiling the Contract 174

    Deploying the Contract 176

    Testing the Contract 177

Making Further Changes to the Smart Contract 180

    Restricting Access to Functions 181

    Accepting Payments in Smart Contracts 182

    Events in Smart Contracts 188

    Cashing Out 191

    Destroying a Contract 193

Summary 194

Chapter 8: Using the web3.js APIs 195

What Is web3.js? 195

    Installing web3.js 196

Testing the web3.js Using MetaMask 197

Interacting with a Contract Using web3.js 202

Summary 214

Chapter 9: Developing Web3 dapps using Python 215

Interacting with Ethereum Using Python 216

Registering with Infura 217

Connecting to Infura 220

Fetching a Block 221

Setting Up the Accounts 223

Getting the Balance of an Account 225

Transferring Ethers Between Accounts 225

Creating a Dapp Using Python 227

Loading the Contract 230

Base64 Encoding 231

Saving Credentials on the Blockchain 231

Verifying the Result 234

Summary 239

Chapter 10: Project: Online Lottery 241

How the Lottery Game Works 241

Defining the Smart Contract 243

Betting a Number 246

Setting the Winning Number and Announcing the Winners 249

Getting the Game Status and Winning Number 253

Cashing Out from the Contract 253

Testing the Contract 254

Announcing the Winner 258

Saving the ABI of the Contract 260

Deploying the Contract to the Testnet 262

Creating the Web Front End 263

Announcing the Winning Number 269

Cashing Out 271

The Complete Contract 272

Summary... 277

Chapter 11: Creating Your Tokens 279

What Are Tokens?.. 279

How Tokens Are Implemented? 281

Minting New Tokens 282

Burning Tokens.. 282

Units Used Internally in Token Contracts 283

ERC-20 Token Standard 285

Creating Token Contracts 287

Overriding the Number of Decimal Places of Precision........................... 288

Deploying the Token Contract.. 289

Adding the Token to MetaMask 291

What Can You Do with the Token? 291

Using Tokens for Smart Contract Payments 292

Selling Tokens Programmatically 300

Calculating the Amount of Tokens Bought... 302

Deploying the Contract 304

Summary... 310

Chapter 12: Creating Non-Fungible Tokens Using ERC-721 311

What Is an NFT?.. 311

Ownership vs. Copyright.. 313

Where Do You Buy or Sell NFTs? 313

Creating NFTs Using Token Contracts 314

Who Deploys the NFT Token Contract?... 315

Using ERC-721 for Creating NFTs.. 315

Deploying the NFT Token Contract.. 316

Testing the NFT Contract 318

Summary... 327

Chapter 13: Introduction to Decentralized Finance **329**

Limitations of Traditional Finance 329

    Decentralized Finance 330

    Components in DeFi 331

Stablecoins 331

    Fiat-Backed Stablecoins 333

    Crypto-Backed Stablecoins 334

    Non-Collateralized Stablecoins 340

Crypto Exchanges 340

    Creating a Decentralized Exchange 342

    Creating the Token Contract 343

    Deploying the Token Contract 343

    Creating the DEX Contract 345

    Funding the DEX 351

    Swapping WML Tokens for LWM Tokens 354

Summary 359

Index **361**

About the Author

 **Wei-Meng Lee** is the founder of Developer Learning Solutions, a technology company specializing in hands-on training of blockchain and other emerging technologies. He has many years of training expertise and his courses emphasize a learn-by-doing approach. He is a master at making learning a new programming language or technology less intimidating and more fun. He can be found speaking at conferences worldwide such as NDC, and he regularly contributes to online and print publications such as *Medium* (https://weimenglee.medium.com) and *CoDe Magazine*. He is active on social media, on his blog calendar.learn2develop.net, on Facebook (www.facebook.com/DeveloperLearningSolutions), on Twitter as @weimenglee, and on LinkedIn (linkedin.com/leeweimeng).

About the Technical Reviewer

 **Prasanth Sahoo** is a Blockchain Certified Professional, Professional Scrum Master, and Microsoft Certified Trainer who is passionate about helping others learn how to use and gain benefits from the latest technologies. He is a thought leader and practitioner in blockchain, cloud, and Scrum. He also handles the Agile methodology, cloud, and blockchain technology community initiatives within TransUnion through coaching, mentoring, and grooming techniques.

Prasanth is an adjunct professor and a technical speaker. He was selected as a speaker at the China International Industry Big Data Expo 2018 by the Chinese government and also to the International Blockchain Council by the governments of Telangana and Goa. He also received accolades for his presentation at China International Industry Big Data Expo 2018 by the Chinese government. Prasanth has published a patent titled "*Digital Educational Certificate Management System using IPFS Based Blockchain.*"

To datc, Prasanth has reached over 50,000 students, mostly within the technical domain. He is a working group member of the CryptoCurrency Certification Consortium, Scrum Alliance, Scrum Organization, and International Institute of Business Analysis.

Acknowledgments

Writing a book is immensely exciting, but along with it comes long hours of hard work and responsibility, straining to get things done accurately and correctly. To make a book possible, a lot of unsung heroes work tirelessly behind the scenes.

For this, I would like to take this opportunity to thank a number of special people who made this book possible. First, I want to thank my acquisitions editor, Joan Murray, for giving me this opportunity. Thanks for suggesting that I update this book with the latest happenings in the crypto world!

Next, a huge thanks to Jill Balzano, my associate editor, who was always very patient with me, even though I missed several of my deadlines for the revision of this book. Thanks, Jill, for your guidance. I could not finish the book without your encouragement and help!

Equally important is my project coordinator, Shobana Srinivasan. Shobana has been very patient with me during the whole project while I struggle between work and writing. Thanks, Shobana, for the assistance rendered during the project!

Last, but not least, I want to thank my parents and my wife, Sze Wa, for all the support they have given me. They have selflessly adjusted their schedules to accommodate my busy schedule when I was working on this book. I love you all!

Introduction

Welcome to *Beginning Ethereum Smart Contracts Programming, Second Edition*!

This book is a quick guide to getting started with Ethereum smart contracts programming. It starts off with a discussion of blockchain and the motivations behind it. You will learn what a blockchain is, how blocks in a blockchain are chained together, and how blocks get added to a blockchain. You will also understand how mining works and discover the various types of nodes in a blockchain network. Since the publication of the first edition of this book, a lot of things have changed. In particular, Ethereum has been updated to use Proof of Stake (PoS) (instead of Proof of Work) as its consensus algorithm. This book has been updated to include a discussion of how PoS works.

Once that is out of the way, you dive into the Ethereum blockchain. You will learn how to use an Ethereum client (Geth) to create a private Ethereum blockchain and perform simple transactions such as sending Ethers to another account.

The next part of this book discusses smart contract programming, a unique feature of the Ethereum blockchain. You will jumpstart on smart contracts programming without needing to wade through tons of documentation. The learn-by-doing approach of this book makes you productive in the shortest amount of time. By the end of this book, you should be able to write smart contracts, test them, deploy them, and create web applications to interact with them. In this second edition, I have added more examples to make it easy for you to explore more complex smart contracts.

The last part of this book touches on tokens and DeFi (decentralized finance), something that has taken the cryptocurrency market by storm. You will be able to create your own tokens, launch your own ICO, and write token contracts that allow buyers to buy tokens using Ethers. As a bonus, I show you how to write a DEX (decentralized exchange) smart contract to exchange two different tokens!

This book is designed for those who want to get started quickly with Ethereum smart contracts programming. Basic programming knowledge and an understanding of Python or JavaScript are recommended.

I hope you enjoy working on the sample projects as much as I enjoyed creating them!

Understanding the Science Behind Blockchain: Cryptography

The reason you are reading this book is because you want to understand what a blockchain is, how it works, and how you can write smart contracts on it to do cool things. And while I perfectly understand that you are excited to get started in this first chapter, we need to take a step back and look at one fundamental technology that makes blockchain possible: *cryptography*.

In this chapter, I will explain what cryptography is, the different types of cryptographic algorithms, how they work, and how they play a vital role in the world of blockchain. I will also show you how to experiment with the various cryptographic algorithms using the Python programming language. Even if you are familiar with cryptography, I suggest scanning through this chapter so that you have a firm foundation for the subsequent chapters.

What Is Cryptography?

Whether you are trying to build a web application to store users' credentials or writing a network application to securely transmit encrypted messages, or even trying to understand how blockchain works, you need to understand one important topic: *cryptography*.

So, what exactly is cryptography? Put simply, cryptography (or cryptology) is the practice and study of hiding information. It is the science of keeping information secret and safe.

© Wei-Meng Lee 2023

W.-M. Lee, *Beginning Ethereum Smart Contracts Programming*, https://doi.org/10.1007/978-1-4842-9271-6_1

One of the simplest and most widely known cryptographic algorithms is the **Caesar Cipher**. It is a very simple algorithm in which each letter in the plaintext is replaced by a letter a fixed number of positions down the alphabet. Consider the example shown in Figure 1-1.

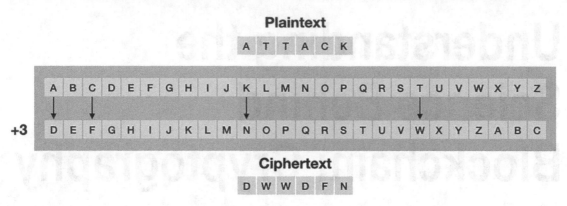

Figure 1-1. *Understanding how the Caesar Cipher works*

As you can observe, each character in the alphabet is shifted down three positions. A becomes D, B becomes E, and so on. If you want to send a sentence (known as the plaintext), say ATTACK, to your recipient, you map each of the characters in the sentence using the above algorithm and derive the encrypted sentence (known as the ciphertext): DWWDFN. When the recipient receives the ciphertext, they reverse the process to obtain the plaintext. While this algorithm may seem impressive (especially in the early days of cryptography), it no longer works as intended as soon as someone knows how the messages are encrypted. Nevertheless, this is a good illustration of the attempt by early inventors of cryptography to hide information. Today, the cryptographic algorithms we use are much more sophisticated and secure.

In the following sections, I will explain the main types of cryptographic functions and how they are used.

Types of Cryptography

There are three main types of cryptography:

- Hash functions

- Symmetric cryptography

- Asymmetric cryptography

In the following sections, I will go through each of the above types in more detail.

Hash Functions

Hashing is the process in which you convert a block of data of arbitrary size to a fixed-size value. The function that performs this process is known as a *hash function* . Figure 1-2 shows the hashing process.

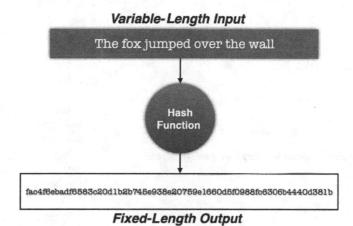

Figure 1-2. *A hash function converts a block of data of variable length to a fixed-length output*

Tip   A commonly-used hash function is **SHA256.** SHA stands for Secure Hash Algorithms.

For example, the **SHA256** hash function converts a block of text into a 256-bit hash output. The resultant hash is usually written in hexadecimal, and since each hexadecimal takes up 4 bits, a 256-bit hash will have 64 characters. To experience how hashing works, go to `https://emn178.github.io/online-tools/sha256.html`, type in a sentence, and observe the result (see Figure 1-3).

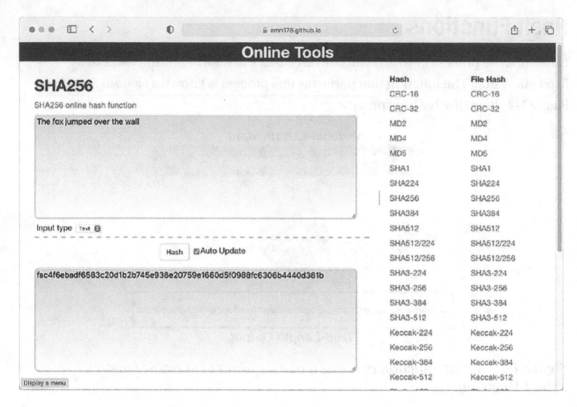

Figure 1-3. *Trying out the SHA256 hash function*

Hashing has the following important properties:

- **Preimage resistant**: Based on the hash created, you cannot obtain the original block of text.

- **Deterministic**: The same block of text will always produce the same hash output.

- **Collision resistant**: It is hard to find two different blocks of text that will produce the same hash.

Another important feature of hashing is that a single change in the original text will cause a totally different hash to be generated. This is also known as the *avalanche effect*. For example, a change in a single character in the input shown in Figure 1-4 will have a totally different output.

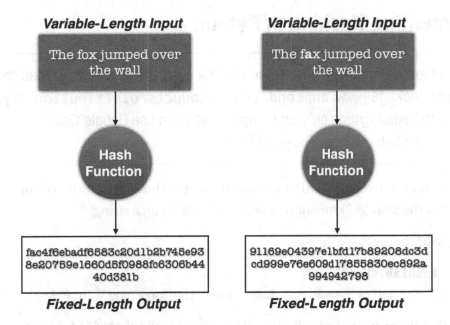

Figure 1-4. *A single change in the input will cause a totally different output hash*

Uses of Hashing

Hashing fulfils some very important roles in computing. For one, websites use hashing to store your password, instead of storing it in plaintext. Storing your password as hashes prevents hackers from reversing the hashes and obtaining your original password (which may very likely be used on other websites as well).

Hashing also plays a very crucial role in blockchain, where each block is "chained" to the previous block using the hash of the previous block. Any modifications to a block will invalidate the hash stored in the next block, and the rest of the blocks will hence be invalid.

Tip   Some commonly used hashing algorithms are MD5, SHA256, SHA512, and Keccak-256.

Implementing Hashing in Python

Note   To install Python on your computer, the easiest way is to download the Anaconda package (www.anaconda.com/products/distribution). If you do not want to install Python on your computer, you can use Google Colab (https://colab.research.google.com).

In Python, you can use the hashlib module to perform hashing. The following code snippet uses the sha256() function to perform hashing on a string:

```
import hashlib

result = hashlib.sha256(
    bytes("The quick brown fox jumps over the lazy dog",'utf-8'))
```

Note that the string to be hashed must be passed to the sha256() function as a byte array. And so you use the bytes() function to convert the string into a byte array. Alternatively, in Python, you can prefix the string with a b to denote a *bytes string literal*:

```
result = hashlib.sha256(
    b'The quick brown fox jumps over the lazy dog')
```

The sha256() function returns a sha256 hash object. To get the resultant hash in hexadecimal, you can call the hexdigest() function of the sha256 hash object:

```
print(result.hexdigest())
```

The hash for the above string is as follows:

```
d7a8fbb307d7809469ca9abcb0082e4f8d5651e46d3cdb762d02d0bf37c9e592
```

If you make a small change to the original string, the output is drastically different from the previous hash:

```
result = hashlib.sha256(
    b'The quick brown fox jumps over the lazy dag')
print(result.hexdigest())
# output:
# 559cc2cb0e1998182b4b6343e38611b3757e8a6279d43e9914d74dfb7e7089e6
```

Symmetric Cryptography

In symmetric cryptography, you use the same cryptographic key (commonly referred to as the *shared key*) for both the encryption of plaintext and the decryption of ciphertext. Figure 1-5 shows the use of the shared key for both encryption and decryption.

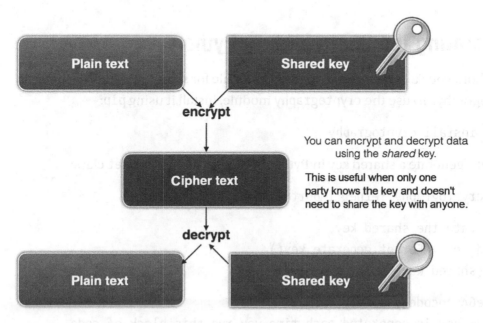

Figure 1-5. *Using a shared key for encryption and decryption*

Symmetric cryptography is fast and simple, but the main problem is how to ensure that the key is kept secret. For example, if Tom wants to send a secret message to Susan, Tom can encrypt the message using the shared key and Susan can decrypt the encrypted message using the same shared key. The problem here is how can Tom securely send Susan the shared key? Can Tom email Susan? Send it through SMS or WhatsApp? How about through the traditional post office? All these methods are not absolutely safe and are subject to eavesdropping. Moreover, there is this popular saying, "Three may keep a secret if two of them are dead." This means, if more than one person knows the secret, it is no longer a secret.

Having said that, symmetric cryptography has its uses and applications. It is useful when you want to protect your private data. For example, say you have some confidential data on your computer that you want to prevent others from seeing. Using symmetric cryptography, you can encrypt and decrypt the data using the same key, which is only known to you and no one else.

Tip   Some examples of symmetric key algorithms are AES (Advanced Encryption Standard, originally known as Rijndael), DES (Data Encryption Standard), and IDEA (International Data Encryption Algorithm).

Generating the Shared Key in Python

In Python, you can use the `cryptography` module for symmetric and asymmetric cryptography. To use the `cryptography` module, install it using `pip`:

```
$ pip install cryptography
```

Let's generate a shared key in Python. To do so, use the `Fernet` class:

```
from cryptography.fernet import Fernet

# generate the shared key
shared_key = Fernet.generate_key()
print(shared_key)

# base64 encoded, binary format
# A new key is generated each time you run this block of code
# e.g. b'ixXEfrz2NTJlxy1OhxXlsCiFfoYcg_GLOCyoMlgTv4U='
```

Tip   The `Fernet` class is an implementation of symmetric (also known as "secret key") authenticated cryptography. Fernet uses the AES algorithm in CBC mode with a 128-bit key for encryption. For more details, refer to `https://github.com/fernet/spec/blob/master/Spec.md`.

The `generate_key()` function returns a shared key in binary format and it is base64 encoded.

Performing Symmetric Encryption

To encrypt your data using the shared key, you first create an instance of the Fernet class using the shared key:

```
# create an instance of the Fernet class
fernet = Fernet(shared_key)
```

You can then use the encrypt() function to encrypt your data:

```
# encrypt the message with the shared key
ciphertext = fernet.encrypt(
    bytes("Secret message!",'utf-8'))
# remember to pass in a byte array
```

You can save the encrypted data into a file:

```
# write the encrypted message to file
with open('message.encrypted', 'wb') as f:
    f.write(ciphertext)
```

And you can save the shared key to file:

```
# write the shared key to file
with open('symmetric_key.crypt', 'wb') as f:
    f.write(shared_key)
```

Performing Symmetric Decryption

Decryption is similar to encryption. First, load the shared key from the file (which you saved previously):

```
with open('symmetric_key.crypt', 'rb') as f:
    shared_key = f.read()
print(shared_key)
```

Then, create an instance of the Fernet class using the shared key and call the decrypt() function to decode the ciphertext:

```
# create an instance of the Fernet class
fernet = Fernet(shared_key)
```

```
# decrypt the encrypted message read from file
with open('message.encrypted', 'rb') as f:
    print(fernet.decrypt(f.read()).decode("utf-8"))
```

Asymmetric Cryptography

Unlike symmetric cryptography, which uses a single shared key, asymmetric cryptography uses a key-pair, one public and one private.

Tip   Asymmetric cryptography is also known as public-key cryptography.

A public key algorithm generates two keys that are mathematically linked:

- **One public and one private**: The public key, as the name implies, should be made public. The private key, on the other hand, absolutely must be kept a secret.

- You can encrypt data with a public key and decrypt with the private key. For example, if Tom wants to send a secret message to Susan, Tom could encrypt the message using Susan's public key and only Susan can decrypt the secret message with her private key.

- You can encrypt data with a private key and decrypt with the public key. At first, this sounds counterintuitive. If one could decrypt using the public key (which is supposed to be public), what's the point of this? Actually, this is useful. Suppose Tom encrypts a message using his own private key and sends it to Susan. When Susan receives the message, she can try to decrypt it using Tom's public key. If the message can be decrypted, this means that the message has not been tampered with and that it indeed comes from Tom. On the other hand, if the message has been tampered with, Susan would not be able to decrypt the message using Tom's public key. This technique is used in creating a *digital signature*.

Tip   Some examples of public key algorithms are RSA (Rivest–Shamir–Adleman), Elliptical Curve Cryptography (ECC), and TLS/SSL protocol.

Figure 1-6 shows the first approach, that of encrypting the data using the public key and then decrypting it using the private key.

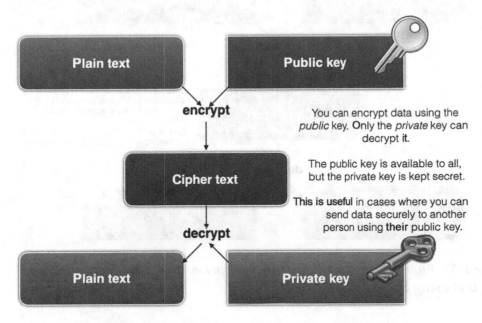

Figure 1-6. *Encrypting data using the public key and then decrypting the ciphertext using the private key*

Figure 1-7 shows the second approach of encrypting the data using the private key and then decrypting it using the public key.

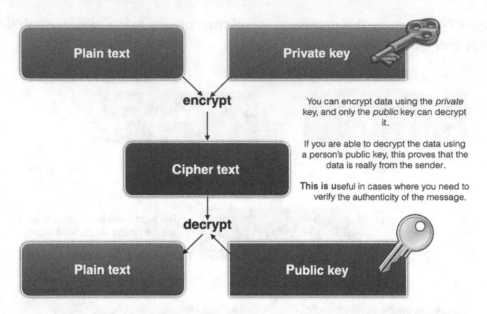

You can encrypt data using the *private* key, and only the *public* key can decrypt it.

If you are able to decrypt the data using a person's public key, this proves that the data is really from the sender.

This is useful in cases where you need to verify the authenticity of the message.

Figure 1-7. Encrypting data using the private key and then decrypting the ciphertext using the public key

Generating and Saving the Public/Private Key Pairs

Let's generate the public/private key pair using the cryptography module with some commonly used parameters:

```
from cryptography.hazmat.backends import default_backend
from cryptography.hazmat.primitives.asymmetric import rsa

# generate the private key
private_key = rsa.generate_private_key(
    public_exponent=65537,
    key_size=2048,
    backend=default_backend()
)

# derive the public key from the private key
public_key = private_key.public_key()
```

In this code snippet, you are using the RSA algorithm to first generate a private key. Using the private key, you can then derive its corresponding public key. Once the keys are generated, it's useful to serialize (flatten) them to files:

```python
from cryptography.hazmat.primitives import serialization

#---serialize the private key as bytes---
pem = private_key.private_bytes(
    encoding = serialization.Encoding.PEM,
    format = serialization.PrivateFormat.PKCS8,
    encryption_algorithm = serialization.NoEncryption()
)
with open('private_key.pem', 'wb') as f:
    f.write(pem)

#---serialize the public key as bytes---
pem = public_key.public_bytes(
    encoding = serialization.Encoding.PEM,
    format = serialization.PublicFormat.SubjectPublicKeyInfo
)
with open('public_key.pem', 'wb') as f:
    f.write(pem)
```

You also need to be able to load them back from files:

```python
with open('private_key.pem', 'rb') as f:
    private_key = serialization.load_pem_private_key(
        f.read(),
        password = None,
        backend = default_backend()
    )

with open('public_key.pem', 'rb') as f:
    public_key = serialization.load_pem_public_key(
        f.read(),
        backend = default_backend()
    )
```

Encrypting Using the Public Key

You are now ready to perform encryption using the *public* key:

```
from cryptography.hazmat.primitives import hashes
from cryptography.hazmat.primitives.asymmetric import padding

plaintext = bytes("This message is secret.",'utf-8')

# encrypt the message using the public key
ciphertext = public_key.encrypt(
    plaintext,
    padding.OAEP(
        mgf = padding.MGF1(algorithm = hashes.SHA256()),
        algorithm = hashes.SHA256(),
        label = None
    )
)
```

Note   The encrypted ciphertext is a byte array.

Decrypting Using the Private Key

With the ciphertext created, you can decrypt it using the *private* key:

```
# decrypt using the private key
plaintext = private_key.decrypt(
    ciphertext,
    padding.OAEP(
        mgf = padding.MGF1(algorithm = hashes.SHA256()),
        algorithm = hashes.SHA256(),
        label = None
    )
)
```

```
# decode the plaintext as it is a byte array
print(plaintext.decode('utf-8'))
# This message is secret.
```

Note   The decrypted plaintext is a byte array.

Digital Signature: Signing Using Private Key

Earlier I mentioned that in a *digital signature* you perform encryption using the private key and then decrypt using the public key. How does this really work and how is it useful? Let's look at the flow of events shown in Figure 1-8.

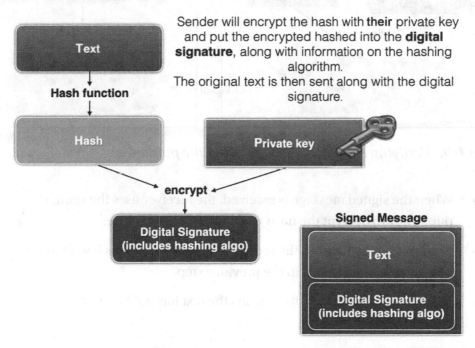

Figure 1-8. *Generating a digital signature using the private key*

- First, the text to be sent is hashed using a hash function.

- The hash is then encrypted using the private key and turned into a *digital signature* (this also includes the information on the hashing algorithm used).

- The original text, together with the digital signature, are then sent to the recipient. This is known as the *signed message*.

Figure 1-9 shows what happens when the signed message is received by the recipient.

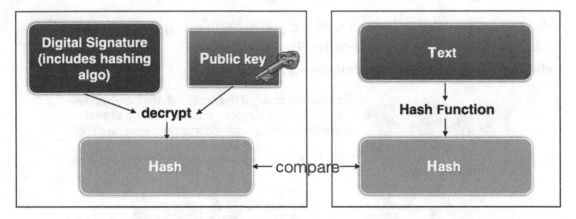

Figure 1-9. *Verifying a digital signature using the public key*

- When the signed message is received, the receiver uses the sender's public key to decrypt the hash from the digital signature.

- The receiver also hashes the received text and compares it with the hash that was decrypted in the previous step.

- If the two hashes match, this means the text has not been tampered with.

Note   A digital signature is a mathematical technique used to validate the authenticity and integrity of a message, software, or digital document.

Let's create a digital signature using the private key.

Technically, you can't call the encrypt() function on the private key:

```
private_key.encrypt(...)     # ERROR
# AttributeError: '_RSAPrivateKey' object has no attribute 'encrypt'
```

Rather, you call the sign() function:

```
import base64

plaintext = bytes("This message is public.",'utf-8')

# sign the message using the private key
signed = private_key.sign(
    plaintext,
    padding.PSS(
        mgf = padding.MGF1(algorithm=hashes.SHA256()),
        salt_length = padding.PSS.MAX_LENGTH
    ),
    hashes.SHA256()
)

# print out the digital signature using base64 encoding
signed_base64 = base64.b64encode(signed).decode('utf-8')
print(signed_base64)
```

Here you use the *private* key to *sign* the message. The sign() function returns the digital signature of the string. It returns the digital signature as a byte array, and in the above code snippet you encode it using base64 encoding and then converted it to string. The output looks like this:

aNUZixxLUiRRpDjm+nqkcaZo5URklvIA/hiSECR+DoLmS+oVb65oIc5/vg6ADmCvi91CSwiXRY
kknDBEr2qTWaK+Fe9UPqukDFx8WwyW7K2NacjS8TiKqAfPPSH4t2l9ohexwTqfih9oZXli57zf
Z4LKaY63iQxXlWKE9S5OZOhWyGUfygEInY8OZerGKWFnmxuXHjWNCpDmzSngPO4MYBBnfoPVps
Dg7vgKLOgpaz1dn2Qg+Ra2GFLmznqjYKq2qP43zLrdYSmzH3MmPAkOOAIh8XaRnHc+qOXYyUGhT
Bm9iIa7rS8eYaB7MD9G18jOHA7lWWVQjqujnFCQNm8Npg==

When you transmit the message (plaintext), you also send the digital signature along with it.

Verifying the Digital Signature Using a Public Key

When the recipient receives the message along with the digital signature, they can simply verify that the message has not been tampered by calling the `verify()` function on the *public* key:

```python
from cryptography.exceptions import InvalidSignature

# decode the digital signature from base64
signed = base64.b64decode(signed_base64)

try:
    public_key.verify(
        signed,
        plaintext,     # from the previous section
        padding.PSS(
            mgf = padding.MGF1(hashes.SHA256()),
            salt_length = padding.PSS.MAX_LENGTH
        ),
        hashes.SHA256()
    )
    print('Signature is valid!')
except InvalidSignature:
    print('Signature is invalid!')
```

Note that you have to catch the exception raised by the `verify()` function. If there is no exception, the signature is deemed to be correct; otherwise, it is invalid.

How Cryptography Is Used in Blockchain

If you have been following up to this point, you should now have a good idea of how cryptography works. You might now be wondering how cryptography plays an important role in blockchain.

The following sections discuss how the various cryptographic algorithms are used in blockchain. If you are new to blockchain, feel free to skip the following sections and read the next chapter. Come back to the next few sections after you have read the following chapters:

- Chapter 2: Hashing is used to "chain" the blocks in a blockchain.

- Chapters 4 and 5: Asymmetric cryptography is used to generate your accounts, and symmetric cryptography is used to secure the accounts you have created in your crypto-wallets.

- Chapter 4 onwards: Asymmetric cryptography is used to create digital signatures for all of your transactions on the blockchain.

Hashing

As mentioned briefly, hashing is used to "chain" the blocks in a blockchain. Each block in a blockchain contains the hash of the previous block. Doing so allows you to ensure that data recorded on the blockchain are immutable and thus prevent tampering.

Another good use case of hashing is when storing data on the blockchain. Since all data on public blockchains are open to scrutiny, you should not store private data on the public blockchain. If you need to store private data on a public blockchain for proofing purposes, you should instead store the hash of the data, since it is not reversible. Chapter 7 provides a good example of this.

Symmetric and Asymmetric Cryptography

Symmetric and asymmetric cryptography are used in generating and securing of accounts in blockchain.

As shown in Figure 1-10, when you create an account in Ethereum, a private key using asymmetric cryptography is first generated.

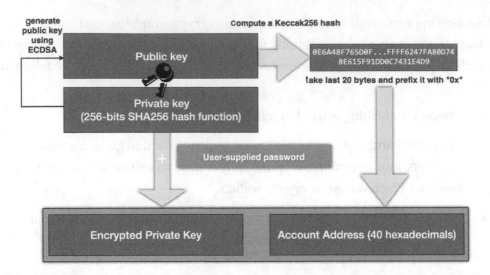

Figure 1-10. *Understanding how an account is generated and secured*

Using this private key, a public key is generated using **ECDSA** (Elliptic Curve Digital Signature Algorithm). This public key is then used to generate the account address using the **Keccak256** hashing algorithm. The last 20 bytes of this output is used as the address of the account.

At the same time, remember that when you create an account you must supply a password. This password is used to encrypt your private key using symmetric cryptography.

Digital Signature

In blockchain, a digital signature is used when creating transactions. In Chapter 4, you will learn how to create a simple transaction by sending some Ethers from one account to another.

When you create a transaction, the transaction is signed using your account's private key to derive the digital signature. The digital signature, together with the details of the transaction, are then broadcasted to the various miners/validators in the blockchain network (see Figure 1-11).

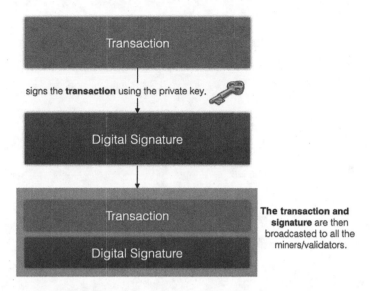

Figure 1-11. *A digital signature is created for a transaction to prove the identity of the creator*

The miners/validators, upon receiving your transaction, verify the authenticity of your transaction using the transaction's digital signature. Once the transaction is verified to be authentic, the miners/validators proceed to verify the content of the transaction.

Summary

In this chapter, you learned about the main science behind blockchain: cryptography. You learned about hashing, symmetric cryptography, and asymmetric cryptography. If you are familiar with Python, I strongly suggest you try out the code samples so that you get first-hand experience with the various cryptographic algorithms. With that, you are now ready to dive into the world of blockchain. See you in Chapter 2!

CHAPTER 2

Understanding Blockchain

One of the hottest technologies of late is *blockchain*. But what exactly is a blockchain? And how does it actually work? In this chapter, you will explore the concept of blockchain, how the concept was conceived, and what problems it aims to solve. By the end of this chapter, the idea and motivation behind blockchain will be crystal clear.

Tip   For the clearly impatient, a blockchain is a digital transaction of records that is arranged in chunks of data called *blocks*. These blocks link with each other through a cryptographic validation known as a *hashing function*. Linked together, these blocks form an unbroken chain, a *blockchain*. A blockchain is programmed to record not only financial transactions but virtually everything of value. Another common name for blockchain is *distributed ledger*.

Hold on tight, as I'm going to discuss a lot of concepts in this chapter. But if you follow along closely, you'll understand the concepts of blockchain and be on your way to creating some really creative applications on the Ethereum blockchain in the upcoming chapters!

Tip   Ethereum is an open-source public blockchain that is similar to the Bitcoin network. Besides offering a cryptocurrency known as Ether (which is similar to Bitcoin), the main difference between it and Bitcoin is that it offers a programming platform on top of the blockchain called Smart Contract. This book focuses on the Ethereum blockchain and Smart Contract.

© Wei-Meng Lee 2023
W.-M. Lee, *Beginning Ethereum Smart Contracts Programming*, https://doi.org/10.1007/978-1-4842-9271-6_2

Motivations Behind Blockchain

Most people have heard of cryptocurrencies, or at least, Bitcoin.

Note   The technology behind cryptocurrencies is blockchain.

To understand why we need cryptocurrencies, you have to first start by understanding a fundamental concept: *trust*. Today, any asset of value or transaction is recorded by a third party, such as a bank, government, or company. We trust banks to not steal our money, and they are regulated by the government. And even if the banks fail, they are backed by the government. We also trust our credit card companies. Sellers trust credit card companies to pay them the money, and buyers trust credit card companies to settle any disputes with the sellers.

Placement of Trust

All of this boils down to one key concept: the placement of trust. And that is, we place our trust in a central body. Think about it. In our everyday life, we place our trust in banks and we place our trust in our governments.

Even for simple mundane day-to-day activities, we place our trust in central bodies. For example, when you go to the library to borrow a book, you trust that the library will maintain a proper record of the books you have borrowed and returned.

The key theme is that we trust institutions but don't trust each other. We trust our government, banks, even our library, but we just don't trust each other. As an example, consider the following scenario. Imagine you work at a cafe, and someone walks up to you and offers you a $10 bill for two cups of coffee. Another person offers to pay you for the two cups of coffee using a handwritten note saying he owes you $10. Which one would you trust? The answer is pretty obvious, isn't it? Naturally you would trust the $10 bill as opposed to the handwritten note. This is because you understand that you can use the $10 bill elsewhere for other goods or services and that it is backed by the US government. In contrast, the handwritten note is not backed by anyone, except perhaps the person who wrote it, and hence it has literally no value.

Now let's take the discussion a bit further. Again, imagine you are trying to sell something. Someone comes up to you and suggests paying for your goods using the currencies shown in Figure 2-1.

Figure 2-1. *Currencies from two countries*

Would you accept the currencies shown in the figure? Here, you have two different currencies, one from Venezuela and one from Zimbabwe. In this case, the first thing you consider is whether these currencies are widely accepted. Then you consider your trust in these governments. You might have read in the news about the hyperinflation in these two countries, and that these currencies might not retain their value over time. So, would you accept these currencies as payment?

Trust Issues

Earlier, I mentioned that people trust institutions and don't trust each other. But even established economies can fail, such as in the case of the financial crisis of the United States in 2007–2008. Investment bank Lehman Brothers collapsed in September 2008 because of the subprime mortgage market. So, if banks from established economies can collapse, how can people in less-developed countries trust their banks and governments? Even if the banks are trusted, your deposits may be monitored by the government, and they could arrest you based on your transactions.

As you saw in the example in the previous section, there are times when people don't trust institutions, especially if the political situation in that country is not stable.

This brings us to the next key issue: even though people trust institutions, institutions can fail. And when people lose trust in institutions, people turn to *cryptocurrencies*. In the next section, I will discuss how to solve the trust issues using *decentralization*, a fundamental concept behind cryptocurrency.

Solving Trust Issues Using Decentralization

Now that you have seen the challenges of trust, who to trust and who not to trust, it is time to consider a way to solve the trust issues. In particular, blockchain uses decentralization to solve the trust issue.

In order to understand decentralization, let's use a very simple example based on our daily lives.

Example of Decentralization

To understand how decentralization solves the trust issue, let's consider a real-life example.

Imagine a situation where you have three persons with DVDs that they want to share with one another (see Figure 2-2).

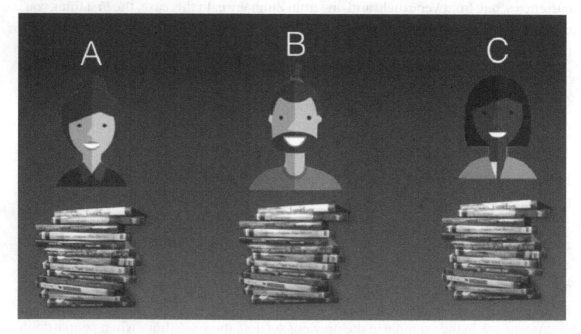

Figure 2-2. *Sharing DVDs among a group of people*

The first thing they need to do is to have someone keep track of the whereabouts of each DVD. Of course, the easiest is for each person to keep track of what they have borrowed and what they have lent, but since people inherently do not trust each other, this approach is not very popular among the three people.

To solve this issue, they decided to appoint one person, say B, to keep a ledger of the whereabouts of each DVD (see Figure 2-3).

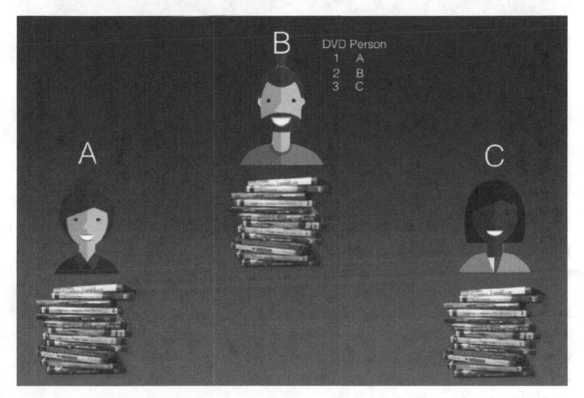

Figure 2-3. *Appointing a particular person to keep the records*

This way, there is a central body to keep track of the whereabouts of each DVD. But wait, isn't this the problem with centralization? What happens if B is not trustworthy? Turns out that B has the habit of stealing DVDs, and he can easily modify the ledger to erase the record of DVDs that he has borrowed. So, there must be a better way.

Then someone has an idea! Why not let everyone keep a copy of the ledger? Whenever someone borrows or lends a DVD, the record is broadcast to everyone, and everyone records the transaction. See Figure 2-4.

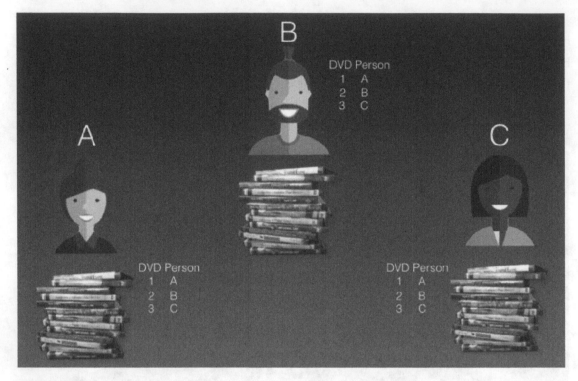

Figure 2-4. *Getting everyone to keep the records*

So now the record keeping is decentralized. Three people now hold the same ledger. But wait a minute. What if A and C conspire to change the ledger so that they can steal the DVDs from B? Since majority wins, as long as there is more than 50% of the people with the same records, the others would have to listen to the majority. And because there are only three people in this scenario, it is extremely easy to get more than 50% of the people to conspire.

The solution is to have a lot more people to hold the ledger, especially people who are not related to the DVD-sharing business (see Figure 2-5).

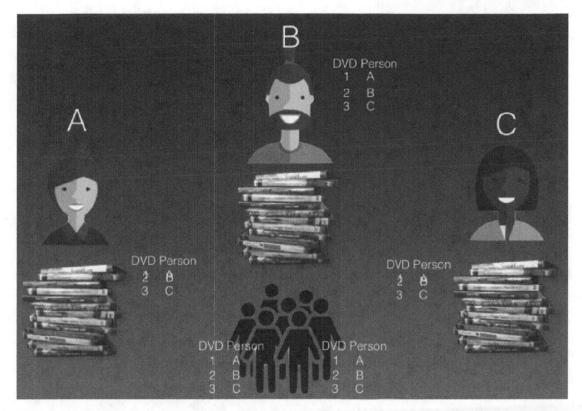

Figure 2-5. *Getting a group of unrelated people to help keep the records*

This way, it makes it more difficult for one party to alter the records in the ledger. In order to alter a record, it would need to involve a number of people to do so all at the same time, which is a time-consuming affair. And this is the key idea behind a *distributed ledger*, commonly known as blockchain.

Blockchain As a Distributed Ledger

Now that you have a better idea of a distributed ledger, you can associate it with the term *blockchain*. Using the DVD exchange example, each time a DVD is borrowed or returned, a transaction is created. A number of transactions are then grouped into a block. As more transactions are performed, the blocks are linked together cryptographically, forming what we now call a blockchain (see Figure 2-6).

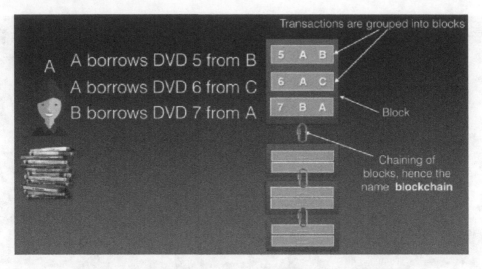

Figure 2-6. *Transactions form a block, and blocks are then chained*

Here's a summary of a few important points:

- Centralized databases and institutions work when there is trust in the system of law, governments, regulatory bodies, and people.

- A decentralized database built on the blockchain removes the need for the trust in a central body.

- A blockchain can be used for anything of value, not just currencies.

How a Blockchain Works

At a very high level, a blockchain consists of a number of blocks. Each block contains a list of transactions and a timestamp (see Figure 2-7).

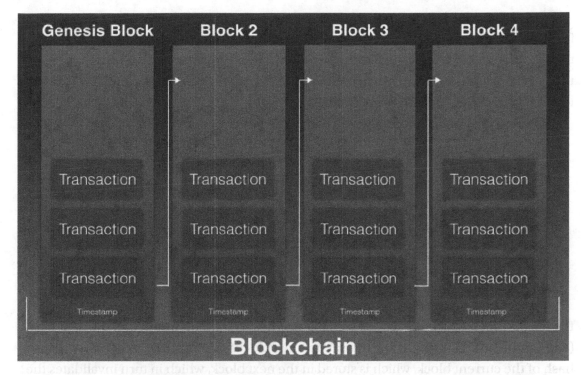

Figure 2-7. *Every blockchain has a beginning block known as the genesis block*

The blocks are connected to each other cryptographically, the details of which I will discuss in the sections ahead. The first block in a blockchain is known as the *genesis* block.

Note   Every blockchain has a genesis block.

So, the next important questions is, how do you chain the blocks together?

Chaining the Blocks

To understand how blocks in a blockchain are chained together, you must understand one key concept: *hashing*.

Tip   Chapter 1 discussed hashing in more detail. Be sure to read it first before continuing with this section.

Recall that a hash function is a function that maps data of arbitrary size to data of fixed size. By altering a single character in the original string, the resultant hash value is totally different from the previous one. Most importantly, observe that a single change in the original message results in a completely different hash, making it difficult to know that the two original messages are similar.

A hash function has the following characteristics:

- **It is deterministic**: The same message always results in the same hash.

- **It is a one-way process**: When you hash a string, it is computationally hard to reverse a hash to its original message.

- **It is collision resistant**: It is hard to find two different input messages that hash to the same hash.

You are now ready to learn how blocks in a blockchain are chained together. To chain the blocks together, the content of each block is hashed and then stored in the next block (see Figure 2-8). This way, if any transaction in a block is altered, this will invalidate the hash of the current block, which is stored in the next block, which in turn invalidates the hash of the next block, and so on.

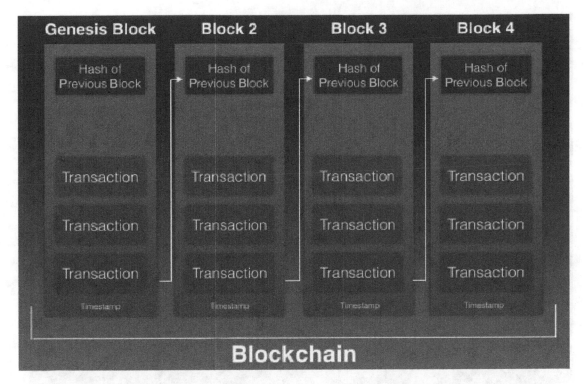

Figure 2-8. *Chaining the blocks with hashes*

Observe that when hashing the content of a block, the hash of the previous block is hashed together with the transactions. However, do take note that this is a simplification of what is in a block. Later on, you will dive into the details of a block and see exactly how transactions are represented in a block.

Storing the hash of the previous block in the current block assures the integrity of the transactions in the previous block. Any modifications to the transaction(s) within a block causes the hash in the next block to be invalidated and also affects the subsequent blocks in the blockchain. If a hacker wants to modify a transaction, not only must they modify the transaction in a block but all other subsequent blocks in the blockchain. In addition, they need to synchronize the changes to all other computers on the network, which is a computationally expensive task to do. Hence, data stored in the blockchain is *immutable*, for they are hard to change once the block they are in is added to the blockchain.

At this juncture, you have a pretty good idea of what a blockchain looks like. In the real world, the blockchain is stored on multiple computers (called nodes) usually scattered geographically around the world (see Figure 2-9).

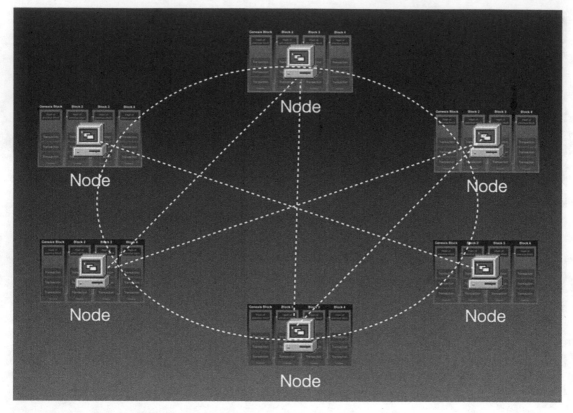

Figure 2-9. *Confirmations of blocks in a blockchain*

Each of these nodes are connected to each other in a peer-to-peer fashion. Nodes that store the entire blockchain are known as *full nodes*.

Immutability of Blockchains

In a blockchain, each block is chained to its previous block through the use of a cryptographic hash. A block's identity changes if the parent's identity changes. This in turn causes the current block's children to change, which affects the grandchildren, and so on. A change to a block forces a recalculation of all subsequent blocks, which requires enormous computation power. This makes the blockchain immutable, a key feature of cryptocurrencies like Bitcoin and Ethereum.

As a new block is added to the blockchain, the block of transactions is said to be *confirmed* by the blockchain. When a block is newly added, it's deemed to have one confirmation. As another block is added to it, its number of confirmation increases. Figure 2-10 shows the number of confirmations for the blocks in a blockchain. The more confirmations a block has, the more difficult it is to remove it from the blockchain.

Tip   In general, once a block has six or more confirmations, it's deemed infeasible for it to be reversed. Therefore, the data stored in the blockchain is immutable.

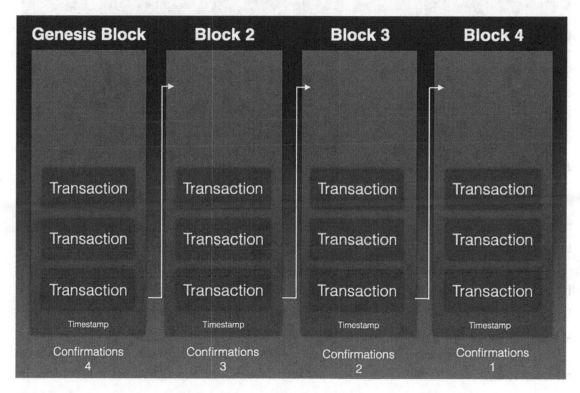

Figure 2-10. Confirmations of blocks in a blockchain

Consensus Protocols

When a transaction is performed, the transaction is broadcasted to the network to be collated into a block so that subsequently the block can be added to the existing blockchain (see Figure 2-11).

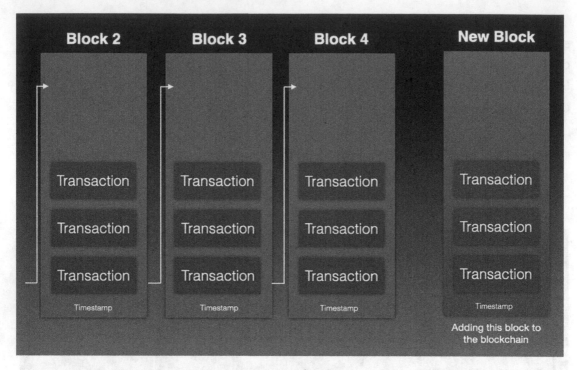

Figure 2-11. *Adding a new block to the blockchain*

So who actually collates the transactions? And since there may be multiple transactions going on at the same time, who gets to add the block to the blockchain? This is where *consensus protocols* (also known as *consensus algorithms*) come in.

A consensus protocol, as its name implies, is a method for all the nodes in a blockchain to reach an agreement. Since transactions are broadcasted to the network, there must be some sort of agreement among all the nodes to decide which transactions go into each block. If not, the blockchain would make no sense.

In the world of blockchain, there are quite a few consensus protocols in use. Here are some of them:

- Proof of Work (PoW)

- Proof of Stake (PoS)

- Delegated Proof of Stake

- Practical Byzantine Fault Tolerance (pBFT)

- Proof of Elapsed Time

For this chapter, I will only focus on the first two consensus protocols stated above.

Bitcoin's implementation of blockchain uses Proof of Work. Ethereum initially used Proof of Work but transitioned in September 2022 to a much more energy-efficient consensus protocol, Proof of Stake.

Proof of Work

In PoW, nodes that collate all the transactions are known as *mining nodes* (or *miner nodes*). When a transaction is performed, the transaction is broadcasted to all mining nodes. Figure 2-12 shows four transactions created by different users on the network broadcasting them to the various mining nodes.

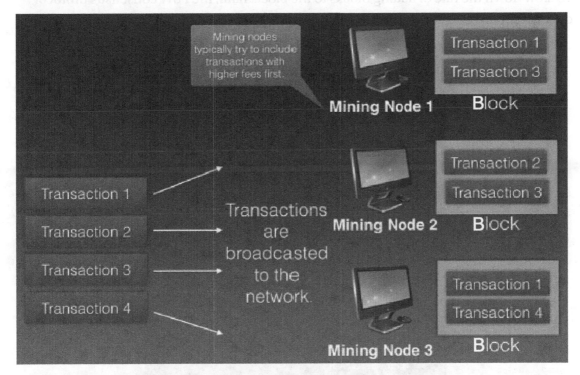

Figure 2-12. *Transactions are broadcasted to mining nodes, which assemble them into blocks to be mined*

Due to network latency, each mining node may receive these transactions at different timings. As a node receives transactions, it will try to include them in a block. Observe that each node is free to include whatever transactions it wants in a block. In practice, which transactions get included in a block depends on several factors, such as transaction fees, transaction size, order of arrival, and so on. The aim of the miner is to try to fill the block with transactions so that it can proceed to the next step, which is adding the block to the blockchain.

At this point, transactions that are included in a block but are not yet added to the blockchain are known as *unconfirmed transactions*. Once a block is filled with transactions, a mining node will attempt to add the block to the blockchain.

Now here comes the problem: with so many miners out there, who gets to add the block to the blockchain first?

The Mining Process

To slow down the rate of adding blocks to the blockchain, the PoW consensus protocol dictates a *network difficulty target* (see Figure 2-13).

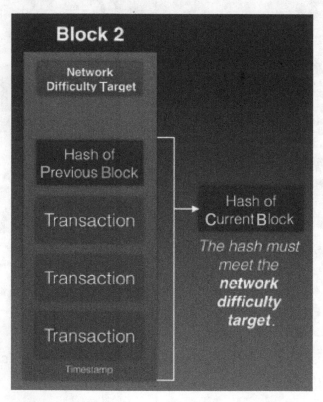

Figure 2-13. *Hashing the block to meet the network difficulty target*

In order to successfully add a block to the blockchain, a miner hashes the content of a block and checks that the hash meets the criteria set by the *difficulty target*. For example, the resultant hash must start with five zeros and so on.

As more miners join the network, the difficultly level increases. For example, the hash must now start with six zeros and so on. This allows the blocks to be added to the blockchain at a consistent rate.

Note   For Bitcoin, the difficulty is adjusted every 2,016 blocks (or every 2 weeks approximately) so that the average time between each block remains 10 minutes.

But wait a minute! The content of a block is fixed, and so no matter how you hash it, the resultant hash is always the same. So how do you ensure that the resultant hash can meet the difficulty target? To do that, miners add a *nonce* to the block, which stands for *number used once* (see Figure 2-14).

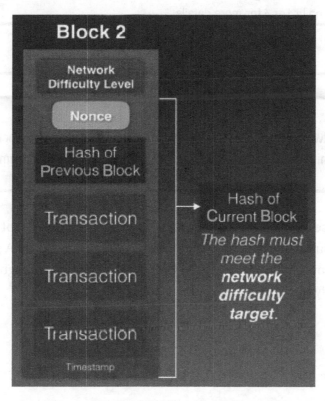

Figure 2-14. *Adding a nonce to change the content of the block in order to meet the network difficulty target*

The first miner who meets the target gets to claim the reward and add the block to the blockchain. They do so by broadcasting the block to other nodes so that they can verify the claim and stop working on their current work of mining their own blocks. These miners drop their current work, and the process of mining a new block starts all over again. The transactions that were not included in the block that was successfully mined are added to the next block to be mined.

REWARDS FOR MINERS

In the case of Bitcoin, the block reward initially was 50 BTC and halved every 210,000 blocks. At the time of writing, the block reward is currently at 6.25 BTC, and it will eventually be reduced to 0 after 64 halving events. For Ethereum, prior to the Merge, the reward for mining a block is 2 ETH (Ether). After the Merge, the rewards are slightly more complicated. You can visit https://ethereum.org/en/developers/docs/consensus-mechanisms/pos/rewards-and-penalties/ for more details.

BLOCKS ADDING RATES

For Bitcoin, the network adjusts the difficulty of the puzzles so that a new block is mined roughly every 10 minutes. For Ethereum using PoW, a block is mined approximately every 14 seconds.

Why is this process called Proof of Work? Well, because it takes a lot of work to find the proof! It is difficult to find the proof but easy to validate the proof. A good example of PoW is cracking a combination lock. It takes a lot of time to find the right combination, but it is easy to verify once the combination is found.

DOUBLE-SPENDING

Double-spending is a problem that arises when you try to spend the same cryptocurrency twice. Double-spending is not a problem when dealing with fiat-currency. Your $100 bill in your hand can not be at another place at the same time. However, it is a potential problem in the crypto world. Suppose you have 1 Bitcoin in your wallet, and you send it to a friend. Immediately after this and before the transaction is confirmed, you send the same Bitcoin to another friend. Essentially, you are trying to spend the same Bitcoin twice. Fortunately, with the consensus protocol in place, miners are able to ensure that the second transaction is not valid because you already spent it in an earlier transaction.

PoW uses tremendous computing resources. GPUs are required (as well as ASICs, application-specific integrated circuits, for some blockchains), while CPU speed is not important. It also uses a lot of electricity, because miners are doing the same work repeatedly, that of finding the nonce to meet the network difficulty for the block.

A common question is why you need to use a powerful GPU instead of CPU for mining. Well, as a simple comparison, a CPU core can execute 4 32-bit instructions per clock, whereas a GPU like the Radeon HD 5970 can execute 3200 32-bit instructions per clock. In short, the CPU excels at doing complex manipulations to a small set of data, whereas the GPU excels at doing simple manipulations to a large set of data. And since mining is all about performing hashing and finding the nonce, it is a highly repetitive task, something that the GPU excels in.

Tip   When a miner has successfully mined a block, they earn mining fees as well as transaction fees. That's what keeps miners motivated to invest in mining rigs and keep them running 24/7, thereby incurring substantial electricity bills.

Proof of Stake (PoS)

With the recent focus on sustainability, PoW is definitely not the way to go if blockchain is to become a long term technology for decentralized solutions. For this reason, a lot of new blockchain implementations are now using other consensus protocols. In particular, Ethereum has migrated from using PoW to a newer protocol called Proof of Stake (PoS).

41

In PoS, what used to be called miners are now known as *validators*. These validators mint (or forge) new blocks. To become a validator, a node must stake (hence its name Proof of Stake) at least 32 Ethers. The size of Ethers staked will affect the chance of a node being selected to be the next validator to mint the next block.

When a node becomes a validator, it will perform the same tasks that miners do: validate all the transactions in the block to ensure that they are valid. When everything checks out, the validator signs off the block, adds it to the blockchain, and then synchronize the blockchain across the network. This validator receive the transaction fees from the block they minted.

Compared with PoW where every miner is doing the same work, PoS seems to be more efficient because only one validator is required. But this raises another issue: what happens if the validator is not trustworthy and purposely allowed fraudulent transactions to be added to a block? This is where the stake that the validator has placed comes in. If it is later found that the validator has allowed fraudulent transactions to be added to the block, the validator will lose a part of his stake. As long as the stake is higher than the transaction fees that the validator can earn, we can trust that the validator will do their job correctly. If the validator does not do their job properly, they will lose more than they gain.

When the validator ceases to be one, all transaction fees plus their stake are released back to them at a later date. This gives the network time to punish the validator in the event that some of the minted blocks were later found to be fraudulent.

Comparing PoW with PoS

Now that you understand how PoS works, it is useful to do a quick comparison with PoW:

- In PoW, every miner node mines! In PoS, only a selected node gets to forge new blocks.

- PoS is more decentralized. PoW utilizes mining pools where people team up to increase their chances of mining new blocks. These pools control large portions of the blockchain (such as Bitcoin) and this is dangerous. If all the large mining pools merge, they can start approving fraudulent transactions.

- PoS makes easier to forge a new block and doesn't need expensive hardware, unlike PoW. This encourages more validators and hence increases the security of the network.

- PoS is also environmentally friendly, consuming much less energy than PoW.

Blockchain in More Detail

In the previous section, you learned that a block contains a nonce, timestamp, and the list of transactions. That was a simplification. In a real implementation, a block consists of

- A block header

- The list of transactions

The block header in turn consists of the following:

- The hash of the previous block

- A timestamp

- The Merkle root

- A nonce

- The network difficulty target

Note that the block header contains the *Merkle root* and not the transactions (see Figure 2-15). The transactions are collectively represented as a Merkle root, the details of which will be discussed in the next few sections.

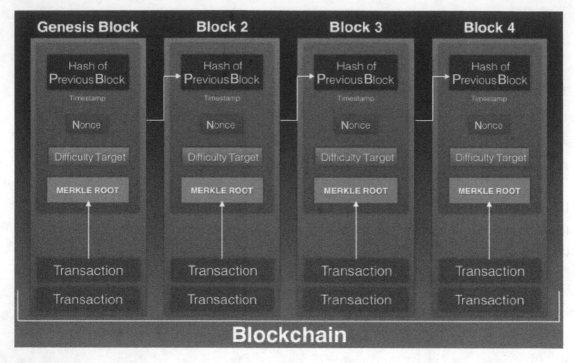

Figure 2-15. *A block contains the block header, which in turns contains the Merkle root of the transactions*

Types of Nodes

Before I address the rationale for storing the Merkle root in the block header, I need to talk about the types of nodes in a blockchain network. Figure 2-16 shows the different types of nodes in a blockchain network.

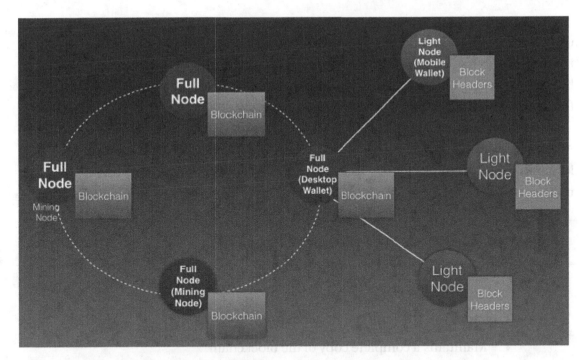

Figure 2-16. *Different types of nodes in a blockchain network*

As mentioned, computers connected to the blockchain network are known as nodes. I have discussed the role of mining/validator nodes, whose key responsibility is to gather transactions into blocks and then try to add the block to the blockchain. Mining/validator nodes are also known as *full nodes*.

Tip   Full nodes are not necessarily mining/validator nodes. However, a mining/validator node needs to be a full node.

The purpose of a full node is to ensure the integrity of the blockchain, and people running full nodes do not get rewards. On the other hand, mining/validator nodes are rewarded when they add a block to the blockchain.

An example of a full node is a desktop wallet, which allows users to perform transactions using the cryptocurrency.

Each full node has a copy of the entire blockchain. Full nodes also validate every block and transactions presented to it.

Besides full nodes, there are also *light nodes*. Light nodes help to verify transactions using a method called *simplified payment verification* (SPV). SPV allows a node to verify if a transaction has been included in a block, without needing to download the entire blockchain. Using SPV, light nodes connect to full nodes and transmit transactions to the full nodes for verifications.

Light nodes only need to store the block headers of all the blocks in the blockchain. An example of a light node is a mobile wallet, such as the Coinbase mobile app for iOS and Android. Using a mobile wallet, a user can perform transactions on the mobile device.

Note   Desktop wallets can be full node or light node.

Here is a summary of the types of nodes discussed thus far.

- **Full node**:

  - Maintains a complete copy of the blockchain

  - Able to verify all transactions since the beginning

  - Verifies a newly created block and adds it to the blockchain

  - Visit the following sites to see the current number of full nodes for the following blockchains:

    - Bitcoin: `https://bitnodes.earn.com`

    - Ethereum: `www.ethernodes.org/network/1`

- **Mining node** (must be a full node):

  - Works on a problem (finding the nonce)

- **Light node** (e.g., wallets):

  - Maintains the headers of the blockchain

  - Uses SPV to verify if a transaction is present and valid in a block

Finally, you'll see the use of representing the transactions as a Merkle root in the block header in the next section.

Merkle Tree and Merkle Root

The list of transactions in a block is stored as a *Merkle tree*. A Merkle tree is a tree data structure in which every leaf node is the hash of a transaction and every non-leaf node is the cryptographic hash of the child nodes. Figure 2-17 shows how the Merkle root is derived from the transactions.

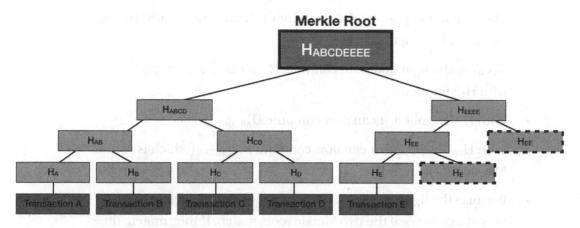

Figure 2-17. *How the Merkle root is derived from the Merkle tree*

As you can see, each transaction is hashed. The hash of each transaction is hashed together with the hash of another node. For example, the hash of transaction A (H_A) is combined with the hash of transaction B (H_B) and hashed to derive H_{AB}. This process is repeated until there's only one resultant hash. This final hash is known as the Merkle root. In this example, because H_E doesn't have another node to pair with, it's hashed with itself. The same applies to H_{EE}.

The Merkle root is stored in the block header, and the rest of the transactions are stored in the block as a Merkle tree. In earlier discussion, I mentioned full nodes. Full nodes download the entire blockchain. There's another type of node (known as a *light node*) that downloads only the blockchain headers. Because light nodes don't download the entire blockchain, they're easier to maintain and run. Using a method called *simplified payment verifications* (SPV), a light node can query a full node to verify a transaction. Examples of light nodes are cryptographic wallets.

Uses of Merkle Tree and the Merkle Root

By storing the Merkle root in the block header and the transactions as a Merkle tree in the block, a light node can easily verify if a transaction belongs to a particular block. This is how it works. Suppose a light node wants to verify that transaction C exists in a particular block.

- The light node queries a full node for the following hashes: H_D, H_{AB}, and H_{EEEE} (see Figure 2-18).

- Because the light node can compute H_C, it can then compute H_{CD} with H_D supplied.

- With H_{AB} supplied, it can now compute H_{ABCD}.

- With H_{EEEE} supplied, it can now compute $H_{ABCDEEEE}$ (which is the Merkle root).

- Because the light node has the Merkle root of the block, it can now check to see if the two Merkle roots match. If they match, the transaction is verified.

As you can see from this simple example, to verify a single transaction out of five transactions, only three hashes need to be retrieved from the full node. Mathematically, for n transactions in a block, it takes $\log_2 n$ hashes to verify that a transaction is in a block. For example, if there are 1,024 transactions in a block, a light node only needs to request 10 hashes to verify the existence of a transaction in the block.

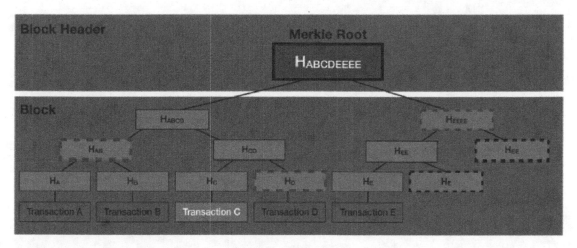

Figure 2-18. *How the Merkle tree and Merkle root are used to validate a transaction*

Summary

In this chapter, you learned the motivations behind blockchain and the problems that it aims to solve. You explored how blocks are added to the blockchain through a process known as mining. In the next chapter, you will learn how to build your own blockchain using Python so that you can see and understand the inner workings of a blockchain.

## CHAPTER 3

Implementing Your Own Blockchain Using Python

In the previous chapter, you learned about the basics of blockchain, the motivations behind blockchains, how transactions are added to blocks, and how blocks are added to the previous blocks to form a chain of blocks called a blockchain. A good way to understand all these concepts is to build one yourself. Implementing your own blockchain offers you a more detailed look at how concepts like *transactions*, *mining*, and *consensus* work.

Obviously, implementing a full blockchain is not for the faint of heart, and that is definitely not your goal in this chapter. What you will try to do in this chapter is implement a conceptual blockchain using Python and use it to illustrate the key concepts.

Your Conceptual Blockchain Implementation

For this chapter, you will build the very simple blockchain shown in Figure 3-1.

© Wei-Meng Lee 2023
W.-M. Lee, *Beginning Ethereum Smart Contracts Programming*, https://doi.org/10.1007/978-1-4842-9271-6_3

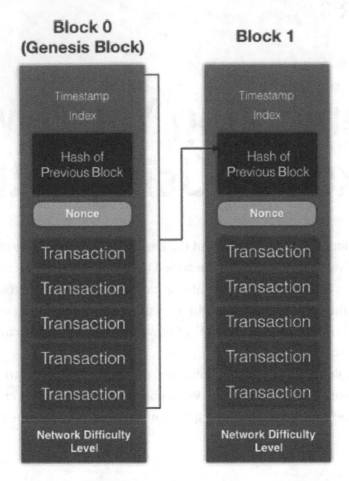

Figure 3-1. *Your conceptual blockchain*

To keep things simple, each block in your blockchain will contain the following components:

- **Timestamp**: The time the block was added to the blockchain

- **Index**: A running number starting from 0 indicating the block number

- **Hash of the previous block**: The hash result of the previous block. As shown in Figure 3-1, the hash is the result of hashing the content of the block consisting of the timestamp, index, hash of the previous block, nonce, and all the transactions.

- **Nonce**: The *number used once*

- **Transaction(s)**: Each block will hold a variable number of transactions.

Note   For simplicity, you are not going to worry about representing the transactions in a Merkle tree, nor are you going to separate a block into block header and content.

The *network difficulty level* is fixed at four zeros; that is, in order to derive the nonce, the result of the hash of the block must start with four zeros.

Tip   Refer to Chapter 2 for the idea behind the nonce and how it relates to network difficulty level.

Obtaining the Nonce

For your sample blockchain implementation, the nonce is found by combining it with the index of the block, the hash of the previous block, and all the transactions, and then checking if the resultant hash matches the network difficulty level (see Figure 3-2).

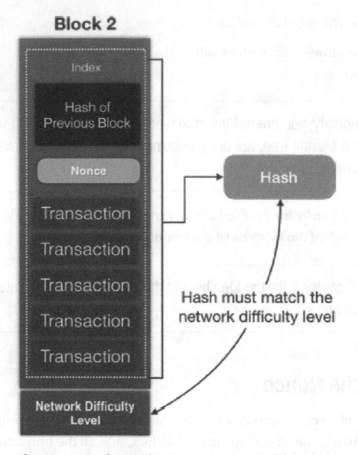

Figure 3-2. How the nonce is derived in your conceptual blockchain

Once the nonce is found, the block gets appended to the last block in the blockchain, with the timestamp added (see Figure 3-3).

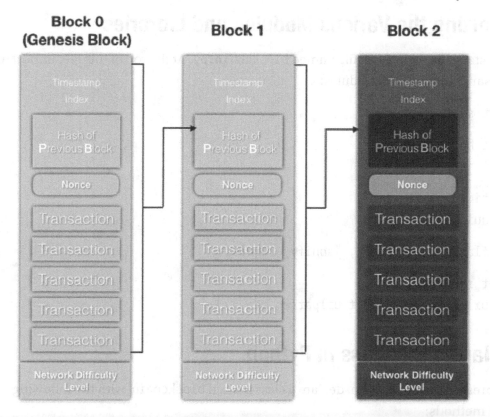

Figure 3-3. *Once a blocked is mined, it will be appended to the blockchain with the timestamp added to the block*

Installing Flask

For your conceptual blockchain, you will run it as a REST API so that you can interact with it through REST calls. For this, you will use the **Flask** microframework. To install Flask, type the following commands in Terminal:

```
$ pip install flask
$ pip install requests
```

These commands install the Flask microframework.

Tip   Flask is a web framework that makes building web applications easy and rapid.

Importing the Various Modules and Libraries

To get started, create a text file named blockchain.py. At the top of this file, import all necessary libraries and modules:

```
import sys

import hashlib
import json

from time import time
from uuid import uuid4

from flask import Flask, jsonify, request

import requests
from urllib.parse import urlparse
```

Declaring the Class in Python

To represent the blockchain, declare a class named blockchain, with the following two initial methods:

```
class Blockchain(object):
    difficulty_target = "0000"

    def hash_block(self, block):
        block_encoded = json.dumps(block,
            sort_keys=True).encode()
        return hashlib.sha256(block_encoded).hexdigest()

    def __init__(self):
        # stores all the blocks in the entire blockchain
        self.chain = []
        # temporarily stores the transactions for the
        # current block
        self.current_transactions = []
        # create the genesis block with a specific fixed hash
        # of previous block genesis block starts with index 0
        genesis_hash = self.hash_block("genesis_block")
```

```
self.append_block(
    hash_of_previous_block = genesis_hash,
    nonce = self.proof_of_work(0, genesis_hash, [])
)
```

This creates a class named `blockchain` with two methods:

- The `hash_block()` method encodes a block into an array of bytes and then hashes it; you need to ensure that the dictionary is sorted or you'll have inconsistent hashes later.

- The `__init__()` function is the constructor for the class. Here, you store the entire blockchain as a list. Because every blockchain has a genesis block, you need to initialize the genesis block with the hash of the previous block, and in this example, you simply use a fixed string called `genesis_block` to obtain its hash. Once the hash of the previous block is found, you need to find the nonce for the block using the method named `proof_of_work()` (which you will define in the next section).

The `proof_of_work()` method (detailed next) will return a nonce that will result in a hash that matches the difficulty target when the content of the current block is hashed.

For simplicity, you fix the `difficulty_target` to a hash result that starts with four zeros ("0000").

Tip   The source code for your blockchain is shown at the end of this chapter. For the impatient, you may wish to look at the code while you go through the various concepts in this chapter.

Finding the Nonce

Now define the `proof_of_work()` method to find the nonce for the block:

```
# use PoW to find the nonce for the current block
def proof_of_work(self, index, hash_of_previous_block,
transactions):
    # try with nonce = 0
    nonce = 0
```

```
# try hashing the nonce together with the hash of the
# previous block until it is valid
while self.valid_proof(index, hash_of_previous_block,
    transactions, nonce) is False:
    nonce += 1
return nonce
```

The proof_of_work() function starts with zero for the nonce and checks if the nonce together with the content of the block produces a hash that matches the difficulty target. If not, it increments the nonce by one and then tries again until it finds the correct nonce.

The next method, valid_proof(), hashes the content of a block and checks to see if the block's hash meets the difficulty target:

```
def valid_proof(self, index, hash_of_previous_block,
    transactions, nonce):
    # create a string containing the hash of the previous
    # block and the block content, including the nonce
    content = \
        f'{index}{hash_of_previous_block}{transactions}{nonce}'.
        encode()
    # hash using sha256
    content_hash = hashlib.sha256(content).hexdigest()
    # check if the hash meets the difficulty target
    return content_hash[:len(self.difficulty_target)] == \
        self.difficulty_target
```

Appending the Block to the Blockchain

Once the nonce for a block has been found, you can write the method to append the block to the existing blockchain. This is the function of the append_block() method:

```
# creates a new block and adds it to the blockchain
def append_block(self, nonce, hash_of_previous_block):
    block = {
        'index': len(self.chain),
```

```
        'timestamp': time(),
        'transactions': self.current_transactions,
        'nonce': nonce,
        'hash_of_previous_block': hash_of_previous_block
    }
    # reset the current list of transactions
    self.current_transactions = []
    # add the new block to the blockchain
    self.chain.append(block)
    return block
```

When the block is added to the blockchain, the current timestamp is also added to the block.

Adding Transactions

The next method to add to the Blockchain class is the add_transaction() method:

```
def add_transaction(self, sender, recipient, amount):
    self.current_transactions.append({
        'amount': amount,
        'recipient': recipient,
        'sender': sender,
    })
    return self.last_block['index'] + 1
```

This method adds a new transaction to the current list of transactions. It then gets the index of the last block in the blockchain and adds one to it. This new index is the block that the current transaction will be added to.

To obtain the last block in the blockchain, define a property called last_block in the Blockchain class:

```
@property
def last_block(self):
    # returns the last block in the blockchain
    return self.chain[-1]
```

Exposing the Blockchain Class as a REST API

Your Blockchain class is now complete, so let's expose it as a REST API using Flask. Append the following statements to the end of the **blockchain.py** file:

```python
app = Flask(__name__)

# generate a globally unique address for this node
node_identifier = str(uuid4()).replace('-', '')

# instantiate the Blockchain
blockchain = Blockchain()
```

Obtaining the Full Blockchain

For the REST API, you want to create a route for users to obtain the current blockchain, so append the following statements to the end of **blockchain.py**:

```python
# return the entire blockchain
@app.route('/blockchain', methods=['GET'])
def full_chain():
    response = {
        'chain': blockchain.chain,
        'length': len(blockchain.chain),
    }
    return jsonify(response), 200
```

Performing Mining

You also need to create a route to allow miners to mine a block so that it can be added to the blockchain:

```python
@app.route('/mine', methods=['GET'])
def mine_block():
    blockchain.add_transaction(
        sender="0",
        recipient=node_identifier,
        amount=1,
    )
```

```
# obtain the hash of last block in the blockchain
last_block_hash = \
    blockchain.hash_block(blockchain.last_block)
# using PoW, get the nonce for the new block to be added
# to the blockchain
index = len(blockchain.chain)
nonce = blockchain.proof_of_work(index, last_block_hash,
    blockchain.current_transactions)
# add the new block to the blockchain using the last block
# hash and the current nonce
block = blockchain.append_block(nonce, last_block_hash)
response = {
    'message': "New Block Mined",
    'index': block['index'],
    'hash_of_previous_block':
        block['hash_of_previous_block'],
    'nonce': block['nonce'],
    'transactions': block['transactions'],
}
return jsonify(response), 200
```

When a miner manages to mine a block, they must receive a reward for finding the proof. Here, you add a transaction to send one unit of reward to the miner to signify the reward for successfully mining the block.

When mining a block, you need to find the hash of the previous block and use it together with the content of the current block to find the nonce for the block. Once the nonce is found, you append it to the blockchain.

Adding Transactions

Another route that you want to add to the API is the ability to add transactions to the current block:

```
@app.route('/transactions/new', methods=['POST'])
def new_transaction():
    # get the value passed in from the client
```

```
values = request.get_json()
# check that the required fields are in the POST'ed data
required_fields = ['sender', 'recipient', 'amount']
if not all(k in values for k in required_fields):
    return ('Missing fields', 400)
# create a new transaction
index = blockchain.add_transaction(
    values['sender'],
    values['recipient'],
    values['amount']
)
response = {'message':
    f'Transaction will be added to Block {index}'}
return (jsonify(response), 201)
```

An example of a transaction is a user sending cryptocurrency from one account to another.

Testing Your Blockchain

You are now ready to test the blockchain. In this final step, add the following statements to the end of **blockchain.py**:

```
if __name__ == '__main__':
    app.run(host='0.0.0.0', port=int(sys.argv[1]))
```

In this implementation, you allow the user to run the API based on the specified port number.

To start the first node, type the following command in terminal:

```
$ python blockchain.py 5000
```

You will see the following output:

```
* Serving Flask app "blockchain" (lazy loading)
 * Environment: production
   WARNING: Do not use the development server in a production environment.
   Use a production WSGI server instead.
```

```
* Debug mode: off
* Running on http://0.0.0.0:5000/ (Press CTRL+C to quit)
```

Your first blockchain on the first node is now running. It is also listening at port 5000, where you can add transactions to it and mine a block.

In another terminal window, type the following command to view the contents of the blockchain running on the node:

$ **curl http://localhost:5000/blockchain**

You will see the following output (formatted for clarity):

```
{
    "chain": [{
        "hash_of_previous_block": "181cfa3e85f3c2a7aa9fb74f992d0d061d3e4a6
        d7461792413aab3f97bd3da95",
        "index": 0,
        "nonce": 61093,
        "timestamp": 1560757569.810427,
        "transactions": []
    }],
    "length": 1
}
```

Note   The first block (index 0) is the genesis block.

Let's try mining a block to see how it affects the blockchain. Type the following command in terminal:

$ **curl http://localhost:5000/mine**

The block that is mined is returned:

```
{
    "hash_of_previous_block": "0e8431c4a7fe132503233bc226b1f68c9d2bd4d30
    af24c115bcdad461dda48a0",
    "index": 1,
    "message": "New Block Mined",
```

```
    "nonce": 24894,
    "transactions": [{
        "amount": 1,
        "recipient": "084f17b6e5364cde86a231d1cc0c9991",
        "sender": "0"
    }]
}
```

Note   Observe that the block contains a single transaction, which is the reward given to the miner.

You can now issue the command to obtain the blockchain from the node:

```
$ curl http://localhost:5000/blockchain
```

You will see that the newly mined block is in the blockchain:

```
{
    "chain": [{
        "hash_of_previous_block": "181cfa3e85f3c2a7aa9fb74f992d0d061d3e4a
        6d7461792413aab3f97bd3da95",
        "index": 0,
        "nonce": 61093,
        "timestamp": 1560757569.810427,
        "transactions": []
    }, {
        "hash_of_previous_block": "0e8431c4a7fe132503233bc226b1f68c9d2bd4d
        30af24c115bcdad461dda48a0",
        "index": 1,
        "nonce": 24894,
        "timestamp": 1560759370.988651,
        "transactions": [{
            "amount": 1,
            "recipient": "084f17b6e5364cde86a231d1cc0c9991",
            "sender": "0"
        }]
```

```
  }],
    "length": 2
}
```

Tip Remember that the default difficulty target is set to four zeros (`difficulty_target = "0000"`). You can change it to five zeros and retest the blockchain. It now takes a longer time to mine a block, since it is more difficult to find a nonce that results in a hash beginning with five zeros.

Let's add a transaction to a block by issuing the following command in terminal:

```
$ curl -X POST -H "Content-Type: application/json" -d '{
"sender": "04d0988bfa799f7d7ef9ab3de97ef481", "recipient":
"cd0f75d2367ad456607647edde665d6f", "amount": 5}' "http://localhost:5000/
transactions/new"
```

Caution Windows does not support single quotes (') when using curl in the command line. Hence, you need to use double quotes and use the slash character (\) to turn off the meaning of double quotes (") in your doublequoted string. The preceding command in Windows would be

```
curl -X POST -H "Content-Type: application/json" -d
"{ \"sender\": \"04d0988bfa799f7d7ef9ab3de97ef481\",
\"recipient\": \"cd0f75d2367ad456607647edde665d6f\",
\"amount\": 5}" "http://localhost:5000/transactions/new"
```

You should see the following result:

```
{"message":"Transaction will be added to Block 2"}
```

You can now mine the block:

```
$ curl http://localhost:5000/mine
```

You should see the following result:

```
{

    "hash_of_previous_block": "282991fe48ec07378da72823e6337e13be8524ced51
    00d55c591ae087631146d",
    "index": 2,
    "message": "New Block Mined",
    "nonce": 61520,
    "transactions": [{
        "amount": 5,
        "recipient": "cd0f75d2367ad456607647edde665d6f",
        "sender": "04d0988bfa799f7d7ef9ab3de97ef481"
    }, {
        "amount": 1,
        "recipient": "084f17b6e5364cde86a231d1cc0c9991",
        "sender": "0"
    }]
}
```

This result shows that Block 2 has been mined and it contains two transactions: one that you added manually and another that is the reward for the miner.

You can examine the contents of the blockchain by issuing this command:

```
$ curl http://localhost:5000/blockchain
```

You will see the newly added block containing the two transactions:

```
{
    "chain": [{
        "hash_of_previous_block": "181cfa3e85f3c2a7aa9fb74f992d0d061d3e4a6
        d7461792413aab3f97bd3da95",
        "index": 0,
        "nonce": 61093,
        "timestamp": 1560757569.810427,
        "transactions": []
    }, {
        "hash_of_previous_block": "0e8431c4a7fe132503233bc226b1f68c9d2bd4d
        30af24c115bcdad461dda48a0",
```

```
        "index": 1,
        "nonce": 24894,
        "timestamp": 1560759370.988651,
        "transactions": [{
            "amount": 1,
            "recipient": "084f17b6e5364cde86a231d1cc0c9991",
            "sender": "0"
        }]
    }, {
        "hash_of_previous_block": "282991fe48ec07378da72823e6337e13be8524
        ced5100d55c591ae087631146d",
        "index": 2,
        "nonce": 61520,
        "timestamp": 1560760629.10675,
        "transactions": [{
            "amount": 5,
            "recipient": "cd0f75d2367ad456607647edde665d6f",
            "sender": "04d0988bfa799f7d7ef9ab3de97ef481"
        }, {
            "amount": 1,
            "recipient": "084f17b6e5364cde86a231d1cc0c9991",
            "sender": "0"
        }]
    }],
    "length": 3
}
```

Synchronizing Blockchains

In real life, a blockchain network consists of multiple nodes maintaining copies of the same blockchain. So, there must be a way for the nodes to synchronize so that every single node is referring to the same identical blockchain.

When you use Python to run the blockchain.py application, only one node is running. The whole idea of blockchain is decentralization. There should be multiple nodes maintaining the blockchain, not just a single one.

For your example, you will modify it so that each node can be made aware of neighboring nodes on the network (see Figure 3-4).

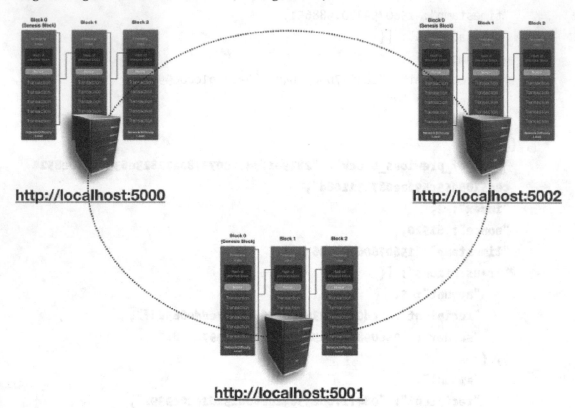

Figure 3-4. *A blockchain network should consist of multiple nodes*

To do that in your example, add a number of methods to the Blockchain class. First, add a nodes member to the constructor of the Blockchain class and initialize it to an empty set:

```
def __init__(self):
    self.nodes = set()
    # stores all the blocks in the entire blockchain
    self.chain = []
    ...
```

This nodes member stores the address of other nodes. Next, add a method called add_node() to the Blockchain class:

```
def add_node(self, address):
    parsed_url = urlparse(address)
    self.nodes.add(parsed_url.netloc)
    print(parsed_url.netloc)
```

This method allows a new node to be added to the nodes member. For example, if "http://192.168.0.5:5000" is passed to the method, the IP address and port number "192.168.0.5:5000" will be added to the nodes member.

The next method to add to the Blockchain class is valid_chain():

```
# determine if a given blockchain is valid
def valid_chain(self, chain):
    last_block = chain[0]    # the genesis block
    current_index = 1        # starts with the second block
    while current_index < len(chain):
        block = chain[current_index]
        if block['hash_of_previous_block'] != \
            self.hash_block(last_block):
            return False
        # check for valid nonce
        if not self.valid_proof(
            current_index,
            block['hash_of_previous_block'],
            block['transactions'],
            block['nonce']):
            return False
        # move on to the next block on the chain
        last_block = block
        current_index += 1
    # the chain is valid
    return True
```

The valid_chain() method validates that a given blockchain is valid by performing the following checks:

- It goes through each block in the blockchain and hashes each block and verifies that the hash of each block is correctly recorded in the next block.

- It verifies that the nonce in each block is valid.

Finally, add the update_blockchain() method to the Blockchain class:

```python
def update_blockchain(self):
    # get the nodes around us that has been registered
    neighbours = self.nodes
    new_chain = None
    # for simplicity, look for chains longer than ours
    max_length = len(self.chain)
    # grab and verify the chains from all the nodes in our
    # network
    for node in neighbours:
        # get the blockchain from the other nodes
        response = \
            requests.get(f'http://{node}/blockchain')
        if response.status_code == 200:
            length = response.json()['length']
            chain = response.json()['chain']
            # check if the length is longer and the chain
            # is valid
            if length > max_length and \
                self.valid_chain(chain):
                max_length = length
                new_chain = chain
    # replace our chain if we discovered a new, valid
    # chain longer than ours
    if new_chain:
        self.chain = new_chain
        return True
    return False
```

The update_blockchain() method works by checking that the blockchain from neighboring nodes is valid and that the node with the longest valid chain is the authoritative one; if another node with a valid blockchain is longer than the current one, it will replace the current blockchain.

With the methods in the Blockchain class defined, you can now define the routes for the REST API:

```python
@app.route('/nodes/add_nodes', methods=['POST'])
def add_nodes():
    # get the nodes passed in from the client
    values = request.get_json()
    nodes = values.get('nodes')
    if nodes is None:
        return "Error: Missing node(s) info", 400
    for node in nodes:
        blockchain.add_node(node)
    response = {
        'message': 'New nodes added',
        'nodes': list(blockchain.nodes),
    }
    return jsonify(response), 201
```

The /nodes/add_nodes route allows a node to register one or more neighboring nodes.

The /nodes/sync route allows a node to synchronize its blockchain with its neighboring nodes:

```python
@app.route('/nodes/sync', methods=['GET'])
def sync():
    updated = blockchain.update_blockchain()
    if updated:
        response = {
            'message':
                'The blockchain has been updated to the latest',
            'blockchain': blockchain.chain
        }
```

```python
    else:
        response = {
            'message': 'Our blockchain is the latest',
            'blockchain': blockchain.chain
        }
    return jsonify(response), 200
```

Testing the Blockchain with Multiple Nodes

In the terminal that is running the blockchain.py application, press Ctrl+C to stop the server. Type the following command to restart it:

```
$ python blockchain.py 5000
```

Open another terminal window. Type the following command:

```
$ python blockchain.py 5001
```

Tip   You now have two nodes running: one listening at port 5000 and another at 5001.

Let's mine two blocks in the first node (5000) by typing the following commands in *another* terminal window:

```
$ curl http://localhost:5000/mine
{
    "hash_of_previous_block": "ac46b1f492997e27612a8b5750e0fe340a217aae89e
    5c0efd56959d87127b4d3",
    "index": 1,
    "message": "New Block Mined",
    "nonce": 92305,
    "transactions": [{
        "amount": 1,
        "recipient": "db9ef69db7764331a6f4f23dbb8acd68",
        "sender": "0"
    }]
}
```

```
$ curl http://localhost:5000/mine
{
    "hash_of_previous_block": "790ed48f5d52b3eacd2f419e6fdfb2f6b3142
    bcfc31943e4857b7ba4df48bd98",
    "index": 2,
    "message": "New Block Mined",
    "nonce": 224075,
    "transactions": [{
        "amount": 1,
        "recipient": "db9ef69db7764331a6f4f23dbb8acd68",
        "sender": "0"
    }]
}
```

The first node should now have three blocks:

```
$ curl http://localhost:5000/blockchain
{
    "chain": [{
        "hash_of_previous_block": "181cfa3e85f3c2a7aa9fb74f992d0d061d3e4a6
        d7461792413aab3f97bd3da95",
        "index": 0,
        "nonce": 61093,
        "timestamp": 1560823108.2946198,
        "transactions": []
    }, {
        "hash_of_previous_block": "ac46b1f492997e27612a8b5750e0fe340a217
        aae89e5c0efd56959d87127b4d3",
        "index": 1,
        "nonce": 92305,
        "timestamp": 1560823210.26095,
        "transactions": [{
            "amount": 1,
            "recipient": "db9ef69db7764331a6f4f23dbb8acd68",
            "sender": "0"
        }]
```

```
    }, {
        "hash_of_previous_block": "790ed48f5d52b3eacd2f419e6fdfb2f6b3142bcf
        c31943e4857b7ba4df48bd98",
        "index": 2,
        "nonce": 224075,
        "timestamp": 1560823212.887074,
        "transactions": [{
            "amount": 1,
            "recipient": "db9ef69db7764331a6f4f23dbb8acd68",
            "sender": "0"
        }]
    }],
    "length": 3
}
```

Since you have not done any mining on the second node (5001), there is only one block in this node:

$ curl http://localhost:5001/blockchain

```
{
    "chain": [{
        "hash_of_previous_block": "181cfa3e85f3c2a7aa9fb74f992d0d061d3e4a6d
        7461792413aab3f97bd3da95",
        "index": 0,
        "nonce": 61093,
        "timestamp": 1560823126.898498,
        "transactions": []
    }],
    "length": 1
}
```

To tell the second node that there is a neighbor node, use the following command:

```
$ curl -H "Content-type: application/json" -d '{"nodes" :
["http://127.0.0.1:5000"]}' -X POST  http://localhost:5001/nodes/add_nodes
{
    "message": "New nodes added",
    "nodes": ["127.0.0.1:5000"]
}
```

Tip   This command registers a new node with the node at port 5001 that there is a neighboring node listening at port 5000.

To tell the first node that there is a neighbor node, use the following command:

```
$ curl -H "Content-type: application/json" -d '{"nodes" :
["http://127.0.0.1:5001"]}' -X POST  http://localhost:5000/nodes/add_nodes
{
    "message": "New nodes added",
    "nodes": ["127.0.0.1:5001"]
}
```

Tip   This command registers a new node with the node at port 5000 that there is a neighboring node listening at port 5001.

Figure 3-5 shows the two nodes aware of each other's existence.

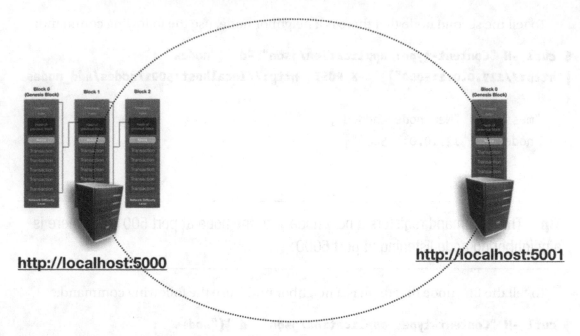

http://localhost:5000   **http://localhost:5001**

Figure 3-5. *The current states of the two nodes in your blockchain network*

With the first node aware of the existence of the second node (and vice versa), synchronize the blockchain starting from the first node:

```
$ curl http://localhost:5000/nodes/sync
{
    "blockchain": [{
        "hash_of_previous_block": "181cfa3e85f3c2a7aa9fb74f992d0d061d3e4a6d
        7461792413aab3f97bd3da95",
        "index": 0,
        "nonce": 61093,
        "timestamp": 1560823108.2946198,
        "transactions": []
    }, {
        "hash_of_previous_block": "ac46b1f492997e27612a8b5750e0fe340a217aae
        89e5c0efd56959d87127b4d3",
        "index": 1,
        "nonce": 92305,
        "timestamp": 1560823210.26095,
        "transactions": [{
```

```
            "amount": 1,
            "recipient": "db9ef69db7764331a6f4f23dbb8acd68",
            "sender": "0"
        }]
    }, {
        "hash_of_previous_block": "790ed48f5d52b3eacd2f419e6fdfb2f6b3142
        bcfc31943e4857b7ba4df48bd98",
        "index": 2,
        "nonce": 224075,
        "timestamp": 1560823212.887074,
        "transactions": [{
            "amount": 1,
            "recipient": "db9ef69db7764331a6f4f23dbb8acd68",
            "sender": "0"
        }]
    }],
    "message": "Our blockchain is the latest"
}
```

As the result shows, the first node has the longest chain (three blocks), so the blockchain is the latest and it remains intact. You can synchronize from the second node:

```
$ curl http://localhost:5001/nodes/sync
{
    "blockchain": [{
        "hash_of_previous_block": "181cfa3e85f3c2a7aa9fb74f992d0d061d3e4
        a6d7461792413aab3f97bd3da95",
        "index": 0,
        "nonce": 61093,
        "timestamp": 1560823108.2946198,
        "transactions": []
    }, {
        "hash_of_previous_block": "ac46b1f492997e27612a8b5750e0fe340a21
        7aae89e5c0efd56959d87127b4d3",
        "index": 1,
        "nonce": 92305,
```

```
        "timestamp": 1560823210.26095,
        "transactions": [{
            "amount": 1,
            "recipient": "db9ef69db7764331a6f4f23dbb8acd68",
            "sender": "0"
        }]
    }, {
        "hash_of_previous_block": "790ed48f5d52b3eacd2f419e6fdfb2f6
        b3142bcfc31943e4857b7ba4df48bd98",
        "index": 2,
        "nonce": 224075,
        "timestamp": 1560823212.887074,
        "transactions": [{
            "amount": 1,
            "recipient": "db9ef69db7764331a6f4f23dbb8acd68",
            "sender": "0"
        }]
    }],
    "message": "The blockchain has been updated to the latest"
}
```

As the second node's blockchain only has one block, it is therefore deemed outdated. It now replaces its blockchain from that of the first node.

Full Listing for the Python Blockchain Implementation

```python
import sys

import hashlib
import json

from time import time
from uuid import uuid4

from flask import Flask, jsonify, request
```

```python
import requests
from urllib.parse import urlparse

class Blockchain(object):
    difficulty_target = "0000"

    def hash_block(self, block):
        block_encoded = json.dumps(block,
            sort_keys=True).encode()
        return hashlib.sha256(block_encoded).hexdigest()

    def __init__(self):
        self.nodes = set()
        # stores all the blocks in the entire blockchain
        self.chain = []
        # temporarily stores the transactions for the
        # current block
        self.current_transactions = []
        # create the genesis block with a specific fixed hash
        # of previous block genesis block starts with index 0
        genesis_hash = self.hash_block("genesis_block")
        self.append_block(
            hash_of_previous_block = genesis_hash,
            nonce = self.proof_of_work(0, genesis_hash, [])
        )

    # use PoW to find the nonce for the current block
    def proof_of_work(self, index, hash_of_previous_block,
    transactions):
        # try with nonce = 0
        nonce = 0
        # try hashing the nonce together with the hash of the
        # previous block until it is valid
        while self.valid_proof(index, hash_of_previous_block,
            transactions, nonce) is False:
            nonce += 1
        return nonce
```

```python
    def valid_proof(self, index, hash_of_previous_block, \
        transactions, nonce):
        # create a string containing the hash of the previous
        # block and the block content, including the nonce
        content = \
            f'{index}{hash_of_previous_block}{transactions}{nonce}'. \
            encode()

        # hash using sha256
        content_hash = hashlib.sha256(content).hexdigest()
        # check if the hash meets the difficulty target
        return content_hash[:len(self.difficulty_target)] == \
            self.difficulty_target

    # creates a new block and adds it to the blockchain
    def append_block(self, nonce, hash_of_previous_block):
        block = {
            'index': len(self.chain),
            'timestamp': time(),
            'transactions': self.current_transactions,
            'nonce': nonce,
            'hash_of_previous_block': hash_of_previous_block
        }
        # reset the current list of transactions
        self.current_transactions = []
        # add the new block to the blockchain
        self.chain.append(block)
        return block

    def add_transaction(self, sender, recipient, amount):
        self.current_transactions.append({
            'amount': amount,
            'recipient': recipient,
            'sender': sender,
        })
        return self.last_block['index'] + 1
```

```python
def add_node(self, address):
    parsed_url = urlparse(address)
    self.nodes.add(parsed_url.netloc)
    print(parsed_url.netloc)

def update_blockchain(self):
    # get the nodes around us that has been registered
    neighbours = self.nodes
    new_chain = None
    # for simplicity, look for chains longer than ours
    max_length = len(self.chain)
    # grab and verify the chains from all the nodes in our
    # network
    for node in neighbours:
        # get the blockchain from the other nodes
        response = \
            requests.get(f'http://{node}/blockchain')
        if response.status_code == 200:
            length = response.json()['length']
            chain = response.json()['chain']
            # check if the length is longer and the chain
            # is valid
            if length > max_length and \
                self.valid_chain(chain):
                max_length = length
                new_chain = chain
    # replace our chain if we discovered a new, valid
    # chain longer than ours
    if new_chain:
        self.chain = new_chain
        return True
    return False

# determine if a given blockchain is valid
def valid_chain(self, chain):
    last_block = chain[0]    # the genesis block
```

```python
            current_index = 1          # starts with the second block
        while current_index < len(chain):
            block = chain[current_index]
            if block['hash_of_previous_block'] != \
                self.hash_block(last_block):
                return False
            # check for valid nonce
            if not self.valid_proof(
                current_index,
                block['hash_of_previous_block'],
                block['transactions'],
                block['nonce']):
                return False
            # move on to the next block on the chain
            last_block = block
            current_index += 1
        # the chain is valid
        return True

    @property
    def last_block(self):
        # returns the last block in the blockchain
        return self.chain[-1]

app = Flask(__name__)

# generate a globally unique address for this node
node_identifier = str(uuid4()).replace('-', '')

# instantiate the Blockchain
blockchain = Blockchain()

# return the entire blockchain
@app.route('/blockchain', methods=['GET'])
def full_chain():
    response = {
        'chain': blockchain.chain,
```

```python
        'length': len(blockchain.chain),
    }
    return jsonify(response), 200

@app.route('/mine', methods=['GET'])
def mine_block():
    blockchain.add_transaction(
        sender="0",
        recipient=node_identifier,
        amount=1,
    )
    # obtain the hash of last block in the blockchain
    last_block_hash = \
        blockchain.hash_block(blockchain.last_block)
    # using PoW, get the nonce for the new block to be added
    # to the blockchain
    index = len(blockchain.chain)
    nonce = blockchain.proof_of_work(index, last_block_hash,
        blockchain.current_transactions)
    # add the new block to the blockchain using the last block
    # hash and the current nonce
    block = blockchain.append_block(nonce, last_block_hash)
    response = {
        'message': "New Block Mined",
        'index': block['index'],
        'hash_of_previous_block':
            block['hash_of_previous_block'],
        'nonce': block['nonce'],
        'transactions': block['transactions'],
    }
    return jsonify(response), 200

@app.route('/transactions/new', methods=['POST'])
def new_transaction():
    # get the value passed in from the client
    values = request.get_json()
```

```python
        # check that the required fields are in the POST'ed data
        required_fields = ['sender', 'recipient', 'amount']
        if not all(k in values for k in required_fields):
            return ('Missing fields', 400)
        # create a new transaction
        index = blockchain.add_transaction(
            values['sender'],
            values['recipient'],
            values['amount']
        )
        response = {'message':
            f'Transaction will be added to Block {index}'}
        return (jsonify(response), 201)

@app.route('/nodes/add_nodes', methods=['POST'])
def add_nodes():
    # get the nodes passed in from the client
    values = request.get_json()
    nodes = values.get('nodes')
    if nodes is None:
        return "Error: Missing node(s) info", 400
    for node in nodes:
        blockchain.add_node(node)
    response = {
        'message': 'New nodes added',
        'nodes': list(blockchain.nodes),
    }
    return jsonify(response), 201

@app.route('/nodes/sync', methods=['GET'])
def sync():
    updated = blockchain.update_blockchain()
    if updated:
        response = {
            'message':
                'The blockchain has been updated to the latest',
```

```python
            'blockchain': blockchain.chain
        }
    else:
        response = {
            'message': 'Our blockchain is the latest',
            'blockchain': blockchain.chain
        }
    return jsonify(response), 200

if __name__ == '__main__':
    app.run(host='0.0.0.0', port=int(sys.argv[1]))
```

Summary

In this chapter, you learned how to build your own blockchain using Python. Through this exercise, you learned the following:

- How blocks are added to the blockchain

- How the nonce in a block is found

- How to synchronize blockchains between nodes

In the next chapter, you will learn how to connect to the real blockchain, the Ethereum blockchain.

CHAPTER 4

Creating Your Own Private Ethereum Test Network

Now that you have a solid understanding of how a blockchain works, you are ready to see how to interact with one. In this chapter, you will learn how to make use of an Ethereum client to create a private Ethereum blockchain network within your local network. Doing this provides you with the chance to learn how to interact with an Ethereum blockchain without needing to worry about synchronizing with the entire mainnet (which may take up more than one terabyte of disk space on your computer).

Downloading and Installing Geth, the Ethereum Client

To get connected to the Ethereum blockchain, you need an Ethereum client, which is an application that runs as an Ethereum node on the blockchain. Using an Ethereum client, you can perform tasks such as the following:

- Mine Ethers
- Transfer Ethers from one account to another
- View block information
- Create and deploy smart contracts
- Use and interact with smart contracts

© Wei-Meng Lee 2023
W.-M. Lee, *Beginning Ethereum Smart Contracts Programming*, https://doi.org/10.1007/978-1-4842-9271-6_4

There are two main Ethereum clients that you can use to interact with the Ethereum blockchain:

- **Geth**: The official Ethereum client implemented using the Go programming language

- **Parity**: An Ethereum client written using the Rust programming language

---

Note   The preceding clients are all CLI (command line interface) clients.

For this chapter, you will use the Geth client. Geth is available for three main platforms:

- Linux

- macOS

- Windows

Also, the source of Geth is available for download at `https://github.com/ethereum/go-ethereum` if you want to learn how Geth is implemented. In the following sections, I will show you how to download and install Geth for the three main platforms.

Installing Geth for macOS

There are two ways to install Geth for macOS. The first is through the command line. To do this, you need to use **Brew**.

Tip   Homebrew (commonly known as Brew) is a free and open-source software package management system that simplifies the installation of software on Apple's macOS operating system and Linux.

If you do not have Brew, you need to install it first. To do so, in terminal, type the following command to install Brew:

```
$ /usr/bin/ruby -e "$(curl -fsSL https://raw.githubusercontent.com/
Homebrew/install/master/install)"
```

Then type the following commands to update and upgrade Brew:

```
$ brew update
$ brew upgrade
```

To install Geth in terminal, type the following commands in Terminal:

```
$ brew tap ethereum/Ethereum
$ brew install ethereum
```

Tip   To upgrade Geth to the latest version, use the command `brew upgrade Ethereum`. To find the current version of Geth installed on your computer, use the command `geth help`.

If you do not want to install Geth from terminal, the second way to install Geth is to go to `https://geth.ethereum.org/downloads/` and download Geth for macOS. Once downloaded, unzip the file and move the Geth file onto your home directory.

Installing Geth for Windows

For Windows users, the easiest way to install Geth is to go to `https://geth.ethereum.org/downloads/` and click the button for the Windows version of Geth. Once downloaded, double-click the .exe to install Geth on your Windows machine.

Tip   For Windows users, if you encounter problems running any of the commands in this book, you should use PowerShell instead of the command prompt.

Installing Geth for Linux

For Linux users, you can install Geth by downloading the version of Geth for Linux from `https://geth.ethereum.org/downloads/` and unzipping the file and moving the geth file onto your home directory.

Alternatively, you can also install Geth through terminal. In terminal, type the following commands:

```
$ sudo apt-get install software-properties-common
$ sudo add-apt-repository -y ppa:ethereum/ethereum
$ sudo apt-get update
$ sudo apt-get install ethereum
```

Geth is now installed.

Creating the Private Ethereum Test Network

In the previous section, you saw how to download and install the Geth client. One useful feature of Geth is that you can use it to create your own private test network in your local setup, without connecting to the real blockchain. This makes the development work much easier and allows you to explore the Ethereum blockchain without needing to pay for real Ether. Hence, in this section you will see how to create your own private Ethereum test network as well as how to connect to peers and perform transactions such as sending Ethers between accounts.

For this example, you are going to create a private test network of two nodes in a single computer, **node1** and **node2**, and a third node, **node3**, on another computer (see Figure 4-1).

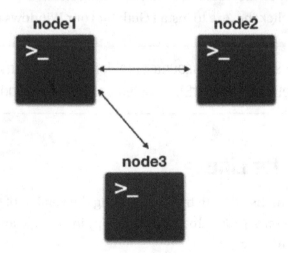

Figure 4-1. *Your private Ethereum test network*

These three nodes will form your own test network where you can do things like mining, transferring Ethers to another account, and (in the next chapter) deploying your smart contracts.

Creating the Genesis Block

Before you create your own private Ethereum test network, you need to create the *genesis block*. The genesis block is the start of the blockchain: the first block (block 0) and the only block that does not point to a predecessor block. The Ethereum protocol ensures that no other node will agree with your version of the blockchain unless they have the same genesis block, so you can make as many private testnet blockchains as you like.

For this chapter, create a folder named MyTestNet on your computer. For simplicity, create this folder in your home directory:

```
$ cd ~
$ mkdir MyTestNet
$ cd MyTestNet
```

Tip   For Windows users, the home directory is typically
C:\users\<user_name>\.

To create the genesis block, create a file named genesisblock.json and populate it as follows:

```
{
  "config": {
      "chainId": 10,
      "homesteadBlock": 0,
      "eip155Block": 0,
      "eip158Block": 0,
      "eip150Block": 0,
      "eip150Hash": "0x0000000000000000000000000000000000000000000000000
                     0000000000000000",
  },
  "alloc"       : {},
```

```
"coinbase"   : "0x0000000000000000000000000000000000000000",
"difficulty" : "0x20000",
"extraData"  : "",
"gasLimit"   : "0x2fefd8",
"nonce"      : "0x0000000000000042",
"mixhash"    : "0x0000000000000000000000000000000000000000000000000
               0000000000000",
"parentHash" : "0x0000000000000000000000000000000000000000000000000
               0000000000000",
"timestamp"  : "0x00"
}
```

Tip   The value of the difficulty key sets the rate at which new blocks will be mined. If you want to slow down the rate of mining, set this value to a higher number.

Creating a Folder for Storing Node Data

Next, you need to create a directory to store the data for all the nodes in your private test network. For this, create a directory named data in the MyTestNet folder:

```
$ cd ~/MyTestNet
$ mkdir data
```

Figure 4-2 shows the directory structure at this point.

Figure 4-2.   *The content of the MyTestNet directory*

Initiating a Blockchain Node

To create a node on the test network, you need to initialize it using the genesis block you created earlier. You can do it using the following command:

```
$ geth --datadir ~/MyTestNet/data/node1 init ~/MyTestNet/genesisblock.json
```

This code creates a node named node1 and saves all its data in the node1 directory. You should see the following response:

```
INFO [06-21|15:41:51.899] Maximum peer count
ETH=50 LES=0 total=50
INFO [06-21|15:41:51.899] Set global gas
cap                                    cap=50,000,000
INFO [06-21|15:41:51.900] Allocated cache and file
handles           database=/Users/weimenglee/MyTestNet/data/node1/geth/
chaindata cache=16.00MiB handles=16
INFO [06-21|15:41:52.009] Opened ancient database
database=/Users/weimenglee/MyTestNet/data/node1/geth/chaindata/ancient
readonly=false
INFO [06-21|15:41:52.010] Persisted trie from memory database        nodes=0
size=0.00B time="94.569µs" gcnodes=0 gcsize=0.00B gctime=0s livenodes=1
livesize=0.00B
INFO [06-21|15:41:52.010] Successfully wrote genesis state
database=chaindata hash=5e1fc7..d790e0
INFO [06-21|15:41:52.010] Allocated cache and file handles
database=/Users/weimenglee/MyTestNet/data/node1/geth/lightchaindata
cache=16.00MiB handles=16
INFO [06-21|15:41:52.121] Opened ancient database
database=/Users/weimenglee/MyTestNet/data/node1/geth/lightchaindata/ancient
readonly=false
INFO [06-21|15:41:52.121] Persisted trie from memory database        nodes=0
size=0.00B time="1.66µs"   gcnodes=0 gcsize=0.00B gctime=0s livenodes=1
livesize=0.00B
INFO [06-21|15:41:52.122] Successfully wrote genesis state
database=lightchaindata hash=5e1fc7..d790e0
```

Figure 4-3 shows the content of **node1** after this command is run.

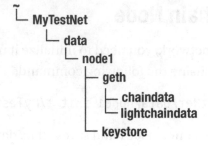

Figure 4-3. *The content of the node1 directory*

The Geth directory contains two folders for storing the blockchains, chaindata and lightchaindata, while the keystore directory contains accounts information (more on this later).

Let's create another node called **node2**:

```
$ geth --datadir ~/MyTestNet/data/node2 init ~/MyTestNet/genesisblock.json
```

Figure 4-4 shows the current state of the MyTestNet directory.

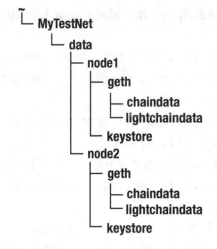

Figure 4-4. *The node2 directory is now added to the data directory*

Starting Up the Nodes

Now that the nodes have been initialized, let's start them up. Let's start up **node1**:

```
$ geth --datadir ~/MyTestNet/data/node1 console 2>console1.log
```

Once **node1** is started up, you will see the Geth JavaScript Console:

```
Welcome to the Geth JavaScript console!

instance: Geth/v1.10.26-stable/darwin-arm64/go1.19.3
at block: 0 (Thu Jan 01 1970 07:30:00 GMT+0730 (+0730))
 datadir: /Users/weimenglee/MyTestNet/data/node1
 modules: admin:1.0 debug:1.0 engine:1.0 eth:1.0 ethash:1.0 miner:1.0
net:1.0 personal:1.0 rpc:1.0 txpool:1.0 web3:1.0

To exit, press ctrl-d or type exit
>
```

Tip   The Geth JavaScript Console provides an interactive console for you to interact with the Ethereum blockchain using the JavaScript language.

The `console 2` option basically redirects the output to a file (named `console1.log` in this example). Without this redirection, Geth would continually generate a lot of output and the Geth JavaScript Console would not be usable.

Creating Accounts

Now that **node1** is started up, you can create a new account in your node using the `personal.newAccount()` function:

```
> personal.newAccount()
Passphrase: <password>
Repeat passphrase: <password>
"0x6e05a61f9414d2ecbe79ae9c70fd4a7f234be7cb"
```

Tip   The web3 object (from the web3.js library) allows you to programmatically interact with the Ethereum blockchain. It also exposes the eth object, which itself also exposes the personal object. Hence the full name for the `personal. newAccount()` function is actually web3.eth.personal.newAccount(). The personal object allows you to interact with the Ethereum node's accounts.

You will be asked to enter a password for the new account. Once that is done, the public address of the account will be displayed.

To show the list of accounts in your node, use the eth.accounts property:

```
> eth.accounts
["0x6e05a61f9414d2ecbe79ae9c70fd4a7f234be7cb"]
```

The list of accounts will be shown as an array. In the example here, there is only one account.

Once the account is created, the account details are stored in a file (named beginning with the UTC word) in the ~/MyTestNet/data/node1/keystore directory. I will talk more about this later in this chapter.

Checking the Balance of an Account

To check the balance of an account, use the eth.getBalance() function:

```
> eth.getBalance(eth.accounts[0])
0
```

Tip   As mentioned, the eth object is derived from the web3 object, so the preceding function is equivalent to web3.eth.getBalance(web3.eth.accounts[0]).

Apparently, at this moment you have no Ethers, so you will see a 0. However, note that the unit displayed for the balance is *Wei*, where 1 Ether is 1000000000000000000 Wei (1 followed by 18 zeros). You may prefer to see the units displayed in *Ether*. To make your life easier, you can use the web3.fromWei() function, like the following command, to convert the balance in Wei to Ether:

```
> web3.fromWei(eth.getBalance(eth.accounts[0]), "ether")
0
```

Table 4-1 shows the different units in Ethereum.

Table 4-1. *Units in Ethereum*

Unit	Wei Value	Wei
Wei	1 Wei	1
Kwei (babbage)	10^3 Wei	1,000
Mwei (lovelace)	10^6 Wei	1,000,000
Gwei (shannon)	10^9 Wei	1,000,000,000
Microether (szabo)	10^{12} Wei	1,000,000,000,000
Milliether (finney)	10^{15} Wei	1,000,000,000,000,000
Ether	10^{18} Wei	1,000,000,000,000,000,000

Stopping the Node

To stop the node, simply use the exit command:

> **exit**

For now, let's stop **node1**.

Starting Another Node

Now that you have started **node1** and then stopped it, let's start **node2**. In a new terminal window, type the following command:

```
$ geth --datadir ~/MyTestNet/data/node2 --port 30304 --nodiscover --networkid
2345 --authrpc.port 8547 console 2>console2.log
```

In this command, you have specified the `--port` option and set the port to 30304. This is because Geth by default uses port 30303, and if you have multiple nodes running on the same computer, each node must use a unique port number. By setting this to port 30304, it will prevent a conflict with another node using the default port. The `--nodiscover` option means that peers will not automatically discover each other and that they need to be added manually. The `--networkid` option specifies the network id so that other nodes can attach to the network with the same network id. Also note the `--authrpc.port` option. For each node, this must be set to a unique number other than the default port number 8551.

Once **node2** is started, restart **node1** with the following command:

```
$ geth --datadir ~/MyTestNet/data/node1 --networkid 2345 console
2>console1.log
```

Notice that **node1** is started with the --networkid option with the value of 2345. This is required so that it can be added as a peer to **node2** later on. Figure 4-5 shows the state of the two nodes at this moment.

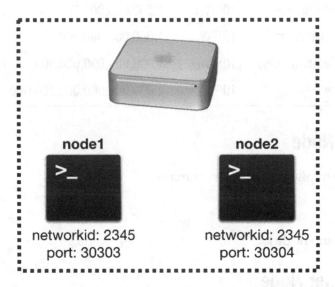

Figure 4-5. *The two nodes currently running within the same computer*

Getting Information About the Node

Now that the two nodes are up and running, let's get some detailed information about each of them. Type the following command in **node1**:

```
> admin.nodeInfo
{
  enode: "enode://970900b3e4c76e9ce2d0a9d592f2f85d89fdd341cf513a352822
  d49f62240a33c9f61423a2793e186b4abb54f6640c07cb90e366df49223888c8de56e
  c6938f7@116.87.74.126:30303",
  enr: "enr:-KO4QG1bMANDGX-m3Ncxs7exhotOWiFMImfymqs27saQ3hZsF7MVWByWplenrpw
  YQmL7ix-xOlaOeJ5OE1n1sGy78t-GAYGFN_fag2VOaMfGhHEBOw2AgmlkgnYOgmlwhHRXSn6
  Jc2VjcDI1NmsxoQOXCQCz5MdunOLQqdWS8vhdif3TQc9ROjUoItSfYiQKM4RzbmFwwINOY3CC
  dl-DdWRwgnZf",
```

```
id: "d5b2504c731b3899c7f92941c0d703477b84c79fd9c0b68d9ebad4e145799079",
ip: "116.87.74.126",
listenAddr: "[::]:30303",
name: "Geth/v1.10.19-stable/darwin-amd64/go1.18.3",
ports: {
  discovery: 30303,
  listener: 30303
},
protocols: {
  eth: {
    config: {
      chainId: 10,
      eip150Block: 0,
      eip150Hash: "0x00000000000000000000000000000000000000000000000000000000
      00000000000",
      eip155Block: 0,
      eip158Block: 0,
      homesteadBlock: 0
    },
    difficulty: 131072,
    genesis: "0x5e1fc79cb4ffa4739177b5408045cd5d51c6cf766133f23f7cd72ee1f
    8d790e0",
    head: "0x5e1fc79cb4ffa4739177b5408045cd5d51c6cf766133f23f7cd72ee
    1f8d790e0",
    network: 2345
  },
  snap: {}
}
}
```

Tip   The admin object is derived from the web3 object. Hence the full name of
admin.addPeer() is web3.admin.addPeer(). The admin object allows you to
interact with the underlying blockchain.

You will find a whole bunch of information. In particular, take note of the enode key (bolded for emphasis). At the end of the enode value, observe the port number 30303 (which port node 1 is using).

Tip   An enode describes a node in the Ethereum network in the form of an URI.

Pairing the Nodes

Copy the value of the enode key in **node1**, and in **node2**, type the following command:

```
> admin.addPeer("enode://970900b3e4c76e9ce2d0a9d592f2f85d89fdd341cf51
3a352822d49f62240a33c9f61423a2793e186b4abb54f6640c07cb90e366df49223888c8de5
6ec6938f7@127.0.0.1:30303")
```

Caution   In this example, the **127.0.0.1** refers to my computer's IP address. When pairing with another node on the same computer/network, it is important to replace this IP address with that of the IP address of your computer. If you don't do this, the two nodes will not be paired correctly.

In this command, the bolded portion is the value of the enode key of **node1**. The `admin.addPeer()` function adds a peer to the current node using the peer's enode value.

To verify that the peer is added successfully, use the `admin.peers` property:

```
> admin.peers
[{
    caps: ["eth/66", "eth/67", "snap/1"],
    enode: "enode://970900b3e4c76e9ce2d0a9d592f2f85d89fdd341cf513a352822
    d49f62240a33c9f61423a2793e186b4abb54f6640c07cb90e366df49223888c8de56e
    c6938f7@127.0.0.1:30303",
    id: "d5b2504c731b3899c7f92941c0d703477b84c79fd9c0b68d9ebad4e145799079",
    name: "Geth/v1.10.19-stable/darwin-amd64/go1.18.3",
    network: {
      inbound: false,
      localAddress: "127.0.0.1:58369",
```

```
    remoteAddress: "127.0.0.1:30303",
    static: true,
    trusted: false
  },
  protocols: {
    eth: {
      difficulty: 131072,
      head: "0x5e1fc79cb4ffa4739177b5408045cd5d51c6cf766133f23f7cd7
      2ee1f8d790e0",
      version: 67
    },
    snap: {
      version: 1
    }
  }
}]
```

If the peer is added successfully, you should see the preceding output. From the output, you can see that the **node1**'s IP address is 127.0.0.1, which is the local IP address of my computer. Figure 4-6 shows the current state of the private test network.

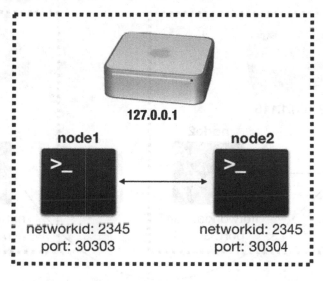

Figure 4-6. *The current state of the private test network, with two peered nodes*

Tip The admin.peers property returns a [ ] if there is currently no peer attached to the node.

So far you have been pairing the nodes within the same computer. How do you pair nodes from another computer?

Note I leave the creation of the third node as an exercise for the reader.

Suppose you have another node called **node3** running on another computer. On the Geth JavaScript Console on that node, you can add **node1** as a peer by using the following command:

```
>admin.addPeer("enode://970900b3e4c76e9ce2d0a9d592f2f85d89fdd341cf513a35282
2d49f62240a33c9f61423a2793e186b4abb54f6640c07cb90e366df49223888c8de56ec693
8f7@192.168.1.116:30303")
```

You just need to replace the IP address and port number of the node with that of the node you are trying to add to. In this example, **node1** is running on port 30303 and its IP address is 192.168.1.116. Figure 4-7 summarizes the state of the nodes at this moment.

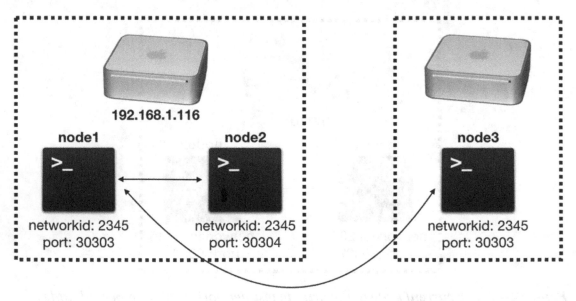

Figure 4-7. *The private test network with three connected nodes*

Performing Mining

With all the nodes connected, you can start to perform some mining operations! Before you do that, let's verify the block numbers for the current blockchain. In any of the nodes, you can use the eth.blockNumber property to display the latest block number in the blockchain:

```
> eth.blockNumber
0
```

As expected, you should see 0. This is because at this moment the blockchain has only one block: the genesis block. To start mining on **node1**, use the miner.start() function:

```
> miner.start(1)
null
```

The number you pass into the start() function is the number of threads you want to use for the mining operation. Don't be alarmed with the null result. The null simply means that the function has nothing to return to you; it does not indicate the failure of the mining operation.

Note   The miner object is derived from the web3 object.

The **node1** will now start the mining operation. On some computers, it will take a few minutes to mine the first block, while on some slower machines, it will take a much longer time. So be patient.

You can verify that a block has been mined by checking the result of the eth.blockNumber property. If the block number is more than 0, you have mined your first block! Congratulations!

And since **node2** is connected to **node1**, you can also verify the block number in **node2**. You should see the same block number.

Caution   If **node2** is not seeing the same block number as **node1**, it means that the two are not paired up correctly.

If you need to stop the mining, you can use the miner.stop() function. For now, leave the mining on.

Tip   This is a good time to check the balance of your account. If you have managed to mine a block, you should have some Ethers in your account now.

Examining a Block

You can examine the contents of a block by using the eth.getBlock() function (e.g., eth.getBlock(22)):

```
{
  difficulty: 132352,
  extraData: "0xd983010a13846765746888676f312e31382e338664617277696e",
  gasLimit: 3209750,
  gasUsed: 0,
  hash: "0xa7a89c8552d7ab22064468fd8ded5ba4759734d9f877a45351e1b00048564e4c",
  logsBloom: "0x000000000000000000000000000000000000000000000000000000000000
000000000000000000000000000000000000000000000000000000000000000000000000000
000000000000000000000000000000000000000000000000000000000000000000000000000
000000000000000000000000000000000000000000000000000000000000000000000000000
000000000000000000000000000000000000000000000000000000000000000000000000000
000000000000000000000000000000000000000000000000000000000000000000000000000
000000000000000000000000000000000000000000000000000000000000000000000000000
0000000000000000000000000",
  miner: "0x6e05a61f9414d2ecbe79ae9c70fd4a7f234be7cb",
  mixHash: "0x938bb57f4f1c68a1760c689028ef02d0ee464ea45ddd7be777205a90a91a9bd9",
  nonce: "0x43b3f9c38f75c685",
  number: 22,
  parentHash: "0xa31e844e09b21b9e2e00c9337b0c127d64b848c71fac5165cfd9b730
30bf460c",
  receiptsRoot: "0x56e81f171bcc55a6ff8345e692c0f86e5b48e01b996cadc001622f
b5e363b421",
  sha3Uncles: "0x1dcc4de8dec75d7aab85b567b6ccd41ad312451b948a7413f0a142fd
40d49347",
```

```
size: 537,
stateRoot: "0xa911ecd43f895f2e01538910d71734cdc149b1b9e0f88815c88438bb
138e81cc",
timestamp: 1655798565,
totalDifficulty: 3028096,
transactions: [],
transactionsRoot: "0x56e81f171bcc55a6ff8345e692c0f86e5b48e01b996cadc0016
22fb5e363b421",
uncles: []
}
```

The eth.getBlock() function takes in a number representing the block number that
you want to examine. One particular interesting point to note: the miner key indicates
the account that successfully mined the block.

Mining on Both Nodes

Up to this point only **node1** is doing the mining and having all the fun (and reaping all
the rewards). Why not get **node2** to do the mining too? If you try to mine on **node2** now,
you will see the following error:

```
> miner.start(1)
Error: etherbase missing: etherbase must be explicitly specified
    at web3.js:6365:9(45)
    at send (web3.js:5099:62(34))
    at <eval>:1:12(4)
```

Why? In order to perform mining, you need to have at least one account in your node
for the rewards to be deposited into. To solve this problem, create a new account using
the personal.newAccount() function. Once the account is created, you can use the
miner.start() function again.

You now have two miners mining at the same time and competing for rewards. To
know which is the miner of the latest block, you can use the eth.getBlock() function
and check its miner property like this: eth.getBlock(eth.blockNumber).miner. The
result is the address of the account that managed to mine the latest block.

Transferring Ethers Between Nodes

In **node1**, let's create another account using the personal.newAccount() function. You should now have two accounts:

```
> eth.accounts
["0x6e05a61f9414d2ecbe79ae9c70fd4a7f234be7cb",
"0xbb6f2406a8a49746f25e5b2230af7ee9d3196e9c"]
```

Let's verify how much you have in each account:

```
> eth.getBalance(eth.accounts[0])
3.376328125e+22
> eth.getBalance(eth.accounts[1])
0
```

To transfer some Ethers from one account to another account, you can use the eth.sendTransaction() function. But before you use it to transfer Ethers, you need to unlock the source account first, using the personal.unlockAccount() function:

```
> personal.unlockAccount(eth.accounts[0])
Unlock account 0x530e822163471b0e65725cbd85dc141ff6b24d59
Passphrase: <password>
true
Once the account is unlocked, you can now transfer the Ether:
> eth.sendTransaction({from: eth.accounts[0], to: eth.accounts[1], value:
web3.toWei(5,"ether")})
"0xbac74dffae71c5532d83ed8ae37ff97d68dd2ab8b7f62fa2b1032f88df8d543c"
```

Tip   If you want to transfer Ethers to another node on another computer, simply specify the address of the account you want to send to, enclosed with a pair of double quotes, like this:

```
eth.sendTransaction({from: eth.accounts[0], to: "0x9ba6f3c9cce2b172d
0a85a50101ae05f3b4c8731", value: web3.toWei(5,"ether")})
```

In this example, you are transferring five Ethers from the first account to the second account within the same node. The output of the function is the transaction ID. If you now check the balance of the two accounts and realize that they are still the same, then one of the following causes is likely:

- You are not currently mining. Remember, mining confirms transactions so that the transactions can be recorded on the blockchain. To resolve this, start mining on the node.

- If you are currently mining, it is likely that the transactions have not be confirmed yet. Wait a while and check the balance again.

After a while, you should see five Ethers in the second account:

```
> eth.getBalance(eth.accounts[1])
5000000000000000000
```

Tip   If you check the balance of the first account, you are likely to see it has less than five Ethers deducted. This is because in spite of the five Ethers deducted, it is also earning rewards doing the mining. Hence, it is easier to verify the balance of the second account.

Managing Accounts

Earlier in this chapter you learned about creating accounts in your node. I also mentioned that the account details are stored in a file with the name starting with "UTC" and saved in the ~/MyTestNet/data/node1/keystore directory. Let's dissect the content of this UTC file:

```
{
  "address": "6e05a61f9414d2ecbe79ae9c70fd4a7f234be7cb",
  "crypto": {
    "cipher": "aes-128-ctr",
    "ciphertext":
    "1f35569e89100cd6d03c7de8780a913f54129cdbce0290a3b39a798391bd2674",
    "cipherparams": {
```

```
      "iv": "0ffbe973059db7a0226cd6fced92e50d"
    },
    "kdf": "scrypt",
    "kdfparams": {
      "dklen": 32,
      "n": 262144,
      "p": 1,
      "r": 8,
      "salt": "d2c73712f61b236beb22c783502a50166049a46b0aa29503a90d2f8a4227741c"
    },
    "mac": "432ab5429c423c3c9e545397f53c64ddc6a900a6ab7dc255a58cf5da9f629242"
  },
  "id": "b9e36890-b2ff-4fdd-af90-f157f352e6bc",
  "version": 3
}
```

This shows the contents of the first account in **node1** with the file name UTC-
-2022-06-21T07-44-59.385557000Z--6e05a61f9414d2ecbe79ae9c70fd4a7f234be7cb.

It contains the following:

- Your encrypted private key (encrypted using your supplied password)

- The public key is not stored in the JSON file as it can be derived
  from the private key. The corresponding public key for the private
  key is derived from the private key using the ECDSA (Elliptic Curve
  Signature) algorithm.

- From the public key derived, compute a keccak256 hash.

- From the keccak256 hash, take the last 20 bytes (which is 40
  hexadecimals), prefix it with "0x", and this is your Ethereum account
  address.

Figure 4-8 summarizes how your account address is derived.

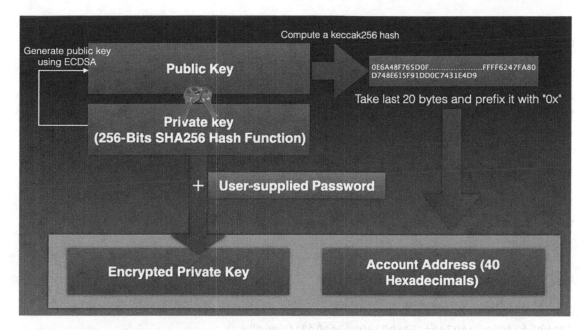

Figure 4-8. *Understanding how the account information is derived*

Tip   Curious about your private key? Import the JSON file into MetaMask and your account will be imported into MetaMask. You can now export the private key of this imported account in MetaMask.

Removing Accounts

Once you use the `personal.newAccount()` function, the account is created. There is no equivalent function to remove the account. The easiest way to delete the account is to go to the ~/MyTestNet/data/node1/keystore directory and delete the UTC file corresponding to the account that you want to delete.

Setting the Coinbase

The `eth.coinbase` property returns the account within the node that all the mining rewards go to. In **node1**, your coinbase is your first account:

```
> eth.coinbase
"0x6e05a61f9414d2ecbe79ae9c70fd4a7f234be7cb"
```

109

To change the coinbase, you can use the `miner.setEtherbase()` function. Let's try it now.

First, print out the accounts you have in **node1**:

```
> eth.accounts
["0x6e05a61f9414d2ecbe79ae9c70fd4a7f234be7cb",
"0xbb6f2406a8a49746f25e5b2230af7ee9d3196e9c"]
```

Let's change the coinbase to the second account:

```
> miner.setEtherbase(eth.accounts[1])
```
true

Once this is done, you can verify if the coinbase has indeed been changed to the second account:

```
> eth.coinbase
"0xbb6f2406a8a49746f25e5b2230af7ee9d3196e9c"
```

Summary

In this chapter, you learned how to use Geth to create your own private Ethereum test network. You learned how to create accounts in your node, connect to other nodes, transfer Ethers between nodes, and more. Deploying your own test network is much more efficient than using one of Ethereum's test network. What's more, it allows you to experiment and have a deeper understanding of Ethereum.

CHAPTER 5

Using the MetaMask Crypto-Wallet

In the previous chapter, you learned how to create your own private Ethereum test network using Geth so that you can try out the various Ethereum transactions, such as transferring Ethers to different accounts and performing mining. You also learned how to create accounts so that you can hold your own Ethers. In this chapter, you will learn how to use a Chrome extension known as **MetaMask**. The MetaMask Chrome extension is an Ethereum crypto-wallet that allows you to hold your Ethereum account(s), and it is an essential tool to help you develop and test smart contracts in the next few chapters.

What Is MetaMask?

MetaMask is a very useful tool that plays a pivotal role in allowing you to make your foray into the world of blockchain. Rather than attempt to define what exactly MetaMask is in one paragraph, I will talk about the role played by MetaMask as we go along.

First and foremost, MetaMask is an Ethereum crypto-wallet. It allows you to do the following:

- Create accounts for use in the various Ethereum networks

- Maintain the private keys for your accounts so you can export them or import new accounts

- Switch between the various Ethereum networks so that your accounts can reflect the correct balance for each network

- Perform transactions between accounts

- Transfer Ethers from one account to another

© Wei-Meng Lee 2023
W.-M. Lee, *Beginning Ethereum Smart Contracts Programming*, https://doi.org/10.1007/978-1-4842-9271-6_5

- Hold tokens in your MetaMask accounts

- View detail transactions on Etherscan, a blockchain explorer

- Swap between Ethers and tokens on decentralized exchanges (DEX)

Note   Besides being an Ethereum wallet, MetaMask also allows you to interact with the Ethereum blockchain by injecting a JavaScript library called web3.js, developed by the Ethereum core team. I will discuss this more in the next chapter when I discuss smart contracts.

How MetaMask Works Behind the Scenes

Behind the scenes, MetaMask connects to a server called INFURA (`https://infura.io/`). INFURA maintains Ethereum nodes that connect to the respective Ethereum networks. Rather than allowing INFURA to keep your private keys (which is always a security risk when your private key is kept in the cloud held by a third party), INFURA allows MetaMask to keep your private keys of your accounts on your local computer and simply relay the transactions to the network. Figure 5-1 shows the relationships between MetaMask, INFURA, and the Ethereum network.

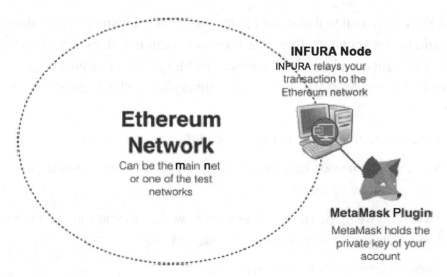

Figure 5-1. *How MetaMask works behind the scene*

When MetaMask connects to one of the Ethereum networks, it connects to one of the respective INFURA nodes through their RPC URLs:

- **Main Ethereum Network:** `https://mainnet.infura.io/v3/`

- **Goerli Test Network:** `https://goerli.infura.io/v3/`

- **Sepolia Test Network:** `https://sepolia.infura.io/v3/`

Caution   Prior to the Merge (where Ethereum switched from using PoW to PoS), most developers used the Ropsten test network. However, the Ropsten test network has been deprecated after the Merge. You should use the Goerli test network instead.

Installing MetaMask

The easiest way to install MetaMask is to use the Chrome browser and install MetaMask as a Chrome extension. To install the MetaMask extension,

---

Note   You can use the MetaMask extension on Chrome, Mozilla Firefox, Brave, and Microsoft Edge browsers.

- Launch Chrome and navigate to the Chrome Web Store at `https://chrome.google.com/webstore/category/extensions`.

- Search for MetaMask.

- You should see the MetaMask extension in the search result. Click **Add to Chrome** (see Figure 5-2).

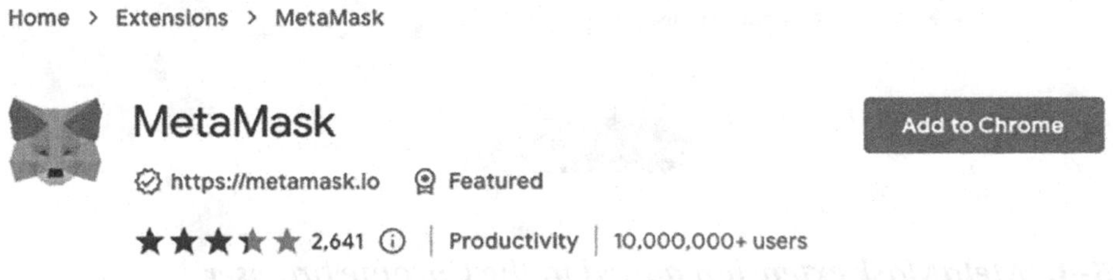

Home > Extensions > MetaMask

MetaMask

⊘ https://metamask.io   ⨀ Featured

★★★☆★ 2,641 ⓘ │ Productivity │ 10,000,000+ users

Add to Chrome

Figure 5-2. Searching for MetaMask in the Chrome Web Store

- You will be prompted to add MetaMask to Chrome. Click **Add extension** (see Figure 5-3).

Figure 5-3. *Adding the MetaMask extension to the Chrome browser*

- Once MetaMask is added to Chrome, you will see the screen shown in Figure 5-4. Click **Get Started**.

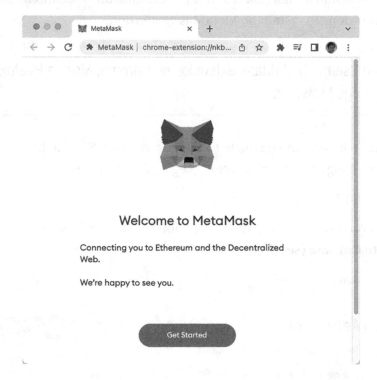

Figure 5-4. *MetaMask extension added to the Chrome browser*

Setting Up the Accounts

If you are using MetaMask for the first time, click **Create a Wallet** (see Figure 5-5).

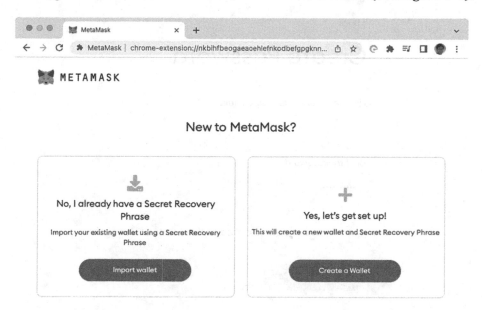

Figure 5-5. *Creating a new wallet*

Read through the terms and conditions and if you are agreeable, click **I agree**. Next, create a password to secure your account. Click **Create** once you are done with this step (see Figure 5-6).

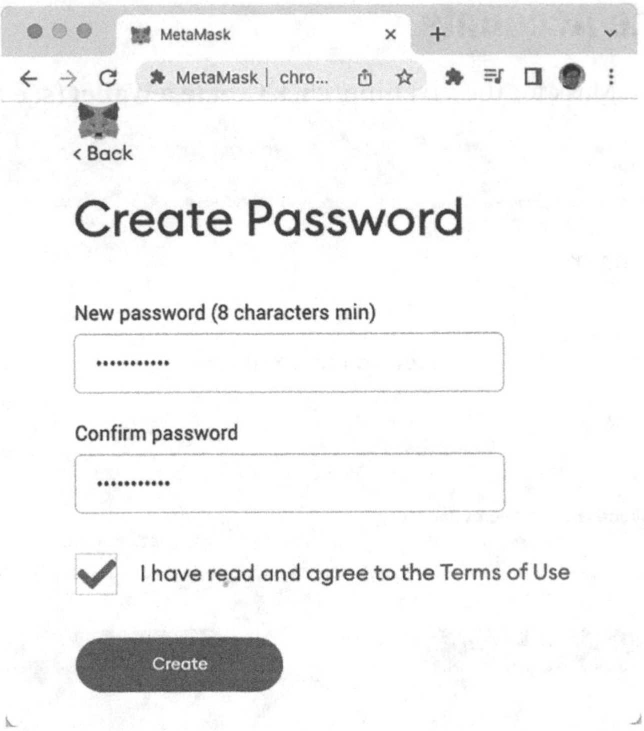

Figure 5-6. *Entering a password to secure your wallet*

You can watch a short video to understand how your account can be recovered if you ever forget your password. Once you are done, click **Next**.

You will be shown your Secret Recovery Phrase. The Secret Recovery Phrase is a set of words that allows you to recover and restore all your accounts. This set of words is something that you need to keep under lock and key. I personally suggest you print it out and lock it in a secure place.

To reveal your Secret Recovery Phrase, click the lock icon (see Figure 5-7).

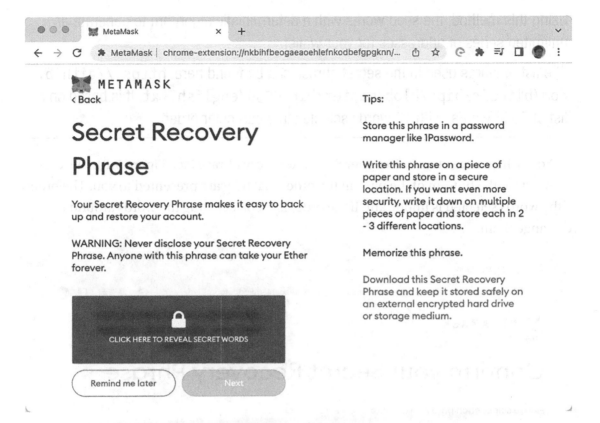

Figure 5-7. *Revealing the 12-word secret phrase*

You can see your Secret Recovery Phrase. Ensure that no one except you knows these 12 words.

Tip   The 12-word secret phrase allows you to recover your account if you forget your password. This 12-word secret phrase is known as the BIP39 (Bitcoin Improvement Proposals) *seed phrase*. MetaMask uses the BIP39 protocol to figure out how to use a 12-word secret phrase to get a *seed*. This seed is used to generate a root key for each cryptocurrency (in the case of Ethereum, it is Ether).

The root key is then hashed to generate a *private key*, which is used to generate a *public key*, which in turn is used to generate the *public address* for an account. To generate a second account (and third account, and so on), the first private key is used to derive a set of child keys, which are then used to generate their respective public keys, and so on.

117

Using this method, the seed works with a deterministic algorithm to generate an unlimited series of addresses for your wallet.

The list of words used in the secret phrase can be found here: `https://github.com/bitcoin/bips/blob/master/bip-0039/english.txt`. It is based on a list of 2048 words, with 12 words selected in a particular order.

You will be asked to confirm your Secret Recovery Phrase (see Figure 5-8). Click on the words at the bottom of the page in the order that they are presented to you. The order of the words selected is important. If the order is incorrect, drag the words around to rearrange them.

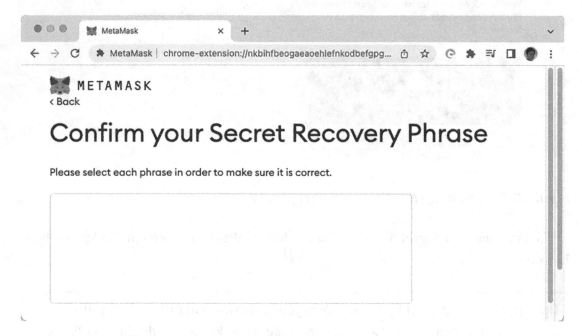

Figure 5-8. *Confirming the Secret Recovery Phrase*

Click **Confirm** when you are done arranging the words. That's it! Your account is now set up!

Using the MetaMask Extension

On the top-right corner of your Chrome browser, you should see the extension icon. Click it (see Figure 5-9).

Figure 5-9. *Locating the extension icon on Chrome*

Click the pin icon displayed next to the MetaMask icon (see Figure 5-10).

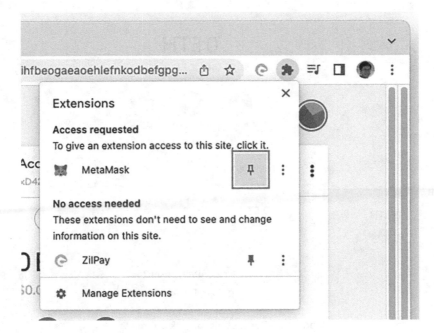

Figure 5-10. *Pinning MetaMask to Chrome*

The MetaMask icon (the icon with the fox) will be pinned on the browser. Click it and you will see the default Account 1 (see Figure 5-11).

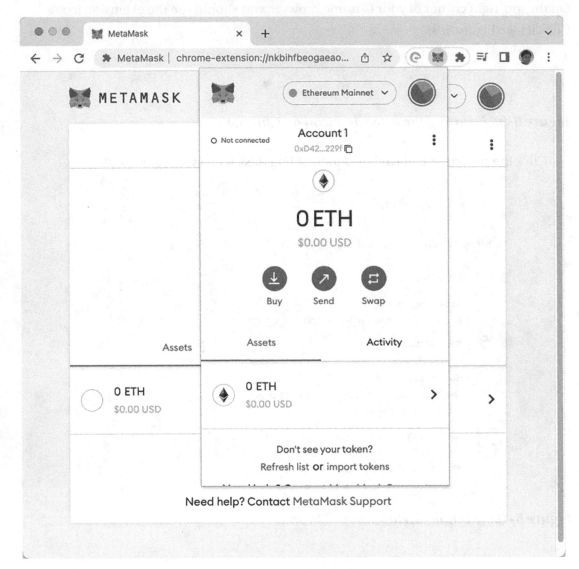

Figure 5-11. *Viewing the MetaMask wallet*

Selecting Ethereum Networks

By default, MetaMask is connected to the Main Ethereum Network. This is the real network where real Ethers are used for transactions, running smart contracts, and so on. For development purposes, you do not want to connect to the real network. Rather, you should connect to one of the test networks available:

- Goerli Test Network

- Sepolia Test Network

MetaMask allows you to connect to either of these test networks (see Figure 5-12).

Tip By default, the test networks are hidden in MetaMask. To view the test networks, click the icon displayed next to the Ethereum Mainnet dropdown list, select Settings | Advanced, and turn on the **Show test networks** option.

In addition, MetaMask also allows you to connect to a local Ethereum node listening at port 8545. It also allows you to connect to a custom RPC host.

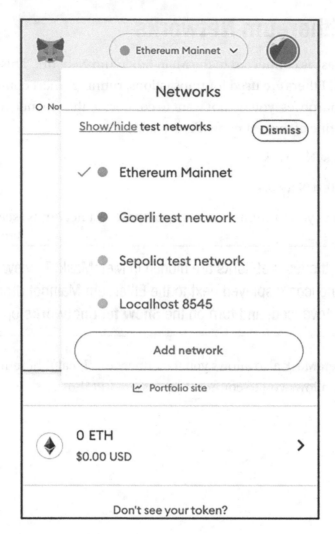

Figure 5-12. *Selecting the Ethereum network to connect to*

For this chapter, you will use the Goerli Test Network, so select it in MetaMask.

Getting Test Ethers

Once you are connected to the Goerli Test Network, the first thing to do is to get some free test Ethers so you can use them to pay for transacting on the network.

To get free Ethers,

- Go to the Goerli Facuet page located at `https://goerlifaucet.com/` (see Figure 5-13).

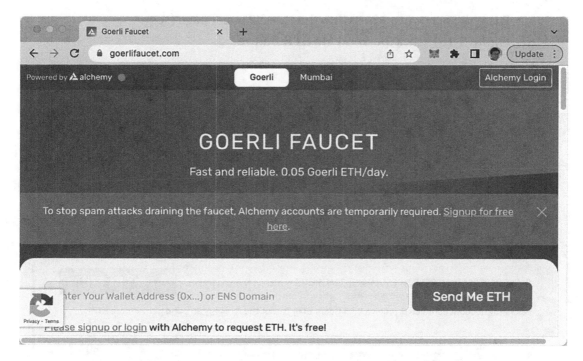

Figure 5-13. *Get free Ethers for your account using the Goerli Faucet page*

- Register for a free Alchemy account at `https://auth.alchemy.com/signup`. Once you have signed up with Alchemy, go back to the Goerli Faucet page and sign in.

- Copy the address of your account in MetaMask (see Figure 5-14).

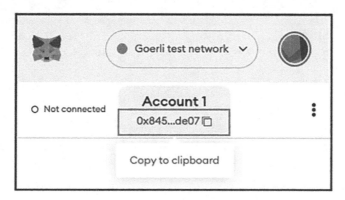

Figure 5-14. *Copying the address of your account in MetaMask*

- Paste the account address into the Goerli Faucet page (see Figure 5-15). Click the **Send Me ETH** button.

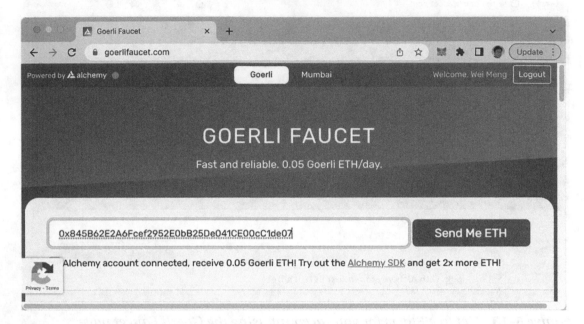

Figure 5-15. *Getting free Ethers from the Goerli faucet*

- At the bottom of the Goerli Faucet page, you will see a transaction hyperlink (see Figure 5-16). Clicking it allows you to see the status of the transaction on Etherscan.

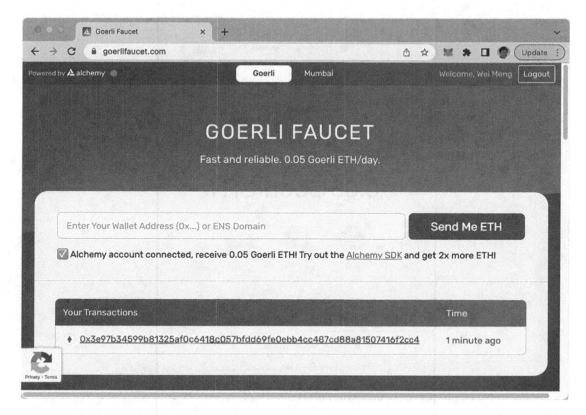

Figure 5-16. *The link to the transaction on Etherscan*

Tip   Etherscan is an Ethereum Blockchain Explorer. It allows you to search the blockchain for transactions, addresses, tokens, prices, and activities happening on the blockchain.

- After a while, you should see 0.05 Ethers deposited into your account (see Figure 5-17).

Tip   You can only request 0.05 free Ethers every 24 hours (this is the policy at the time of writing). If you want more, try setting up MetaMask on multiple computers and create additional Alchemy accounts.

Figure 5-17. *The free Ether(s) credited into your account*

It is important to remember that the amount of Ethers in your account is valid only for the particular Ethereum network that you have obtained it from. For example, if you switch to another test network, say the Sepolia Test Network, you should see 0 for your account balance.

Creating Additional Accounts

MetaMask allows you to create multiple accounts. This is useful when you want to learn how to transfer Ethers from one account to another. It is also useful when testing and debugging your smart contracts.

To create additional accounts in MetaMask,

- Click the colored icon located at the top right corner of MetaMask (see Figure 5-18).

Figure 5-18. *Creating new accounts in MetaMask*

- Click the **Create account** item.

- In the NEW ACCOUNT screen, click **Create**.

- You will see the new account created (Account 2, see Figure 5-19).

Figure 5-19. *The second newly created account*

Tip   You can create as many accounts as you want. In fact, for testing your smart contracts, you should create at least three accounts for testing purposes.

- To switch between accounts, click the colored icon (see Figure 5-20) and select the account you want to switch to.

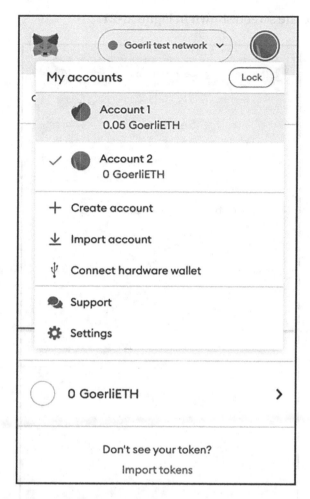

Figure 5-20. *Switching between accounts in MetaMask*

Transferring Ethers

MetaMask allows you to transfer Ethers from one account to another very easily. You can transfer to another account within MetaMask or an external account using its public address.

To transfer Ethers from one account to another,

- Switch to Account 1.

- Click the **SEND** button.

- You will see the screen shown in Figure 5-21.

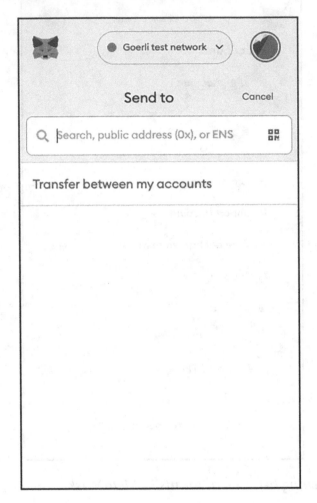

Figure 5-21. *Sending Ethers to another account*

- To send Ethers to another local account, click the **Transfer between my accounts** item. Select Account 2 in this example (see Figure 5-22).

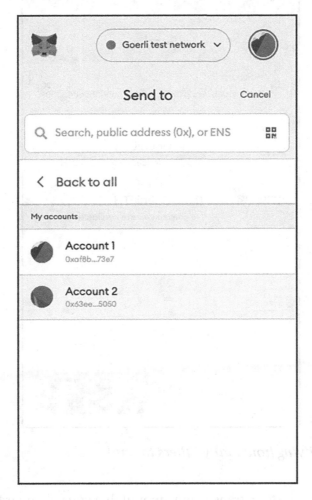

Figure 5-22. *Selecting which account to send the Ethers to*

Tip   To send Ethers to an external account, enter the account address of the recipient, or click the QR code icon and you will be able to use your Webcam to scan the QR code of the public address of the external account.

- Specify how many Ethers you want to send (0.01 in this example; see Figure 5-23). Click **Next**.

Figure 5-23. *Specifying how many Ethers to send*

- You will see the total transaction amount that you will incur for this transaction (see Figure 5-24). Click **Confirm** (you need to scroll down the page).

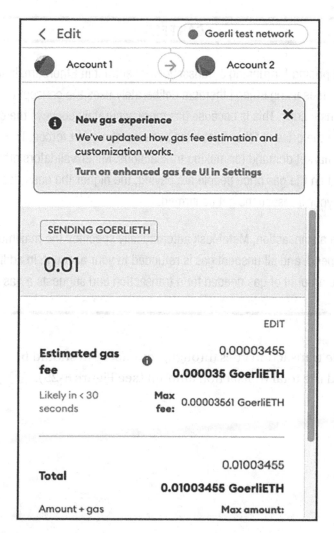

Figure 5-24. *Confirming the transaction*

Note   The total transaction amount is the amount of Ethers you are transferring plus the transaction fee. The transaction fee is also known as the *gas fee*.

GAS FEES

Gas is the internal pricing for running a transaction or contract in Ethereum. Instead of pricing transaction fees using Ether, Ethereum deliberately uses the concept of gas as the unit for pricing transactions. This is because gas more accurately conveys the complexity of computation, while the price of Ether fluctuates because of market forces. The price of gas is decided by the market demand for making transactions. Miner/validators often process transactions based on the gas price people are paying; the higher the gas price you are paying, the faster your transactions get confirmed.

When you perform a transaction, MetaMask automatically specifies the maximum amount of gas you want to spend, and all unspent gas is refunded to your account. In addition, MetaMask also calculates the amount of gas needed for a transaction and suggests a gas price for your transaction.

- When the transaction goes through, your account should be deducted the total transaction amount (see Figure 5-25).

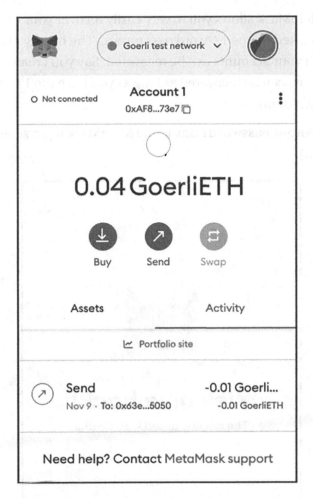

Figure 5-25. *Your account balance after the transfer*

- You can verify that the Ethers have been transferred to Account 2 by switching to Account 2.

Recovering Accounts

MetaMask has an inbuilt system that allows you to recover your accounts safely and securely. There are a few possible scenarios when you would need to recover your accounts:

- You forgot your password to log into MetaMask.

- You need to transfer your account from one computer to another (perhaps you have a new computer or lost your old one).

In either case, MetaMask allows you to very easily recover your existing accounts provided you have backed up the 12-word pass phrase. The beauty of using the 12-word pass phrase is that all your accounts can be recovered. Say you created three accounts in MetaMask. All accounts can be recovered as long as you have the 12-word pass phrase.

To recover your accounts,

- Click the **Forgot password?** link in the MetaMask login screen (see Figure 5-26).

Figure 5-26. *Recovering your account(s) using the 12-word secret seed phrase*

- You will be redirected to a web page that allows you to reset your wallet.

- Enter the 12-word seed phrase in the exact order provided to you (see Figure 5-27). You also need to assign a new password to protect your account. Click **Restore**.

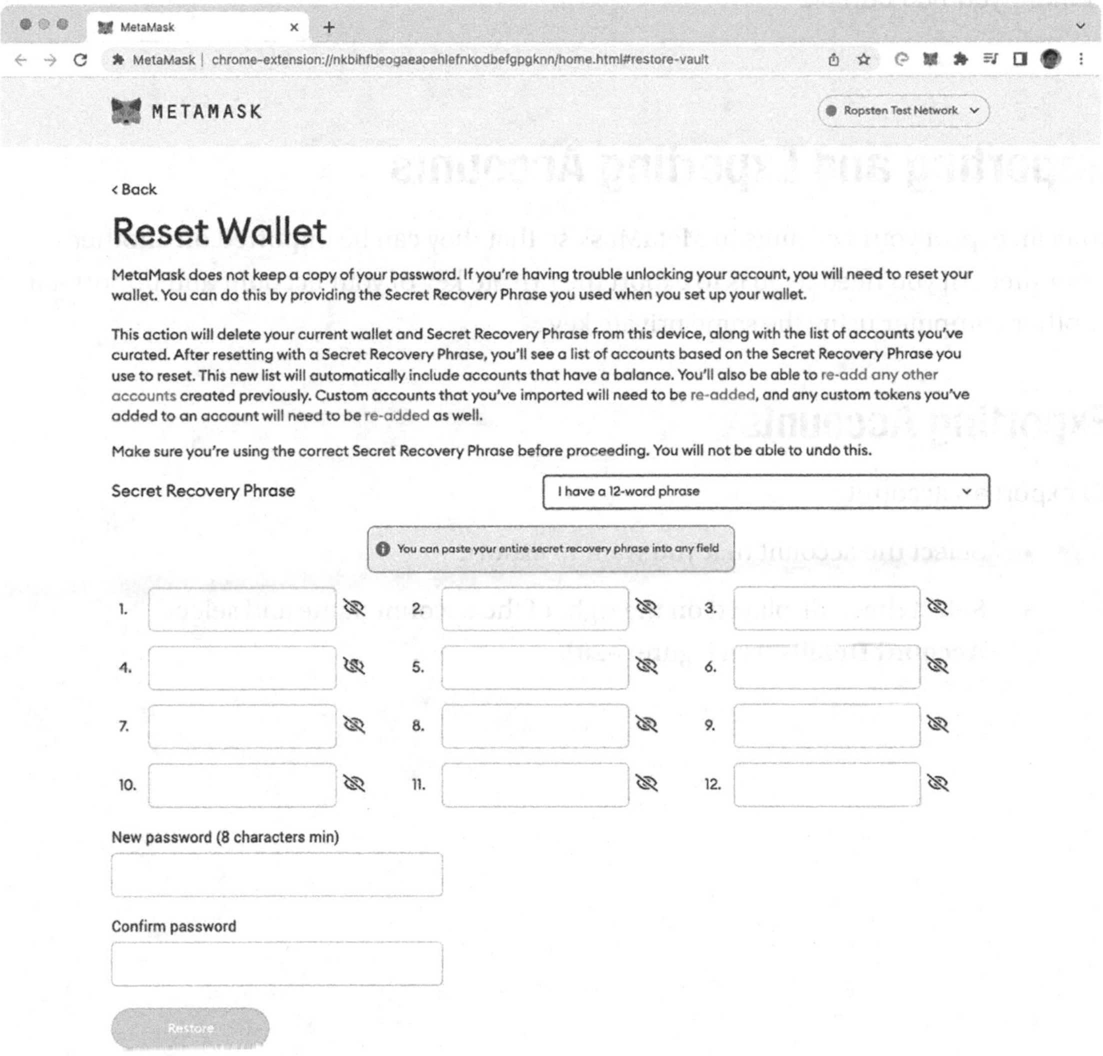

Figure 5-27. Restoring your accounts and resetting your password

- You will now find your original Account 1 and Account 2. In fact, all accounts you created earlier that had a non-zero balance are recovered automatically.

Note   You should see the Account 1 and Account 2 with the same amount of Ethers you had earlier.

Importing and Exporting Accounts

You can export your accounts in MetaMask so that they can be imported on another computer. All you need to do is to export the private key of your account and import it in another computer using the same private key.

Exporting Accounts

To export an account,

- Select the account that you want to export.

- Select the ... displayed on the right of the account name and select **Account Details** (see Figure 5-28).

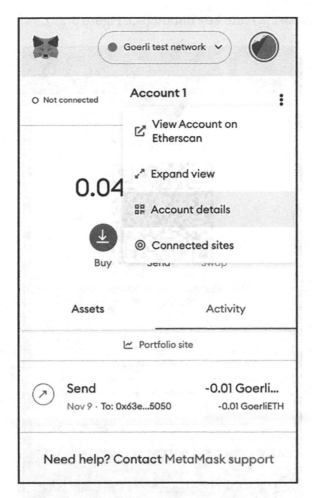

Figure 5-28. *Viewing your account details*

- Click the **Export private key** button (see Figure 5-29).

Figure 5-29. *Exporting the private key for your account*

- Enter your MetaMask password and click **Confirm** (see Figure 5-30).

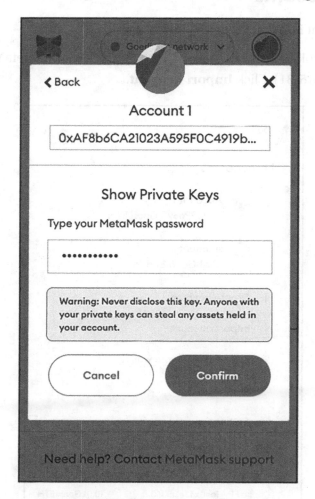

Figure 5-30. *Viewing the private key for your account*

- You should now see your private key. Click it to copy it to the clipboard and save it securely to a text file.

Caution   When dealing with accounts in the Main Ethereum Network, do be very cautious when exporting your private key and be sure to save it in a secure location. Once the private key is leaked, the assets in your account can be stolen easily. Of course, when dealing with one of the test networks, it is far less important because the assets in the test networks have no monetary value.

Importing Accounts

To import an account into MetaMask,

- Click the colored icon located at the top right corner of MetaMask (see Figure 5-31). Click **Import Account**.

Figure 5-31. Importing an existing account

- Paste the private key into the text box as shown in Figure 5-32. Click **Import**. The account is now be imported into MetaMask.

Tip   You can only import a new account based on a private key that is not already in your MetaMask. If not, the import will not be successful. Also, for accounts that you have imported using their private keys, they are not recoverable using the 12-word secret phrase. To restore these accounts, you have to use their private key or JSON file.

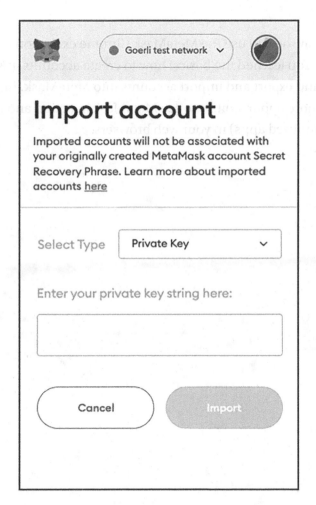

Figure 5-32. *Pasting the private key to import the account*

Tip   There are two ways to import accounts into MetaMask: using private key or JSON File. In Chapter 4, you learned about the accounts stored in the JSON files. This is what you can use to import the accounts in Geth into the MetaMask.

Summary

In this chapter, you saw how to use the MetaMask Chrome extension to manage your Ethereum accounts. You learned the basics: how to create accounts, transfer Ethers between accounts, and export and import accounts into MetaMask. In the following chapters, you have more opportunities to see MetaMask in action and how it helps you to run dapps (decentralized apps) in your web browsers.

CHAPTER 6

Getting Started with Smart Contracts

In the previous chapter, you learned how to manage your Ethers using the MetaMask Chrome extension and how to get test Ethers from the Goerli testnet. In this chapter, you will learn about one of the most interesting and exciting features of Ethereum: smart contracts. You will get a quick look at what a smart contract looks like as well as how to test it. In the next few chapters, you will dive into the details of smart contracts.

What Is a Smart Contract?

A smart contract is essentially an application residing on the blockchain that can write values onto the blockchain itself. As all the data recorded on the blockchain are immutable and traceable, smart contracts allow you to make use of the blockchain as a backing store for storing data that are permanent (such as student examination results) so that you can use it as a form of proof later on.

© Wei-Meng Lee 2023
W.-M. Lee, *Beginning Ethereum Smart Contracts Programming*, https://doi.org/10.1007/978-1-4842-9271-6_6

Figure 6-1 shows the conceptual idea behind smart contracts.

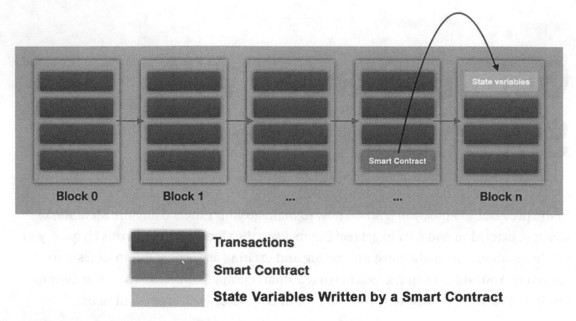

Figure 6-1. *Besides storing transactions, a blockchain also contains smart contracts, which can write values onto the blockchain itself*

Besides storing transactions, a programmable blockchain (such as Ethereum) can also store smart contracts. When a smart contract is invoked (every smart contract deployed onto the blockchain has an address), the smart contract can execute code much like an application can (though there are several restrictions on what a smart contract can and cannot do). Typically, a smart contract can write values (commonly referred to as **state variables**) onto the blockchain.

Besides writing values onto the blockchain, smart contracts can also transfer funds (such as tokens and cryptos) between accounts. This opens a lot of possibilities for developers to write interesting applications that run on the blockchain. Decentralized lottery apps, anyone?

How Smart Contracts Are Executed

A smart contract basically has two main types of functions:

- Functions that write values onto the blockchain and hence change the state of the blockchain

- Functions that read from the blockchain

Note   When you call a smart contract function that writes to the blockchain, you are essentially performing a transaction that changes the state of the storage on the blockchain.

When you call a function that changes the state of the blockchain (such as saving the examination result of a student onto the blockchain), all miners/validators will execute the smart contract function (using the EVM; more on this in the sidebar) and add the state changes onto the block so that it can be prepared for mining/validation and ultimately be added onto the blockchain.

Note   Essentially, when you call a function that changes the state of the blockchain, multiple nodes will run the same function and try to add the state changes into the block. Ultimately, only the winning miner/validator will add the block to the blockchain.

For functions that read from the blockchain and do not make any state changes to the blockchain, the node that is connected to the caller of the function executes the function and directly reads the value from its local copy of the blockchain and then returns the value back to the caller. This is more straightforward and only involve one node.

ETHEREUM VIRTUAL MACHINE (EVM)

The EVM is a sandboxed execution environment on nodes that run smart contracts. The EVM is *turing-complete*, which means that it is capable of running any programs that can (for the most part) solve any reasonable computational problems.

Today, you will often hear the phrase *EVM compatibility*. It means that a particular blockchain supports smart contracts that are compatible with Ethereum virtual machines. This allows your smart contract written in Solidly (or any other languages supported by Ethereum) to run on other blockchains without modifications.

Your First Smart Contract

You are now ready to write your first smart contract. To do this, you can use any of your favorite code editors, such as Visual Studio Code or even vi.

Tip   Visual Studio Code has several Solidity extensions that you can install to make the writing of smart contracts easy.

My personal favorite is the **Remix IDE**. The Remix IDE is a suite of tools for interacting with the Ethereum blockchain. It can compile your smart contract into bytecode, generate the ABI (application binary interface), and deploy your contracts into the various Ethereum test networks (as well as the real Ethereum blockchain). The ability to compile the contract on the fly makes it a very handy tool for learning smart contract programming. Hence, I strongly recommend that you use it to write your contracts.

For this book, use the Remix IDE for writing smart contracts.

Note   To compile a Solidity smart contract, you need to use the **solc** compiler. But if you use the Remix IDE, you don't have to explicitly use it to compile your contract.

Using the Remix IDE

To use the Remix IDE, launch the Chrome browser and load the following URL: https://remix.ethereum.org/. You will see the Remix IDE as shown in Figure 6-2.

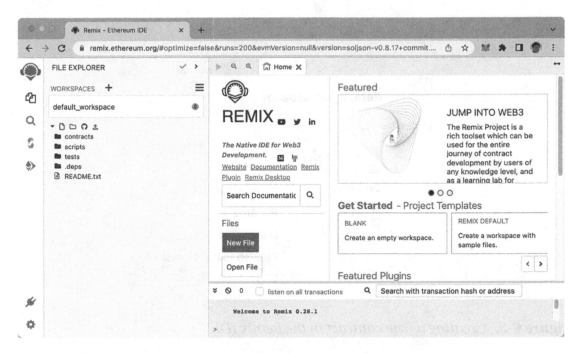

Figure 6-2. *Using the Remix IDE to create your smart contract*

Tip   All contracts created using the Remix IDE are stored locally in your browser cache.

To create a new contract, right-click the contracts item and select New File (see Figure 6-3). You will be asked to give a new name to your newly created contract. Name it as **calculator.sol** and press Enter.

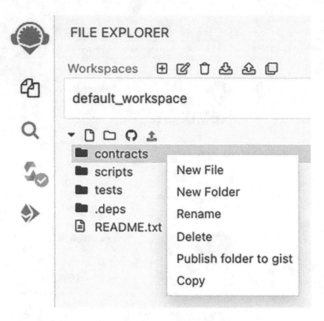

Figure 6-3. *Creating a new contract in the Remix IDE*

Let's now create a simple contract named `Calculator`. Populate the Remix IDE with the following:

```
// SPDX-License-Identifier: MIT
pragma solidity ^0.8;

contract Calculator {
  function arithmetics(uint num1, uint num2) public
    pure returns (uint sum, uint product) {
    sum = num1 + num2;
    product = num1 * num2;
  }

  function multiply(uint num1, uint num2) public
    pure returns (uint) {
    return num1 * num2;
  }
}
```

Let's dissect the code and see how it works, and then you can run it and see the result.

The first line in the contract specifies the type of license the contract uses. This was introduced in Solidity 0.6.8. The MIT License is a permissive free software license originating at the Massachusetts Institute of Technology in the late 1980s. As a permissive license, it puts only very limited restrictions on reuse and has, therefore, high license compatibility.

Next, the `pragma solidity` statement is a directive that tells the compiler that the source code is written for a specific version of Solidity. In this case, it is compatible with version 0.8.x (e.g., versions 0.8.1, 0.8.17, etc.). However, it is not compatible with versions such as 0.7 or 0.9.

Next, the `contract` keyword (think of it as the `class` keyword in languages like C# and Java) defines the contract named `Calculator`. It contains two functions:

- `arithmetics`: This function takes in two arguments, `num1` and `num2`, of type `uint` (unsigned integer). It has a `public` access modifier, and it returns a tuple containing two members, `sum` and `product`, each of type `uint`. The two statements within the function compute the sum and products of the two arguments, and their values are automatically returned from the function.

- `multiply`: This function is similar to the preceding function, except that the return statement is a little different. Here, you specify that you want to return a single value of type `uint`, but you do not specify the name of the variable to return. Instead, you use the `return` keyword to return the specific variable.

Notice that both functions have the `pure` keyword in their declaration. The `pure` keyword indicates that the function will not access nor change the value of *state variables*. The use of this keyword is important; as no modification is made to the blockchain, values can be returned without network verifications. As such, it is also free to call this function without needing any gas.

Note   State variables are storage on the blockchain used to store values, such as the variables you declare in your contract. I will discuss more about state variables in the next chapter.

Compiling the Contract

The Remix IDE allows you to automatically compile the code as you type. To enable this, select the **Compile** tab on the left side of the screen and check the **Auto compile** option, as shown in Figure 6-4. If there are any warnings, you will see them here.

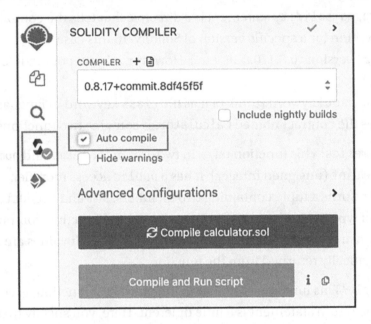

Figure 6-4. *The Remix IDE automatically compiles your code as you type*

If there is a syntax error, an error will appear under the **Compile** tab (see Figure 6-5). Clicking the error brings you to the code. In this example, a statement is missing a semicolon (;) at the end of the line, which can be fixed easily.

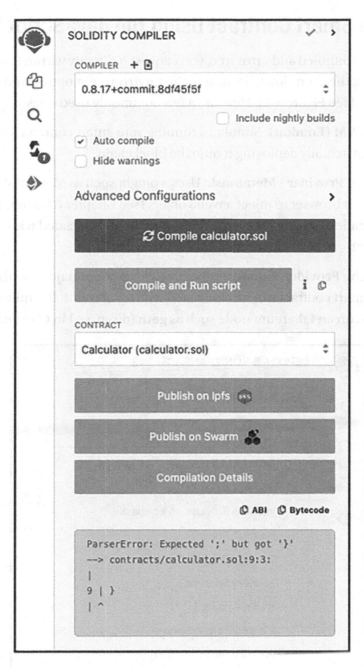

Figure 6-5. *Viewing the syntax error*

Testing the Smart Contract Using the JavaScript VM

Once the code is compiled and error free, you can test it directly within Remix IDE. Click the **Run** tab. Click the drop-down list next to the **Environment** option and you should see a few options (see Figure 6-6). Here are a few commonly used ones:

- **Remix VM (London)**: Simulates running your smart contract locally without actually deploying it onto the blockchain.

- **Injected Provider - Metamask**: Uses a plugin such as MetaMask in your web browser to inject a **web3** object (see Chapter 8 for more information) so that your smart contract can be associated with an account.

- **Ganache Provider**: Connects directly to an Ethereum node so that your smart contract can be associated with an account. It requires you to run an Ethereum node such as **geth** (discussed in Chapter 4).

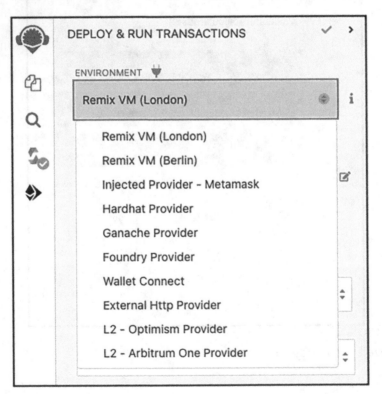

Figure 6-6. *The Remix VM allows you to test your code directly*

Tip   Notice that there is a Remix VM (London) and Remix VM (Berlin). They are flavors of the JavaScript VM built into the Remix IDE. Berlin was released earlier than London and hence Remix VM (London) is much more supported.

Select Remix VM (London) so you can test the contract without deploying it to a blockchain.

Next, click the **Deploy** button (see Figure 6-7). You should see your contract under the **Deployed Contracts** section.

Figure 6-7. *Deploying and testing your smart contract in the Remix IDE*

Click the arrow icon displayed to the left of the Calculator contract to reveal the two functions in your contract, each displayed in a blue box.

Enter the text as shown in Figure 6-8 and click the **arithmetics** button. The result will be displayed underneath it.

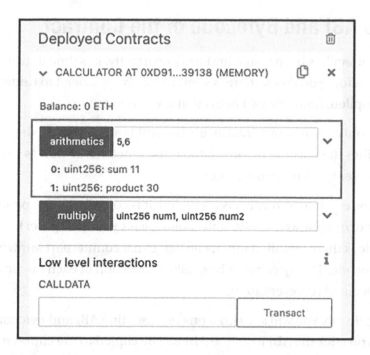

Figure 6-8. *Testing the first function in the smart contract*

Tip   The color of the button serves a purpose. A blue button means that it is free to call the function. A red button, on the other hand, means that you need to incur gas to call it. You will see a red button in the next chapter.

Enter the numbers for the next button and click it (Figure 6-9). You will see its output.

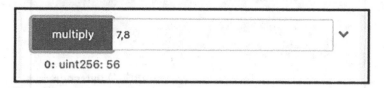

Figure 6-9. *Testing the second function in the smart contract*

Getting the ABI and Bytecode of the Contract

Now that the contract has been tested and works correctly, it is time to test it on a real blockchain. But before you do so, there is something else you need to understand. When a contract is compiled, there are two items that are generated:

- **ABI** (application binary interface): The ABI is a JSON string that describes the makeup of the contract: the functions as well as the parameter types of each function.

- **Bytecode**: When a contract is compiled, it is compiled into opcodes (think of opcode as the assembly language for your computer). Each opcode is then compiled into its hexadecimal counterpart known as bytecode. The bytecode is basically a collection of each opcode's hexadecimal representation.

In the **Compile** tab, you will see two icons representing ABI and bytecode (see Figure 6-10). If you click the ABI icon, the ABI will be copied to the clipboard.

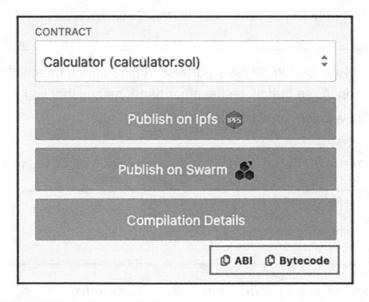

Figure 6-10. *The ABI and Bytecode buttons provide easy access to the ABI and bytecode of the contract*

The ABI looks like the following:

```
[
    {
        "inputs": [
            {
                "internalType": "uint256",
                "name": "num1",
                "type": "uint256"
            },
            {
                "internalType": "uint256",
                "name": "num2",
                "type": "uint256"
            }
        ],
        "name": "arithmetics",
        "outputs": [
            {
                "internalType": "uint256",
                "name": "sum",
                "type": "uint256"
            },
            {
                "internalType": "uint256",
                "name": "product",
                "type": "uint256"
            }
        ],
        "stateMutability": "pure",
        "type": "function"
    },
    {
        "inputs": [
            {
                "internalType": "uint256",
```

```
                    "name": "num1",
                    "type": "uint256"
            },
            {
                    "internalType": "uint256",
                    "name": "num2",
                    "type": "uint256"
            }
        ],
        "name": "multiply",
        "outputs": [
            {
                    "internalType": "uint256",
                    "name": "",
                    "type": "uint256"
            }
        ],
        "stateMutability": "pure",
        "type": "function"
    }
]
```

Likewise, click the **Bytecode** button and paste it onto a text editor. It will look like Figure 6-11.

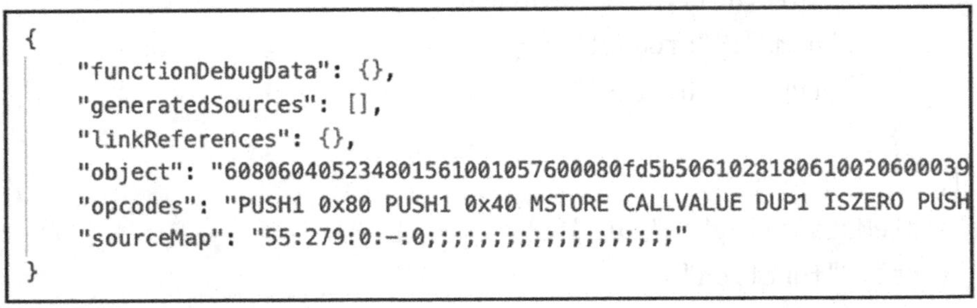

```
{
    "functionDebugData": {},
    "generatedSources": [],
    "linkReferences": {},
    "object": "60806040523480156100105760008f d5b5061028180610020600039
    "opcodes": "PUSH1 0x80 PUSH1 0x40 MSTORE CALLVALUE DUP1 ISZERO PUSH
    "sourceMap": "55:279:0:-:0;;;;;;;;;;;;;;;;;;;;;"
}
```

Figure 6-11. *The bytecode*

Specifically, the value of the **object** key contains the actual bytecode (think of it as machine language) of the contract that will be deployed onto the blockchain. Figure 6-12 shows the steps performed by the Remix IDE when it compiles your smart contract.

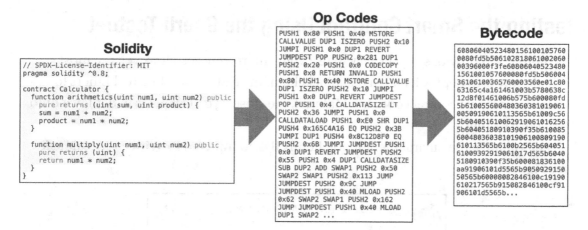

Figure 6-12. *How the Remix IDE compiles your smart contract*

For your reference, the bytecode for your smart contract looks like this:

```
60806040523480156100105760080fd5b506102818061002060000396000f3fe6080604052
34801561001057600080fd5b50600436106100365760003560e01c8063165c4a161461003
b5780638c12d8f01461006b575b600080fd5b610055600480360381019061005091906101011
3565b61009c565b6040516100629190610162565b60405180910390f35b610085600480360
0381019061008091906101013565b6100b2565b6040516100939291906101017d565b604051
80910390f35b600081836100aa91906101d5565b905092915050565b60008082846100c19
190610217565b915082846100cf91906101d5565b905092509290505565b600080fd5b60008
190509190505565b6100f0816100dd565b81146100fb57600080fd5b50565b600081359050
6101010d816100e7565b92915050565b6000806040838503121561012a576101296100d8565b5b
600061013885828601610100fe565b92505060602061014985828601610100fe565b915050925 09
29050565b61015c816100dd565b82525050565b6000602082019050610177600083018461
0153565b92915050565b600060408201905061019260008301856101 53565b61019f602083
0184610153565b9392505050565b7f4e487b710000000000000000000000000000000000000000
00000000000000000000060005260116004526024 6000fd5b60006101e0826100dd565b9
1506101eb836100dd565b92508282026101f9816100dd565b91508282048414831517610
2105761020f6101a565b5b50929150505565b600061022282610 0dd565b915061022d8361
00dd565b925082820190508082111561024557610244 6101a6565b5b92915050 56fea26
```

161

4697066735822122004d196373364650f382fd98a5ee0b1fecb87b1868f9231
59b9aa09076d53beb164736f6c63430008110033

Testing the Smart Contract Using the Goerli Testnet

The Remix VM provides a quick way to test your smart contract. However, the most realistic way is to deploy it onto a real blockchain. Instead of spending real Ethers to deploy your smart contract onto the Mainnet, the closest you can get is to deploy it onto the Goerli testnet.

Let's change the environment in the Remix IDE to **Injected Provider – MetaMask** (see Figure 6-13).

Figure 6-13. *Changing the environment in the Remix IDE*

When you change the environment in the Remix IDE, MetaMask will prompt you to connect to your account (see Figure 6-14). This is to ensure that when you deploy your smart contract to the Goerli testnet, the account will be used to pay for the transaction fee. Click **Connect** in MetaMask to connect the account to the Remix IDE.

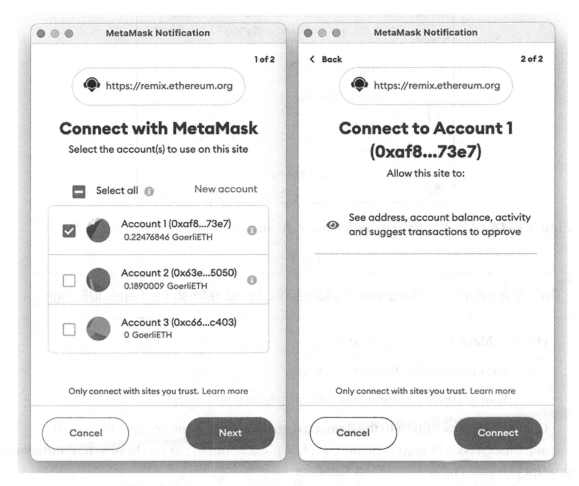

Figure 6-14. *Connect one or more accounts in MetaMask to the Remix IDE*

If MetaMask is connected successfully to the Remix IDE, you will see the address of the account displayed under the ACCOUNT section (see Figure 6-15).

Figure 6-15. *The Remix IDE will display the account that is connected to it*

Tip   If you don't see the account address displayed, refresh the Remix IDE page.

On MetaMask, ensure the following:

- It is connected to the Goerli testnet.

- Your account has some test Ethers (at least 0.02 Ethers).

Click the **Deploy** button in the Remix IDE to deploy the contract onto the Goerli testnet. MetaMask will automatically calculate the amount of gas you have to pay and prompt you (see Figure 6-16). Click **Confirm**.

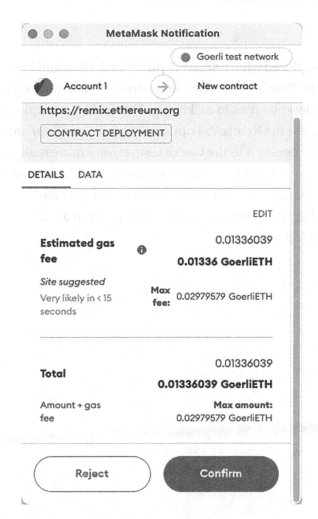

Figure 6-16. *Paying the gas for the contract deployment*

Note   The amount of gas to pay for the deployment of your smart contract is dependent on the size and complexity of your contract.

When the contract is deployed, you will be able to interact with your contract just like you did earlier.

Summary

In this chapter, you explored what a smart contract looks like and how it works. You learned how to use the Remix VM to test the contract locally, without deploying to the blockchain. You also learned how to make use of MetaMask to deploy to the Goerli testnet. In summary, use the Remix VM option to quickly test your smart contract for its functionality and then deploy it to the Goerli testnet for a more realistic feel of how it will work in real life. I strongly suggest that you use the Remix IDE for developing and testing your smart contracts because it makes your life so much simpler.

In the next few chapters, you will dive into the details of a smart contract and the various ways you can interact with it.

CHAPTER 7

Storing Proofs Using Smart Contracts

In the previous chapter, you saw what a smart contract is, how it works, and how to create one. In this chapter, you will learn one good use case of a smart contract and at the same time learn some advanced techniques in Solidity.

A Smart Contract as a Store of Proofs

Recall from Chapter 2 that data stored on the blockchain is immutable. Therefore, the blockchain is a good *store of proofs*. A good use case is storing educational credentials of students on the blockchain.

Recently, there have been many cases of job applicants submitting fake degree qualifications to employers. Employers have no easy way to verify if an applicant's qualification is genuine and must spend precious time verifying the authenticity of the qualification. If an institution is able to record the educational credentials obtained by students onto the blockchain, it will make it easier for employers (or anyone) to verify the authenticity of potential employees' qualifications.

Consider the following simplified example of a student's examination result represented as a JSON string:

```
{
  "id": "1234567",
  "result": {
    "math": "A",
    "science": "B",
    "english": "A"
  }
}
```

© Wei-Meng Lee 2023
W.-M. Lee, *Beginning Ethereum Smart Contracts Programming*, https://doi.org/10.1007/978-1-4842-9271-6_7

The idea is to store the examination result onto the blockchain. However, it is not advisable to store the JSON string directly onto the blockchain for two key reasons:

- Storing the plain text onto the blockchain is expensive. Every additional character stored on the blockchain incurs additional gas fees. The aim is to only store only the absolute essential data.

- You should never store personally identifiable data on public blockchains (such as Ethereum). On public blockchains, all data is up for public scrutiny, so storing the result in plain text will violate privacy regulations and laws.

Considering the privacy concerns, you should instead store the hash of the credentials onto the blockchain.

Caution   Never store encrypted data on the blockchain as they are susceptible to hacking. Storing the hash of the data is much safer.

To verify that the education credential is authentic, pass in the JSON string representing the result and check if the hash exists on the blockchain. If it exists, then the result is authentic.

Creating the Smart Contract

For operational reasons you will see later in this chapter, you first encode the JSON string using base64 encoding before hashing it and storing the hash on the blockchain. To try base64 encoding, you can use the following site: `https://codebeautify.org/json-to-base64-converter`. The above JSON string yields the following base64-encoded output:

ewogICJpZCI6ICIxMjM0NTY3IiwKICAicmVzdWx0IjogewogICAgIm1hdGgiOiAiQSIsCiAg ICAic2NpZW5jZSI6ICJCCIiwKICAgICJlbmdsaXNoIjogIkEiCiAgfQp9Cg==

As usual, use the Goerli testnet.

Note   Recall that the Goerli testnet is the testnet that you should use after the Merge (when Ethereum transitioned from Proof of Work to Proof of Stake). Other testnets such as Ropsten have since been deprecated.

Using the Remix IDE, right-click the **contracts** item and select **New File** (see Figure 7-1).

Figure 7-1. *Creating a new contract file in the Remix IDE*

Name the contract **EduCredentialsStore.sol**. Populate it with the following statements:

```
// SPDX-License-Identifier: MIT
pragma solidity ^0.8;

contract EduCredentialsStore {
  //---store the hash of the strings and their
  // corresponding block number---

  // key is bytes32 and val is uint
  mapping (bytes32 => uint) private proofs;

  //-----------------------------------------------
  // Store a proof of existence in the contract state
  //-----------------------------------------------
```

```solidity
  function storeProof(bytes32 proof) private {
    // use the hash as the key
    proofs[proof] = block.number;
  }

  //-----------------------------------------------
  // Calculate and store the proof for a document
  //-----------------------------------------------
  function storeEduCredentials(string calldata
  document) external {
    // call storeProof() with the hash of the string
    storeProof(proofFor(document));
  }

  //-----------------------------------------------
  // Helper function to get a document's sha256
  //-----------------------------------------------
  // Takes in a string and returns the hash of the
  // string
  function proofFor(string calldata document) private
  pure returns (bytes32) {
    // converts the string into bytes array and
    // then hash it
    return sha256(bytes(document));
  }

  //-----------------------------------------------
  // Check if a document has been saved previously
  //-----------------------------------------------
  function checkEduCredentials(string calldata
  document) public view returns (uint){
    // use the hash of the string and check the
    // proofs mapping object
    return proofs[proofFor(document)];
  }

}
```

The contract is now much more significantly complex that the one you saw in the previous chapter. Here is a summary of this contract:

- The contract has two private functions named `storeProof()` and `proofFor()`. Private functions are denoted with the `private` keyword. Private functions are only callable within the contract and not by users.

- The contract has one external function named (`storeEduCredentials()`) and one public function named (`checkEduCredentials()`). Public and external functions are both visible outside the contract and can be called directly by the user. The key difference between public and external is that public functions are also visible to subclasses of the contract while external functions are not visible to subclasses of the contract.

- Notice the use of the `calldata` keyword in the function parameter declaration. Besides the `calldata` keyword, you can also use the `memory` keyword. The `memory` and `calldata` keywords indicate that the parameter holds a temporary value and it won't be persisted onto the blockchain. The key difference between the two keywords is that parameter prefixed with the `calldata` keyword is immutable (i.e., cannot be changed) while parameters prefixed with `memory` are mutable.

- You will also notice that one function has the `pure` keyword while another has the `view` keyword. The `pure` keyword (as explained in the previous chapter) indicates that the function does not read or write values onto the blockchain. The `view` keyword indicates that the function will read values from the blockchain.

- The contract has a `mapping` object named `proofs`. A `mapping` object in Solidity is like a dictionary object: it holds key/value pairs. The value of `Proofs` is persisted on the blockchain and is known as a *state variable*.

171

With all the different keywords for function access modifiers and parameter declarations, which should you use? Here is a rule of thumb:

- Use `calldata` for parameter declaration if the data passed into the function need not be modified. Declaring a function with a `calldata` parameter will save on gas fees.

- Use `external` instead of `public` if there is no need for your functions to be called by subclasses of the contract. Due to the way arguments in public functions are accessed, declaring functions as external will incur lesser gas fees.

Figure 7-2 shows the conceptual flow of how your smart contract can be used.

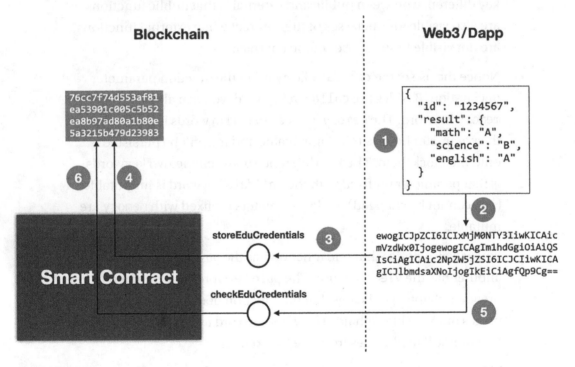

Figure 7-2. *How the smart contract interacts with the user*

1. The examination result of a student is represented as a JSON string.

2. The JSON string is encoded using base64 encoding.

3. The base64-encoded string is passed into the storeEduCredentials() function of the smart contract.

4. The storeEduCredentials() function hashes the base64-encoded string and then stores the hash together with the block number (that contains the transaction) onto the blockchain.

5. To check if an educational credential is authentic, the based64-encoded string of the student's result is passed into the checkEduCredentials() function.

6. The checkEduCredentials() function hashes the base64-encoded string and then checks if the hash already exists on the blockchain. The block number that contains the hash is returned. If the hash is not found, a value of 0 is returned.

Tip   A dapp (decentralized application) is an application (such as web or mobile application) that communicates with a smart contract in the back end. The next chapter will discuss dapps in more detail.

Figure 7-3 shows how the smart contract stores the hash of the exam results onto the blockchain. The state variable is a *mapping* object containing key/value pairs. The keys are the hashes and the values are the block numbers in which the hashes are written onto the blockchain.

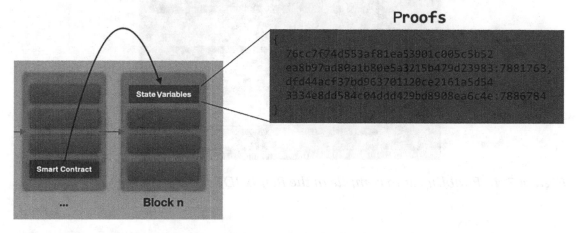

Figure 7-3. *How the mapping object records the hashes and block numbers*

Compiling the Contract

With the smart contract written, it is now time to compile it. In the Remix IDE, click the **Compiler** tab (see Figure 7-4, step 1) and check **Auto compile**. Doing so will enable the Remix IDE to automatically compile your code every time you make changes to it.

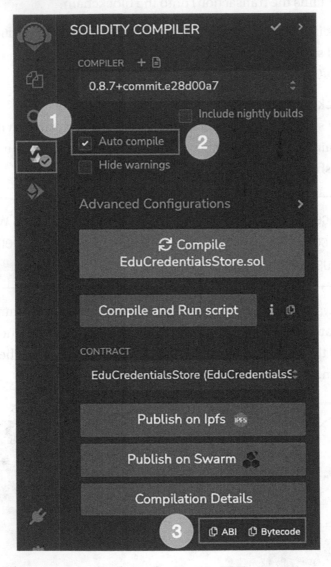

Figure 7-4. *Enabling auto compile in the Remix IDE*

At the bottom, you will see two items: **ABI** and **Bytecode**. Clicking **ABI** will copy the application binary interface (ABI) to the clipboard. Paste it onto a text editor and it will look like this:

```
[
  {
    "inputs": [
      {
        "internalType": "string",
        "name": "document",
        "type": "string"
      }
    ],
    "name": "checkEduCredentials",
    "outputs": [
      {
        "internalType": "uint256",
        "name": "",
        "type": "uint256"
      }
    ],
    "stateMutability": "view",
    "type": "function"
  },
  {
    "inputs": [
      {
        "internalType": "string",
        "name": "document",
        "type": "string"
      }
    ],
```

```
    "name": "storeEduCredentials",
    "outputs": [],
    "stateMutability": "nonpayable",
    "type": "function"
  }
]
```

If you remove the formatting of the ABI and store it as a single line, you will see the following:

```
[    {        "inputs": [         {               "internalType": "string",
"name": "document",          "type": "string"         }       ],       "name":
"checkEduCredentials",       "outputs": [          {          "internalType":
"uint256",           "name": "",              "type": "uint256"          ]       ],
"stateMutability": "view",       "type": "function"      },      {
"inputs": [        {         "internalType": "string",
"name": "document",          "type": "string"         }       ],
"name": "storeEduCredentials",       "outputs": [],       "stateMutability":
"nonpayable",        "type": "function"     }   ]
```

Deploying the Contract

You are now ready to deploy the smart contract to the Goerli testnet. In the Remix IDE, click the **Deploy** icon (see Figure 7-5, step 1). Make sure the environment is **Injected Provider – Metamask** (step 2). By selecting MetaMask, this means that the contract will deploy to whichever network MetaMask is connected to (make sure MetaMask is connected to Goerli). Finally, click the **Deploy** button (step 3).

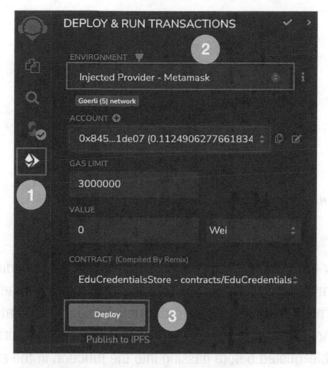

Figure 7-5. *Deploying the contract in the Remix IDE*

MetaMask will prompt you to pay for the transaction. Click **Confirm** and wait a while for the transaction to confirm.

Testing the Contract

Once the smart contract is deployed, you will see the contract under the **Deployed Contracts** section of the Remix IDE. You will also see the address of the contract displayed next to the contract name.

Note   To call a smart contract on the blockchain, your dapp needs the address of the contract as well as its ABI.

Let's now try to store the hash of the base64-encoded JSON string representing the result of a student onto the blockchain. Once the base64-encoded string is pasted into the textbox, click the **storeEduCredentials** button (see Figure 7-6).

Figure 7-6. *Viewing the deployed contract in the Remix IDE*

Tip   Remember I mentioned the need to perform a base64 encoding on the JSON string before computing its hash? If you directly copy and paste the JSON string into the text box next to the **storeEduCredentials** button, this creates problem as keys and string values in JSON are double-quoted, and the entire JSON string needs to be double-quoted before passing into the function in the smart contract. To solve this problem, it is easier to simply base64 encode your JSON string and then pass the function the base64-encoded result.

MetaMask will prompt you to pay for the transaction. Click **Confirm** (see Figure 7-7).

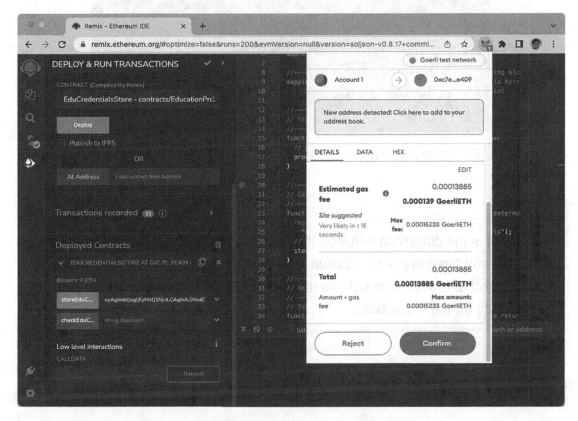

Figure 7-7. *Paying for the transaction using MetaMask*

After a while, the transaction will be confirmed. You can now paste the same base64-encoded string into the textbox displayed next to the **checkEduCredentials** button (see Figure 7-8). Clicking the **checkEduCredentials** button will display the block number (7881763, in this example) in which the hash of the base64-encoded string was stored on the blockchain. If you see a result of 0, it means that the hash was not found on the blockchain.

Figure 7-8. *Verifying that the educational credential was previously stored on the blockchain*

Tip   What is the difference between the colors of the buttons? Orange buttons mean that you need to pay transaction fees (because you are modifying the state of the blockchain) while blue buttons mean that you don't have to pay (you are just reading data off the blockchain).

Making Further Changes to the Smart Contract

Your basic educational credentials smart contract is now up and running. Users are now able to store educational credentials onto the blockchain and use it to verify education qualifications. However, there are a number of improvements that can be made to the contract. In the following sections, you will learn the following:

- How to restrict access to certain functions in your smart contract

- How to accept payments in your smart contract

- How to fire events in your smart contract

- How to transfer funds in your smart contract to another account

- How to destruct a smart contract so that it is no longer available for use

Restricting Access to Functions

Apparently, not everyone should be allowed to store the educational credentials of students on the blockchain. Realistically, only an educational institution (usually the one that deploys the smart contract) should be allowed to do so. You can make some changes to the smart contract to ensure that only the contract owner (the one that deploys the contract) is allowed to call the **storeEduCredentials()** function.

First, add in the following statements in bold to the contract:

```
contract EduCredentialsStore {
  // store the owner of the contract
  address owner = msg.sender;
```

The owner variable automatically stores the address of the account (msg.sender) that deploys it. Then, in the storeEduCredentials() function, add in the require() function, as follows:

```
  function storeEduCredentials(string calldata document) external {
    require(msg.sender == owner,
      "Only the owner of contract can store
        the credentials");

    // call storeProof() with the hash of the string
    storeProof(proofFor(document));
  }
```

The require() function first checks that whoever is calling this function (msg. sender) must be the owner, or else it returns an error message ("Only the owner of contract can store the credentials"). If the condition is met, execution will continue; if not, the execution halts.

In the Remix IDE, you can try out the above modifications by first deploying the contract using Account 1. After the contract is deployed, switch to another account in MetaMask and try to call the storeEduCredentials() function. You will see an error, as shown in Figure 7-9.

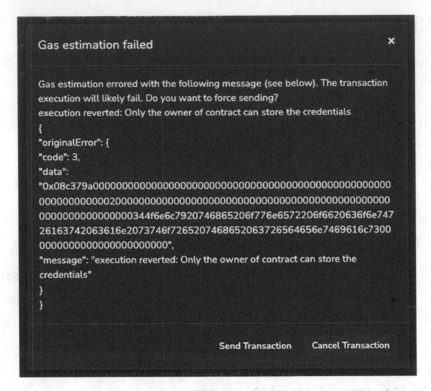

Gas estimation failed   ✕

Gas estimation errored with the following message (see below). The transaction
execution will likely fail. Do you want to force sending?
execution reverted: Only the owner of contract can store the credentials
{
"originalError": {
"code": 3,
"data":
"0x08c379a00000000000000000000000000000000000000000000000000000000
0000000000000200000000000000000000000000000000000000000000000000000
0000000000000000344f6e6c7920746865206f776e6572206f6620636f6e747
26163742063616e2073746f726520746865206372656564656e7469616c7300
00000000000000000000000",
"message": "execution reverted: Only the owner of contract can store the
credentials"
}
}

                                    Send Transaction   Cancel Transaction

Figure 7-9. *The Remix IDE refusing the function call*

Caution   Note that a smart contract is not alterable. Once it is deployed, you
won't be able to make any changes to it. Hence when you redeploy a contract, a
new contract is stored on the blockchain; you will not be able to access any of the
state variables of the old contract in the new one.

Accepting Payments in Smart Contracts

Now that you have written a smart contract that allows educational credentials to be
written to the blockchain, you may want to see how you can financially benefit from
such a contract. How about earning some Ethers whenever someone needs to verify the
educational credential of a potential employee? Well, that's easy.

Add the payable keyword to the checkEduCredentials() function and delete the
view keyword:

```
function checkEduCredentials(string calldata document) public payable
returns (uint) {
  require(msg.value == 1000 wei,
    "This call requires 1000 wei");

  // use the hash of the string and check the proofs mapping object
  return proofs[proofFor(document)];
}
```

At the same time, add the require() function to indicate that the caller must send in 1000 Wei (represented in msg.value).

Tip   1 Ether is equal to 1,000,000,000,000,000,000 Wei (18 zeros). Wei is the smallest denomination of Ether.

Table 7-1 shows the various denominations in Ethereum. For example, 1 Ether is equal to 1,000,000,000,000,000,000 Wei (18 zeros) and 1 Ether is equal to 0.001 Kether.

Table 7-1. The Various Denominations in Ether

Unit	Value (in Ether)
Wei	1,000,000,000,000,000,000 (18 zeros)
Kwei	1,000,000,000,000,000 (15 zeros)
Mwei	1,000,000,000,000 (12 zeros)
Gwei	1,000,000,000 (9 zeros)
Szabo	1,000,000 (6 zeros)
Finney	1,000 (3 zeros)
Ether	1
Kether	0.001 (3 decimal places)
Mether	0.000001 (6 decimal places)
Gether	0.000000001 (9 decimal places)
Tether	0.000000000001 (12 decimal places)

Tip   Some of the denominations in Ether are named after famous people in the crypto world. For example, **Finney** was named after *Hal Finney*, who was an early Bitcoin contributor and received the first bitcoin transaction from Bitcoin's creator, Satoshi Nakamoto. **Szabo** was named after *Nick Szabo*, who first came out with the concept of smart contracts. **Wei** was named after *Wei Dai*, a cryptographer who came up with "b-money," a concept referenced in section 2 of the Bitcoin paper.

SPECIFYING UNITS OF ETHERS IN SOLIDITY

In Solidity, the variable `msg.value` is always expressed in Wei. In the above statement, you could also rewrite the comparison simply as

```
msg.value == 1000
```

However, Solidity allows you to compare units of Ether using the special syntax used above:

```
msg.value == 1000 wei
```

This syntax is useful when you are comparing larger amounts of Ether. For example, if you want to check if the incoming amount is 1 Ether, instead of doing this:

```
msg.value == 1000000000000000000
// OR
msg.value == 1e18
```

you could simply do this using a simpler syntax:

```
msg.value == 1 ether
```

In Solidity 0.7 onwards, you can do this for the following units: `Gwei`, `Ether`, and `Wei`.

When you deploy this contract, observe that the checkEduCredentials button is now red (see Figure 7-10). This is due to the payable keyword in the checkEduCredentials() function.

Figure 7-10. *The checkEduCredentials button is now red*

Tip   If a function button is red, it indicates that besides paying for transaction fees, it may also require you to send Ethers to it.

As you did previously, go ahead and paste the base64-encoded string into the texbox next to the checkEduCredentials button and then click the storeEduCredentials button. When you click the checkEduCredential button, you will see the error message shown in Figure 7-11.

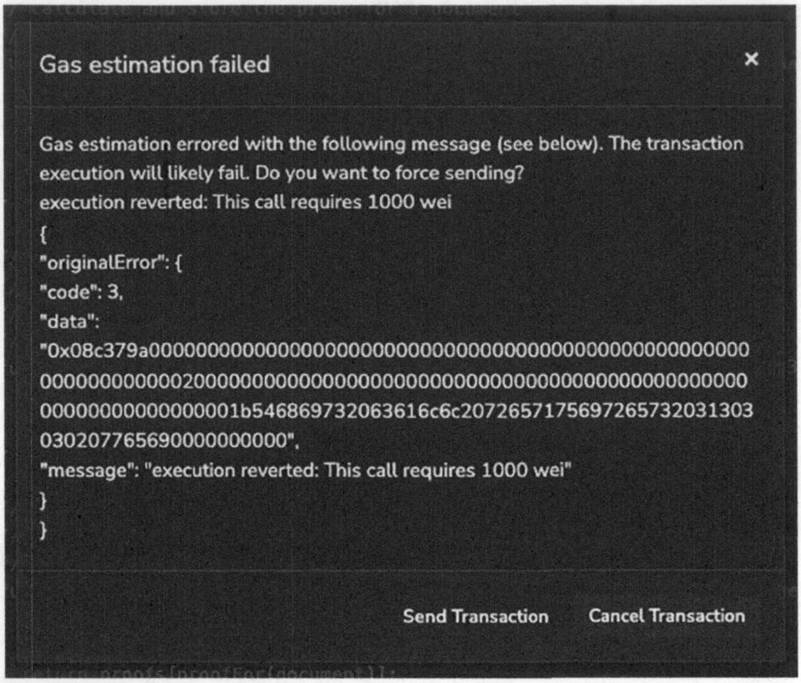
Gas estimation failed
×
Gas estimation errored with the following message (see below). The transaction execution will likely fail. Do you want to force sending?
execution reverted: This call requires 1000 wei
{
"originalError": {
"code": 3,
"data":
"0x08c379a000000000000000000000000000000000000000000000000000
0000000000020000000000000000000000000000000000000000000000000
00000000000000001b546869732063616c6c207265717569726573203130303
0302077656900000000000",
"message": "execution reverted: This call requires 1000 wei"
}
}
Send Transaction
Cancel Transaction

Figure 7-11. *Remix refuses the transaction becuase the function expects Ethers to be sent to it*

Apparently, this is because you did not send 1000 Wei to the contract. To fix this in the Remix IDE, specify 1000 Wei before you click the `checkEduCredential` button, as shown in Figure 7-12.

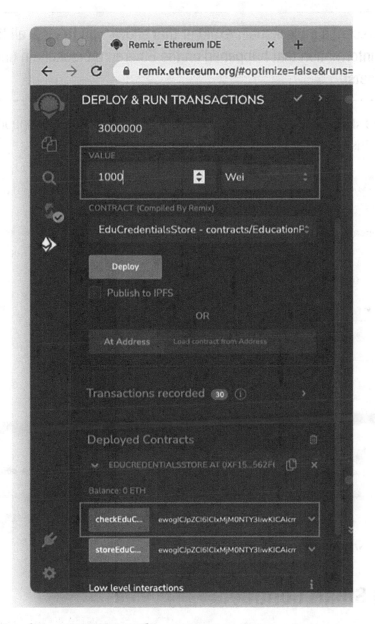

Figure 7-12. *Sending 1000 Wei to the contract*

When the transaction is confirmed, you can go to Etherscan and view the balance of the contract. For example, the address of my contract is 0xf15e70a24a50ef1b2c3bed0d3b033e35233562f6. Hence, the details of my contract on Etherscan (for the Goerli testnet) are https://goerli.etherscan.io/address/0xf15e7 0a24a50ef1b2c3bed0d3b033e35233562f6.

Note   Etherscan is a blockchain explorer that allows you to view all the detailed transaction information that happened on the Ethereum blockchain (including the various testnets).

Figure 7-13 shows that the contract has a balance of 0.000000000000001 Ether (which is 1000 Wei). This proves that a smart contract can hold Ethers.

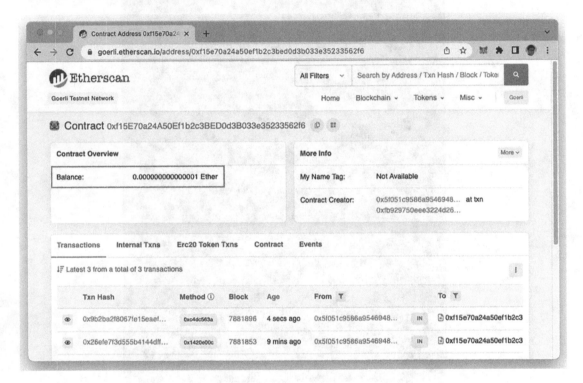

Figure 7-13. *Smart contracts can also hold Ethers*

Events in Smart Contracts

Recall that the checkEduCredential() function returns the block number in which the hash of the base64-encoded string was stored on the blockchain. In the previous section, you modified the function so that it accepts payment. If you tried the smart contract, you would have noticed that after sending the 1000 Wei to the contract, the checkEduCredential() function does not return any value anymore. This is because the function is now performing a transaction, so it is not capable of returning you the result immediately (it needs to wait for the block to be added to the blockchain). So how do you solve this issue? You can solve this using *events*.

In Solidity, a function can return a value back to the caller either directly or through events. Events are usually used by smart contracts to keep front-end applications updated on what is happening to the smart contract.

Let's define an event for your contract using the following statements in bold:

```solidity
// SPDX-License-Identifier: MIT
pragma solidity ^0.8;

contract EduCredentialsStore {
  // store the owner of the contract
  address owner = msg.sender;

  //---store the hash of the strings and their
  // corresponding block number---
  // key is bytes32 and val is uint
  mapping (bytes32 => uint) private proofs;

  //---define an event---
  event Result(
    address from,
    string document,
    uint blockNumber
  );
```

These statements defined an event named Result with three parameters: from, hash, and blockNumber. To fire this event, use the emit keyword. You will fire this event in the checkEduCredentials() function:

```solidity
//-------------------------------------------------
// Check if a document has been saved previously
//-------------------------------------------------
function checkEduCredentials(string calldata document) public payable {
  require(msg.value == 1000 wei ,
    "This call requires 1000 wei");
```

```
    // use the hash of the string and check
    // the proofs mapping object, then fire the event
    emit Result(msg.sender,
                document,
                proofs[proofFor(document)]);

    // return proofs[proofFor(document)];
}
```

Note   There is now no need to return a value from this function, so modify the signature of the checkEduCredentials() function and comment out the return statement.

To try out the updated smart contract, deploy it and then call its checkEduCredentials() function (remember to send it 1000 Wei). The Remix IDE will listen for the event and you will be able to see it after the transaction is confirmed (see Figure 7-14).

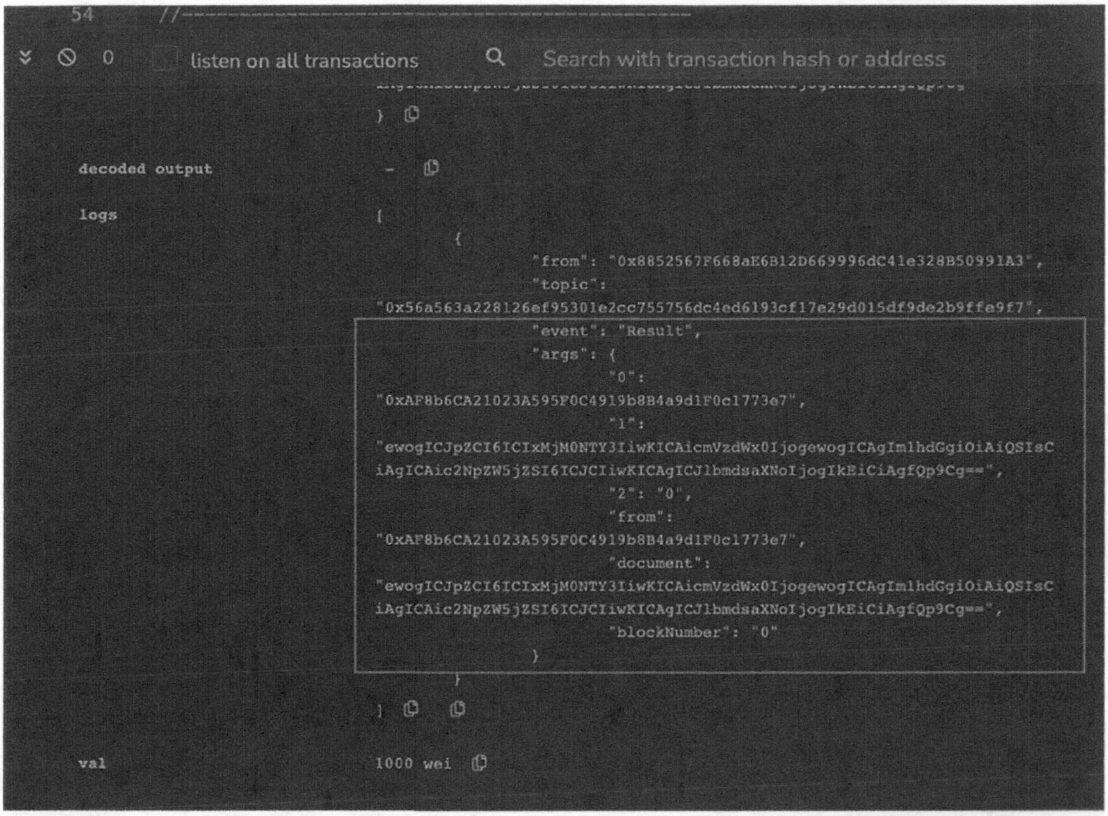

Figure 7-14. *You can use the Remix IDE to examine the events fired by smart contracts*

Cashing Out

Now that your smart contract holds Ether, you have a problem. The Ethers are stuck forever in the contract because you did not make any provisions to transfer them out. To be able to get Ethers out of a contract, there are two main ways:

- Immediately transfer the Ethers to another account the moment they are received in the checkEduCredentials() function.

- Add another function to transfer the Ethers to another account (such as the owner).

For this example, you will use the second approach by adding a new `cashOut()` function to the contract:

```
function cashOut() public {
  require(msg.sender == owner,
    "Only the owner of contract can cash out!");
  payable(owner).transfer(address(this).balance);
}
```

In the `cashOut()` function, you first need to ensure that only the owner can call this function. Once this is verified, you transfer the entire balance of the contract to the owner using the `transfer()` function.

Once again, deploy the contract and then call the `checkEduCredentials()` function so that you can send 1000 Wei to the contract. Then, click the **cashOut** button in the Remix IDE to transfer the Ethers back to the owner. On Etherscan, you can see that there is a transfer of the balance to the owner of the contract (see Figure 7-15).

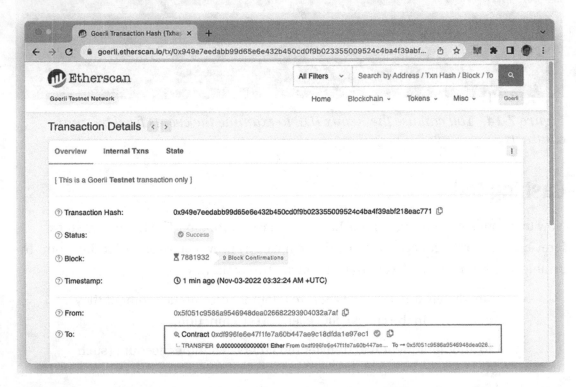

Figure 7-15. *Etherscan records the internal transfers of Ethers to another account*

Destroying a Contract

There will be a time when your smart contract has reached its end of life and needs to be shut down. To disable your smart contract so that it is no longer callable, you can use the selfdestruct() function.

Let's add a kill() function to the contract now:

```
/* self-destruct function */
function kill() public {
  require(msg.sender == owner, "Only owner can kill this contract");
  selfdestruct(payable(owner));
}
```

As usual, you need to ensure that only a specific user (usually the owner of the contract) can kill the contract. The selfdestruct() function sends all remaining Ethers stored in the contract to a designated address, which in this case is owner.

Tip   The selfdestruct() function was introduced in Solidity 0.5.0 as a way to an exit door in case of security threats in your smart contract.

Finally, deploy the contract and observe the new kill button (see Figure 7-16).

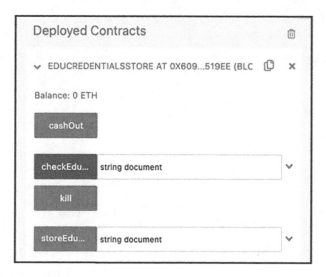

Figure 7-16. *The* kill() *function deletes the contract from the blockchain*

WHAT HAPPENS AFTER SELFDESTRUCT IS CALLED?

After you call the `selfdestruct()` function on the smart contract, it will continue to accept transactions, but no processing will be done and the transaction status is always a success. For example, if you now call the `storeEduCredentials()` function, it can still be called and you still need to pay a gas fee. However, nothing gets stored on the blockchain. Also, you can still send Ethers to the contract and it will hold the Ethers sent. However, you will no longer be able to get the Ethers out from the contract.

After you have deployed this contract, record its deployed contract address and ABI. You will make use of these two pieces of information in the next chapter when you build a Web3 dapp (a front end to the smart contract).

Summary

In this chapter, you learned how to create a smart contract to store proofs of educational credentials. You also learned a few tricks that you can implement in your Solidity smart contracts, such as accepting payments and the ability to kill a smart contract. In the next chapter, you will learn how to build a front-end Web3 dapp to interact with the smart contract.

## CHAPTER 8

Using the web3.js APIs

In previous chapters, you learned the basics of smart contracts and how to deploy them onto the blockchain. So far, all interactions with smart contracts have been through the Remix IDE. While the Remix IDE provides an easy way for developers to test their smart contracts, it is not suitable for use by end users. To allow end users to interact with your smart contracts, you need to build front end that hides the complexity of interacting with the smart contracts in the back end. For this purpose, you need a Web3 API.

In this chapter, you will learn how to interact with smart contracts using the web3. js APIs. Using the web3.js APIs, you can build front ends (such as web pages, Node.js applications, etc.) to interact with smart contracts.

What Is web3.js?

web3.js is a collection of libraries that allows you to interact with a local or remote Ethereum node using HTTP, WebSocket, or IPC. Through the web3.js APIs, your front end can then interact with the smart contracts. The web3.js APIs contain the following modules:

- `web3-eth`: For the Ethereum blockchain and smart contracts
- `web3-shh`: For the whisper protocol to communicate p2p and broadcast
- `web3-bzz`: For the swarm protocol, the decentralized file storage
- `web3-utils`: Contains useful helper functions for dapp developers

For this book, you will only focus on the first module, `web3-eth`.

© Wei-Meng Lee 2023
W.-M. Lee, *Beginning Ethereum Smart Contracts Programming*, https://doi.org/10.1007/978-1-4842-9271-6_8

Installing web3.js

Installing web3.js requires Node.js. Specifically, you will make use of npm to download the web3.js APIs onto your local computer.

Tip   The easiest way to install Node.js is to use nvm (Node Version Manager). To learn how to use nvm to install Node.js, check out my article at `https://bit.ly/3QqyEBR`.

For this chapter, create a folder named web3projects to store the web3.js APIs. In terminal, type the following commands:

```
$ cd ~
$ mkdir web3projects
$ cd web3projects
```

Before you download the web3.js APIs, you want to create an empty Node.js project:

```
$ npm init --yes
```

This command creates a file named package.json. This file contains the dependencies required by a Node.js application. To download the web3.js APIs, type the following command:

```
$ npm install web3 --save
```

Tip   Creating the package.json file will prevent npm (Node Package Manager) from showing pages of warning and error messages when you install web3.js.

The --save option informs npm to modify the package.json file and add the web3.js as a dependency for the application.

The web3projects folder should now have a folder named node_modules. Within this node_modules folder, you will see several folders, all of which make up the suites of APIs that is web3.js.

Testing the web3.js Using MetaMask

With web3.js downloaded, let's now test it and understand how it works. Create a text file named TestWeb3.html and save it in the web3projects folder. Populate it as follows:

```
<!DOCTYPE html>
<html lang="en">
<script src="./node_modules/web3/dist/web3.min.js"></script>
<body>
    <script>
        async function loadWeb3() {
            //---if MetaMask is available on your web browser---
            if (window.ethereum) {
                web3 = new Web3(window.ethereum);

                //---connect to account---
                const account = await window.ethereum.request(
                    {method: 'eth_requestAccounts'});
                console.log(account);
            } else {
                //---set the provider you want from Web3.providers---
                web3 = new Web3(
                    new Web3.providers.HttpProvider(
                        "http://localhost:8545"));
            }
        }

        //---get the current account in MetaMask---
        async function getCurrentAccount() {
            const accounts = await web3.eth.getAccounts();
            console.log(accounts)
            return accounts[0];
        }

        async function load() {
            await loadWeb3();
            alert(await getCurrentAccount());
        }
```

```
        load();
    </script>
</body>
</html>
```

In terminal, type the following command:

```
$ npm install -g serve
```

Tip   Installing the `serve` application globally using the `-g` option may require `sudo` permission. Alternatively, you can install it locally within the current directory without using the `-g` option.

This command installs a web server on the local computer. Typing the `serve` command in any directory enables the directory to serve its content through the web server.

In the `web3projects` folder, type the following command:

```
$ cd ~/web3projects
$ serve
```

Using the Chrome browser (with MetaMask installed), load the following URL: `http://localhost:3000/TestWeb3.html`.

You will see the alert shown in Figure 8-1. Select the account that you want to connect in MetaMask, click **Next**, and then **Connect**.

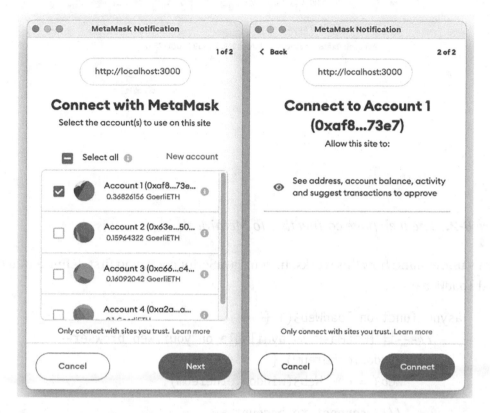

Figure 8-1. *You need to give permission to the page to allow it to access your MetaMask account(s)*

You should now see the alert showing the address of the account that is connected to your web page, as shown in Figure 8-2.

Figure 8-2. *The web page connecting to MetaMask*

Let's understand how this works. In your JavaScript code, you first define a function named loadWeb3:

```
async function loadWeb3() {
    //---if MetaMask is available on your web browser---
    if (window.ethereum) {
        web3 = new Web3(window.ethereum);

        //---connect to account---
        const account = await window.ethereum.request(
            {method: 'eth_requestAccounts'});
        console.log(account);
    } else {
        //---set the provider you want from Web3.providers---
        web3 = new Web3(
            new Web3.providers.HttpProvider(
                "http://localhost:8545"));
    }
}
```

If you load this page through HTTP on a browser with MetaMask installed, MetaMask automatically injects an API through window.ethereum. This window.ethereum allows you to interact with an Ethereum node. In this case, it connects to the

MetaMask extension on your Chrome browser. You make use of `window.ethereum` to create an instance of the `Web3` object, which allows you to connect to user accounts in MetaMask, connect to smart contracts on the blockchain, and more.

If MetaMask is not detected on the browser (due to the absence of `window.ethereum`), you can connect to your own node. In this example, you connect to a local node listening at port 8545 (`http://localhost:8545`). You can run your own local node, such as Ganache (see Figure 8-3).

Figure 8-3. *Ganache allows you to simulate an Ethereum blockchain locally on your computer*

Note   Ganache is a simulated Ethereum blockchain that you can use to deploy contracts, develop your applications, and run tests. It is part of the Truffle Suite of tools for Ethereum development. You can download Ganache from `https://trufflesuite.com/ganache/`.

The next function you define is the getCurrentAccount() function:

```
//---get the current account in MetaMask---
async function getCurrentAccount() {
    const accounts = await web3.eth.getAccounts();
    console.log(accounts)
    return accounts[0];
}
```

In this function, you fetch all the accounts from the connected node (either MetaMask or a node like Ganache) and return the first account.

Finally, you define the load() function so that you can call the loadWeb3() and getCurrentAccount() functions asynchronously:

```
async function load() {
    await loadWeb3();
    alert(await getCurrentAccount());
}

//---call the load function to connect to the node and display
// the first account---
load();
```

Interacting with a Contract Using web3.js

The most common use of the web3.js APIs is to build front ends so that users can interact with your smart contract directly. In this section, you will learn how to use web3.js to interact with your newly deployed contract. You will build a web front end.

Create a new text file and name it as main.css. Populate the file with the following:

```
body {
    background-color:#F0F0F0;
    padding: 2em;
    font-family: 'Raleway','Source Sans Pro', 'Arial';
}
.container {
    width: 90%;
    margin: 0 auto;
}
```

```
label {
    display:block;
    margin-bottom:10px;
}
input {
    padding:10px;
    width: 100%;
    margin-bottom: 1em;
}
button {
    margin: 2em 0;
    padding: 1em 4em;
    display:block;
}

#result {
    padding:1em;
    background-color:#fff;
    margin: 1em 0;
}
```

This file serves as the CSS (Cascading Style Sheet) for the web front end that you will build next.

Create a new text file and name it as index.html (save it in the web3projects folder). Populate it with the following statements:

```
<!DOCTYPE html>
<html lang="en">
<head>
    <meta charset="UTF-8">
    <meta name="viewport" content="width=device-width, initial-scale=1.0">
    <meta http-equiv="X-UA-Compatible" content="ie=edge">
    <title>Document</title>
    <link rel="stylesheet" type="text/css" href="main.css">
    <script src="./node_modules/web3/dist/web3.min.js"></script>
</head>
```

```
<body>
    <div class="container">
        <h1>Educational Credentials Notarizer</h1>
        <label for="document" class="col-lg-2 control-label">
            Credential to store
        </label>
        <input id="document" type="text">
        <button id="btnStore">Store</button>
        <label for="document2" class="col-lg-2 control-label">
            Check Credential
        </label>
        <input id="document2" type="text">
        <button id="btnCheck">Check</button>
        <label for="document2" class="col-lg-2 control-label">
            Status
        </label>
        <h2 id="result"></h2>
    </div>
    <script src="https://code.jquery.com/jquery-3.2.1.slim.min.js"></script>
    <script>
        async function loadWeb3() {
            //---if MetaMask is available on your web browser---
            if (window.ethereum) {
                web3 = new Web3(window.ethereum);

                //---connect to account---
                const account = await window.ethereum.request(
                    {method: 'eth_requestAccounts'});
                console.log(account)
            } else {
                //---set the provider you want from Web3.providers---
                web3 = new Web3(
                    new Web3.providers.HttpProvider(
                        "http://localhost:8545"));
            }
        }
```

```
//---load the smart contract---
async function loadContract() {
    abi = [ { "anonymous": false, "inputs": [ { "indexed":
    false, "internalType": "address", "name": "from", "type":
    "address" }, { "indexed": false, "internalType": "string",
    "name": "document", "type": "string" }, { "indexed": false,
    "internalType": "uint256", "name": "blockNumber", "type":
    "uint256" } ], "name": "Result", "type": "event" },
    { "inputs": [], "name": "cashOut", "outputs": [],
    "stateMutability": "nonpayable", "type": "function" }, {
    "inputs": [ { "internalType": "string", "name": "document",
    "type": "string" } ], "name": "checkEduCredentials", "outputs":
    [], "stateMutability": "payable", "type": "function" }, {
    "inputs": [], "name": "kill", "outputs": [], "stateMutability":
    "nonpayable", "type": "function" }, { "inputs": [ {
    "internalType": "string", "name": "document", "type":
    "string" } ], "name": "storeEduCredentials", "outputs": [],
    "stateMutability": "nonpayable", "type": "function" } ];

    address = '0x450FdF943afec4036787f4deDA11A34526c53921'
    return await new web3.eth.Contract(abi,address);
}

//---get the current account in MetaMask---
async function getCurrentAccount() {
    const accounts = await web3.eth.getAccounts();
    console.log(accounts)
    return accounts[0];
}

async function load() {
    await loadWeb3();

    //---load the contract---
    notarizer = await loadContract();

    //---get the account---
    const account = await getCurrentAccount();
```

```
//---handle the Result event fired by the smart contract---
notarizer.events.Result()
    .on('data', function(event){
        if (event.returnValues[0] == account) {
            console.log(event.returnValues[0]);  // from
            console.log(event.returnValues[1]);  // text
            console.log(event.returnValues[2]);  // blocknumber

            //---if the blocknumber is 0, this means
            // credential is not found---
            if (event.returnValues[2] > 0) {
                $("#result").html("Credential is valid");
            } else {
                $("#result").html("Credential is NOT valid");
            }
        }
    });

//---store the credential onto the blockchain---
$("#btnStore").click(async function() {
    notarizer.methods.storeEduCredentials($("#document").val())
        .send({from:account})
        .then(function (tx) {
            $("#result").html(tx.transactionHash);
        });
});

//---check the credential on the blockchain---
$("#btnCheck").click(async function() {
    notarizer.methods.checkEduCredentials($("#document2")
    .val())
        .send({from:account, value:1000});
});
    }
    load();
    </script>
</body>
</html>
```

In terminal, ensure that the serve command is still running (if not, type serve in the web3projects folder). Load the Chrome web browser with the following URL: http://localhost:3000/index.html. You should see the page shown in Figure 8-4.

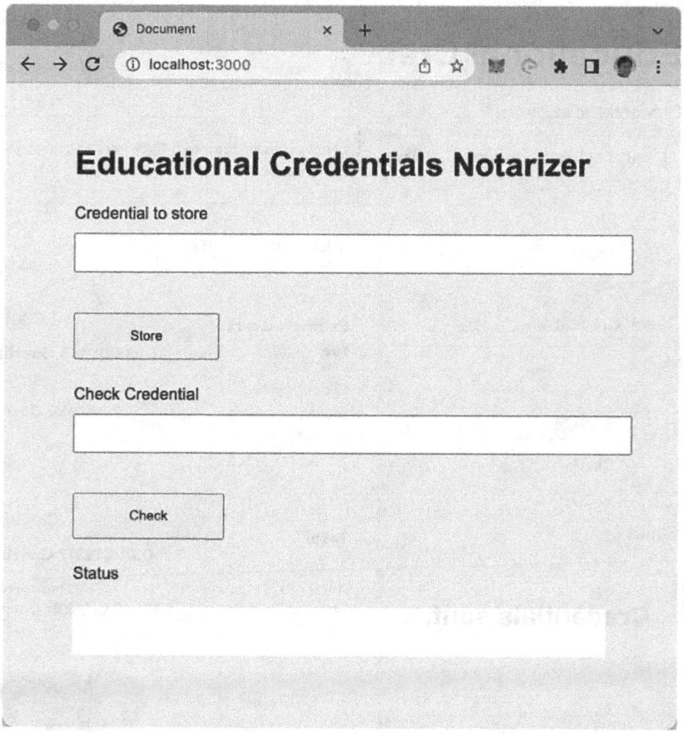

Figure 8-4. *The web front end to interact with the smart contract*

Enter a string such as { "id": "1234567", "result": { "math": "A", "science": "B", "english": "A" } } in the first text box and then click the **Store** button. You should see the popup by MetaMask (see Figure 8-5).

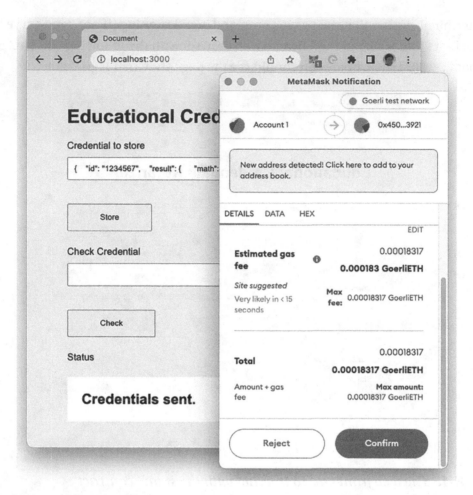

Figure 8-5. *Confirming the transaction to send the credential to the smart contract for notarization*

Click **Confirm** to confirm the transaction. When the transaction is sent, you will immediately see the transaction hash displayed at the bottom of the page (see Figure 8-6).

Figure 8-6. *The transaction hash is displayed at the bottom of the page*

Once the block containing the transaction is mined, you will be able to type the same credential in the second text box and then click the **Check** button to verify if the same credential was previously stored on the blockchain (see Figure 8-7).

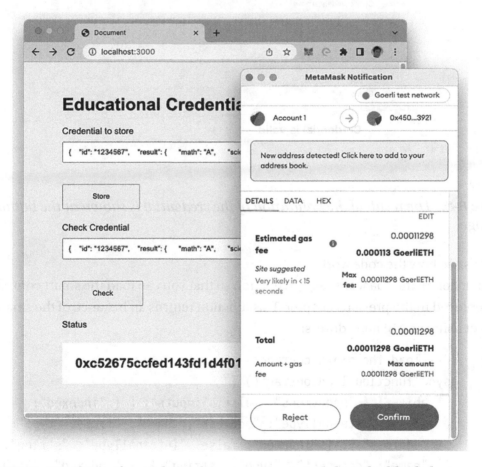

Figure 8-7. *Verifying if a credential was previous stored on the blockchain*

If the credential was stored previously, you should see **Credential is valid** at the bottom of the screen (see Figure 8-8).

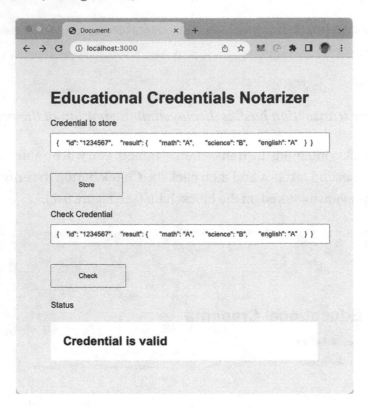

Figure 8-8. *The result of the validation of the credential is shown at the bottom of the page*

Let's see how the code works.

First, define the loadContract() function so that you can load the smart contract you deployed in the previous chapter. This function returns an instance of the smart contract using its ABI and address:

```
//---load the smart contract---
async function loadContract() {
    abi = [ { "anonymous": false, "inputs": [ { "indexed":
    false, "internalType": "address", "name": "from", "type":
    "address" }, { "indexed": false, "internalType": "string",
    "name": "document", "type": "string" }, { "indexed": false,
    "internalType": "uint256", "name": "blockNumber", "type":
```

```
          "uint256" } ], "name": "Result", "type": "event" },
          { "inputs": [], "name": "cashOut", "outputs": [],
          "stateMutability": "nonpayable", "type": "function" }, {
          "inputs": [ { "internalType": "string", "name": "document",
          "type": "string" } ], "name": "checkEduCredentials", "outputs":
          [], "stateMutability": "payable", "type": "function" }, {
          "inputs": [], "name": "kill", "outputs": [], "stateMutability":
          "nonpayable", "type": "function" }, { "inputs": [ {
          "internalType": "string", "name": "document", "type":
          "string" } ], "name": "storeEduCredentials", "outputs": [],
          "stateMutability": "nonpayable", "type": "function" } ];

      address = 'Ox450FdF943afec4036787f4deDA11A34526c53921'

      return await new web3.eth.Contract(abi,address);
  }
```

Tip   Change the highlighted contract address with your own deployed contract address.

In the load() function, you call the loadContract() function and at the same time listen for the events that will be fired by the smart contract when it returns the result of the checks of credentials:

```
      async function load() {
          await loadWeb3();

          //---load the contract---
          notarizer = await loadContract();

          //---get the account---
          const account = await getCurrentAccount();

          //---handle the Result event fired by the smart contract---
          notarizer.events.Result()
              .on('data', function(event){
                  if (event.returnValues[0] == account) {
```

```
console.log(event.returnValues[0]);   // from
console.log(event.returnValues[1]);   // text
console.log(event.returnValues[2]);   // blocknumber

//---if the blocknumber is 0, this means
// credential is not found---
if (event.returnValues[2] > 0) {
    $("#result").html("Credential is valid");
} else {
    $("#result").html("Credential is NOT valid");
}
    }
});
    ...
```

Using the smart contract loaded, you can now call the storeEduCredentials() function of the smart contract through the **Store** button:

```
//---store the credential onto the blockchain---
$("#btnStore").click(async function() {
    notarizer.methods.storeEduCredentials($("#document").val())
        .send({from:account})
        .then(function (tx) {
            $("#result").html(tx.transactionHash);
        });
});
```

Notice that after the storeEduCredentials() function you use the send() function. The send() function is used when you need to perform a transaction on the smart contract (e.g., when the smart contract changes state variables). When the transaction is performed, you display the transaction hash onto the label named #result on the web page.

Likewise, to verify a credential, you call the checkEduCredentials() function with the credential to verify, together with a value of 1000 Wei:

```
//---check the credential on the blockchain---
$("#btnCheck").click(async function() {
    notarizer.methods.checkEduCredentials($("#document2").val())
        .send({from:account, value:1000});
});
```

When the result is returned to you via events, you display it in the label:

```
//---handle the Result event fired by the smart contract---
notarizer.events.Result()
    .on('data', function(event){
        if (event.returnValues[0] == account) {
            console.log(event.returnValues[0]);   // from
            console.log(event.returnValues[1]);   // text
            console.log(event.returnValues[2]);   // blocknumber

            //---if the blocknumber is 0, this means
            // credential is not found---
            if (event.returnValues[2] > 0) {
                $("#result").html("Credential is valid");
            } else {
                $("#result").html("Credential is NOT valid");
            }
        }
    });
```

Recall that all function calls on the smart contract that require payments (either required by the smart contract or required due to the smart contract making changes to state variables) are transactional, so you need to use the send() function when calling these smart contract functions. What happens if you call non-transactional functions? In this case, you can use the call() function.

Suppose the checkEduCredentials() function does not require a payment and simply returns the result directly:

```
// In EduCredentialsStore.sol
//-----------------------------------------------
// Check if a document has been saved previously
//-----------------------------------------------
function checkEduCredentials(string calldata
document) public view returns (uint){
  // use the hash of the string and check the
  // proofs mapping object
  return proofs[proofFor(document)];
}
```

To call this function using the web3.js API, use the call() function, like this:

```
        notarizer.methods.checkEduCredentials($("#document2").val())
            .call(function(error, result) {
            if(!error) {
                console.log("result is " + result);
                if (result > 0) {
                    $("#result").html("Credential is valid");
                } else {
                    $("#result").html("Credential is NOT valid");
                }
            } else
                console.error(error);
        });
```

Summary

In this chapter, you learned how to use the web3.js APIs to interact with your smart contracts. You learned how to use the web3.js APIs to build a web front end and how to interact with different types of smart contract functions. In the next chapter, you will learn how to interact with smart contracts using Python.

CHAPTER 9

Developing Web3 dapps using Python

In the previous chapter, you learned about creating Web3 decentralized applications (dapps) using the web3.js library. When developing your dapp using a web browser, you can conveniently integrate your app with MetaMask, which holds the various accounts you have on the Ethereum blockchain. When you need to perform a transaction, your dapp will rely on MetaMask to sign the transactions. Behind the scenes, MetaMask connects to a node known as **Infura**.

Infura is a full node that is connected to the Ethereum blockchain. It provides an easy way for apps to get connected to the Ethereum blockchain without needing developers to set up their own node, which can be very costly and requires a lot of effort. Figure 9-1 shows the flow between the dapp, MetaMask, Infura, and the Ethereum blockchain.

© Wei-Meng Lee 2023
W.-M. Lee, *Beginning Ethereum Smart Contracts Programming*, https://doi.org/10.1007/978-1-4842-9271-6_9

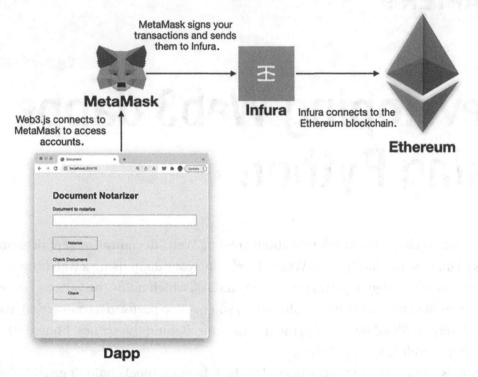

Figure 9-1. *How MetaMask connects to Infura in the backend*

But what if the dapp you are creating is not web-based? How do you pay for the transaction then? This is the topic I will address in this chapter.

Interacting with Ethereum Using Python

In this chapter, I will talk about how you can write a Web3 dapp using Python. For Python, you will use the web3.py library, which allows you to interact with the Ethereum blockchain using Python.

Tip   web3.py is inspired by web3.js, so you will find many functions similar to those you see in web3.js.

When you develop a Python dapp, you do not have the luxury of connecting to MetaMask to access your accounts and use it to sign your transactions. Instead, you need to import your own accounts, sign your own transactions, and then connect it to a full node (such as Infura) yourself, as shown in Figure 9-2.

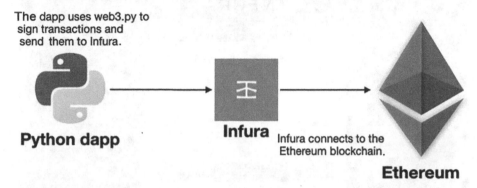

Figure 9-2. *Connecting your Python-based dapp to Infura*

In the following sections, you will learn how to use the web.py library to connect to the Erherum blockchain through Infura.

Registering with Infura

Now that you understand how your Python dapp is going to work, create a free account at `https://infura.io` (see Figure 9-3).

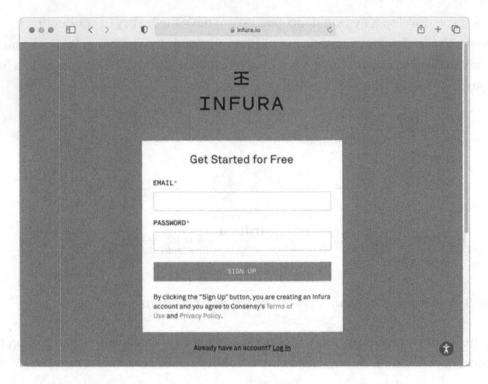

Figure 9-3. *Signing for a free account at Infura*

Once you have verified your email, you will be able to log into Infura. Create your first project (make sure you select **Ethereum** under PRODUCT) and give your project a name (see Figure 9-4).

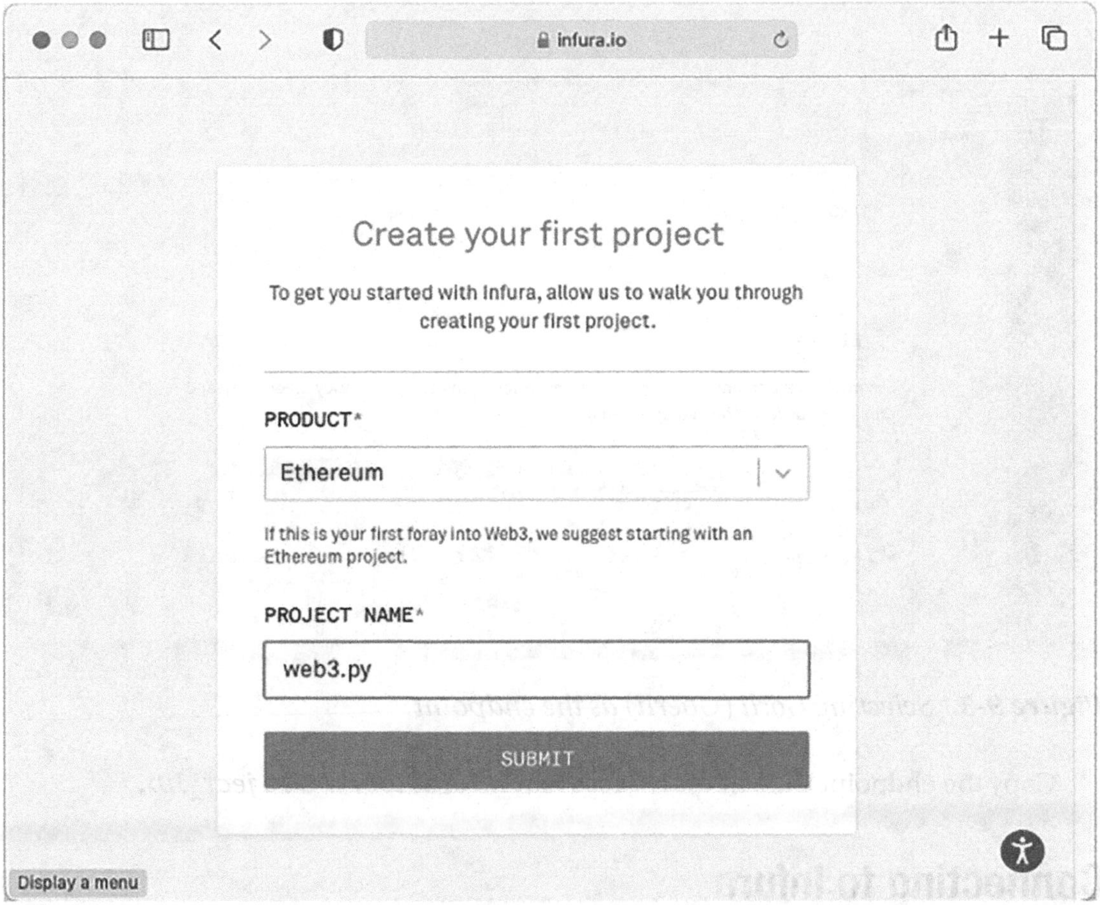

Figure 9-4. *Give your project a name*

You will now be given your project ID, project secret, and endpoints for your application to connect to. For this article, select Görli as the endpoint (see Figure 9-5).

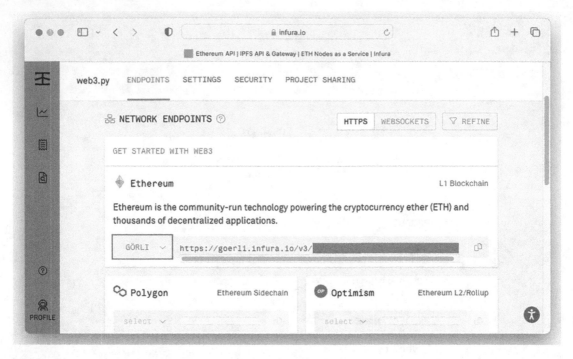

Figure 9-5. *Selecting Görli (Goerli) as the endpoint*

Copy the endpoint URL: `https://ropsten.infura.io/v3/<Project_ID>`.

Connecting to Infura

For the following sections, you will be using Jupyter Notebook. Go ahead a create a new Jupyter Notebook.

Tip   If you are new to Jupyter Notebook, check out this introduction: `https://jupyter.org/try-jupyter/retro/notebooks/?path=notebooks/Intro.ipynb`.

To install web3.py, type the following command in Jupyter Notebook:

```
!pip install web3
```

With the Infura endpoint URL obtained, see if you can connect it using the web3.py library:

```
from web3 import Web3

w3 = Web3(Web3.HTTPProvider(
    'https:// goerli.infura.io/v3/<Project_ID>'))
w3.isConnected()
```

Caution   Be sure to replace the **<Project_ID>** with your own.

The Web3 class returns an instance of a Web3 provider (a full node). The Web3. HTTPProvider class is a convenience API to access an RPC HTTP provider (which in this case is Infura).

Tip   RPC stands for remote procedure call.

If you see True as the output, it means you have connected to Infura successfully.

Fetching a Block

Using the Web3 object, let's now check the latest block number in the Goerli testnet:

```
w3.eth.get_block_number()
# 7978182
```

At the time of writing, the latest block number in the Goerli testnet is 7978182. You can also fetch the last block from the Goerli test network:

```
w3.eth.get_block('latest')
```

You will see the something like the following (an array of transaction hashes):

```
AttributeDict({'baseFeePerGas': 86766563290,
 'difficulty': 0,
 'extraData': HexBytes('0x'),
 'gasLimit': 30000000,
```

```
'gasUsed': 7186794,
'hash': HexBytes('0x6ab97e687ce253a6e4ada4c05166a47315e60447263e510bb1e5
ad85b9eab8b4'),
'logsBloom': HexBytes('0x20040c00c0000824028000180240000400004
840202010120000000000020410040000400201120040098 5
0000820000000000118000002400000028986240050005150 20
04200c08480000080808800000200 0c00016821001102000408
0404002041001220010802001038100010894 0c1000500041120
400001011800100800824008480204010000210000010090000
201400280000810008008000200040020380 00c000021000002
8700610008024002000009000040440005210800 0200840d20a1
00228042e001c00180000002182000400408800408600000000
60201910210802400200001300280000 0018000800084800c01
20040000000000000008'),
'miner': '0x4D496CcC28058B1D74B7a19541663E21154f9c84',
'mixHash': HexBytes('0x8710279fe41af813c450d778c81cff9401e429974249f98cd7
fa02f9788f7c25'),
'nonce': HexBytes('0x0000000000000000'),
'number': 7969293,
'parentHash': HexBytes('0xe1de6d5fe21da88f730faef1c39c6fcf58d3899729218c6e
8abf58b7163322ad'),
'receiptsRoot': HexBytes('0x4be7e89e6fe203768fa2899c7363944d913d7b915d7
5b382a5f871e7d4d39f0f'),
'sha3Uncles': HexBytes('0x1dcc4de8dec75d7aab85b567b6ccd41ad312451b948a741
3f0a142fd40d49347'),
'size': 109385,
'stateRoot': HexBytes('0x78c30965c1020934b6a3cfe784b00a3fbf25106c79818a66
fc21af676b608ca4'),
'timestamp': 1668684708,
'totalDifficulty': 10790000,
'transactions': [HexBytes('0x8fef9975fcc704e4a518370517d10563ea0a3d3edfa31
b5c1bb71fa42fd0a91d'),
 HexBytes('0x0a195f8876d642bbef524c4aa09df48c01471809df9614ea47a692e
 9f4832f7f'),
```

```
HexBytes('0x5fa6e3cb6230c97555391c85d449b6af60af1d4473cfb98a6cb19
  4b97668110c'),
... HexBytes('0xe60ae4a1b51cb89bd238499c471f1df6e34eaac64ab39b7c7a0258c
    3c5996bfa')],
'transactionsRoot': HexBytes('0x8e20604657f9bf48b2ed24ed38c27a6f507dda3e6d
  8b72e56e47754954398dcf'),
'uncles': []})
```

Setting Up the Accounts

Now, set up your Ethereum accounts. You will use the two accounts you created in MetaMask. Since you need to load the private key in your Python program, it is advisable to store the private key in an environment file so that you don't expose it in your Python code. For this, install the **python-dotenv** module:

```
!pip install python-dotenv
```

Once the python-dotenv module is installed, create a file named .env and save it in the same directory as your Jupyter notebook. Populate it with the following:

```
account1_private_key = '<private_key_of_account1>'
```

Note   Replace *<private_key_of_account1>* with the private key of Account 1.

To get the private key of Account 1, go to MetaMask and follow the steps outlined in Figure 9-6.

Figure 9-6. *Getting the private key of Account 1*

Caution   When dealing with the private keys of your accounts, ensure that no one else has access to them.

Once the private key is obtained, you can paste it inside the **.env** file.

Next, use the following code snippet to set up the details for Account 1 and 2:

```
from dotenv import load_dotenv
import os

load_dotenv()

# Account 1
account1_address = '0xa18A8E5c8242EF0DF08538C4870C638dD4667815'
account1_private_key = os.environ.get('account1_private_key')

# Account 2
account2_address = '0x1cc025d9A1741b51FD5dE6003884dc264F149AdC'
```

You are only going to use Account 1 to sign transactions later, so you only need to load up the private key for Account 1.

Caution   Be sure to replace 0xB35b89eE8AAc5C3ea6cd5C9080E8c66
Cb17ca2CC and 0x1cc025d9A1741b51FD5dE6003884dc264F149AdC with the
address of your Account 1 and Account 2, respectively.

Ensure that Account 1 and Account 2 already have some test Ethers in the Goerli test
network. If not, go to `https://goerlifaucet.com/` to get some test Ethers.

Getting the Balance of an Account

The first task you want to do after setting up your account is check the balance of
Account 1:

```
w3.eth.get_balance(account1_address)
```

You will get the result in Wei. Suppose you have 6.2468 ETH. You will get the
following output (in Wei):

```
6246772509923908581
```

Transferring Ethers Between Accounts

Let's now transfer 1 ETH from Account 1 to Account 2. This is a good chance for you to
learn how to perform a transaction manually using web3.py. For this,

- First, use the `eth.get_transaction_count()` function to get the
  number of transactions that have been sent from the specified
  account. This will be used as the *nonce* for the transaction:

  ```
  nonce = w3.eth.get_transaction_count(account1_address)
  ```

- Then, create a dictionary containing the transaction details:

  ```
  tx = {
      'nonce': nonce,                    # transaction count
      'to': account2_address,            # who to send the ETH to
      'value': w3.toWei(1000, 'wei'),    # the amount to transfer
      'gasPrice': w3.eth.gas_price,      # get the price of gas
  }
  ```

In this code, you are transferring 1000 Wei from Account 1 to Account 2. You use the `eth.gas_price` attribute to fetch the current gas price.

- Next, estimate how much gas is needed for this transaction using the `eth.estimate_gas()` function and then insert the amount into the transaction dictionary:

```
gas = w3.eth.estimate_gas(tx)
tx['gas'] = gas
print(tx)
```

You should see the transaction details as follows:

```
{
    'nonce': 4,
    'to': '0x1cc025d9A1741b51FD5dE6003884dc264F149AdC',
    'value': 1000,
    'gasPrice': 114287036513,
    'gas': 21000
}
```

- You can now sign the transaction with the private key using the `eth.account.sign_transaction()` function:

```
signed_tx = w3.eth.account.sign_transaction(tx,account1_
private_key)
```

- To send the transaction to Infura, use the `eth.send_raw_transaction()` function:

```
tx_hash = w3.eth.send_raw_transaction(signed_tx.rawTransaction)
print(w3.toHex(tx_hash))
```

The function will return with a hash, like this:

```
0xc23d15f14f20f51b083fe6dab8f953e76b80ce6a3b4c43bfe336d02576eba1da
```

- The transaction will take some time to confirm. If you want to wait for the transaction to complete, use the eth.wait_for_transaction_receipt() function (this is a blocking call):

```
receipt = w3.eth.wait_for_transaction_receipt(tx_hash)
```

- Finally, to verify that the transfer is indeed performed correctly, check the balance for Account 1 and 2:

```
print(w3.eth.get_balance(account1_address))
print(w3.eth.get_balance(account2_address))
```

The entire code snippet to transfer 1 ETH from Account 1 to Account 2 looks like this:

```
nonce = w3.eth.get_transaction_count(account1_address)
tx = {
    'nonce': nonce,
    'to': account2_address,
    'value': w3.toWei(1000, 'wei'),
    'gasPrice': w3.eth.gas_price,
}
gas = w3.eth.estimate_gas(tx)
tx['gas'] = gas
signed_tx = w3.eth.account.sign_transaction(tx,account1_private_key)
tx_hash = w3.eth.send_raw_transaction(signed_tx.rawTransaction)
print(w3.toHex(tx_hash))
receipt = w3.eth.wait_for_transaction_receipt(tx_hash)
```

Creating a Dapp Using Python

Using Python to sign transactions is useful, but the more important thing you want to do with the web3.py library is interact with your smart contracts. For this purpose, you are going to use Python to interact with the smart contract you created in Chapter 7. Here is the full smart contract for your reference:

```
// SPDX-License-Identifier: MIT
pragma solidity ^0.8;
```

```solidity
contract EduCredentialsStore {
  // store the owner of the contract
  address owner = msg.sender;

  //---store the hash of the strings and their
  // corresponding block number---
  // key is bytes32 and val is uint
  mapping (bytes32 => uint) private proofs;

  //---define an event---
  event Result(
    address from,
    string document,
    uint blockNumber
  );

  //-------------------------------------------------------
  // Store a proof of existence in the contract state
  //-------------------------------------------------------
  function storeProof(bytes32 proof) private {
    // use the hash as the key
    proofs[proof] = block.number;
  }

  //----------------------------------------------
  // Calculate and store the proof for a document
  //----------------------------------------------
  function storeEduCredentials(string calldata
  document) external {
    require(msg.sender == owner,
      "Only the owner of contract can store the credentials");

    // call storeProof() with the hash of
    // the string
    storeProof(proofFor(document));
  }
```

```solidity
  function cashOut() public {
    require(msg.sender == owner,
      "Only the owner of contract can cash out!");
    payable(owner).transfer(
      address(this).balance);
  }

  //---------------------------------------------
  // Helper function to get a document's sha256
  //---------------------------------------------
  // Takes in a string and returns the hash of the
  // string
  function proofFor(string calldata document) private
  pure returns (bytes32) {
    // converts the string into bytes array and
    // then hash it
    return sha256(bytes(document));
  }

  //-----------------------------------------------
  // Check if a document has been saved previously
  //-----------------------------------------------
  function checkEduCredentials(string calldata document) public payable {
    require(msg.value == 1000 wei ,
      "This call requires 1000 wei");

    // use the hash of the string and check
    // the proofs mapping object, then fire the event
    emit Result(msg.sender,
                document,
                proofs[proofFor(document)]);
  }

  /* self-destruct function */
  function kill() public {
    require(msg.sender == owner, "Only owner can kill this contract");
    selfdestruct(payable(owner));
  }

}
```

Tip   If you can't remember the address of this contract you previously deployed on the Goerli testnet, deploy it one more time and take note of its address.

For demonstration, the address of my contract on the Goerli testnet is 0xC1B4338a54bE220672600bbA1e0B6F3d5c1E2E330. Also, you need to get the ABI of the contract. For your convenience, here it is:

```
[ {   "inputs": [],   "name": "cashOut",   "outputs": [],
"stateMutability": "nonpayable",   "type": "function" }, {   "inputs":
[   {     "internalType": "string",     "name": "document",     "type":
"string"   } ],   "name": "checkEduCredentials",   "outputs": [],
"stateMutability": "payable",   "type": "function" }, {   "inputs": [],
"name": "kill",   "outputs": [],   "stateMutability": "nonpayable",
"type": "function" }, {   "anonymous": false,   "inputs": [   {
"indexed": false,     "internalType": "address",     "name": "from",
"type": "address"   },   {     "indexed": false,     "internalType":
"string",     "name": "document",     "type": "string"   },   {
"indexed": false,     "internalType": "uint256",     "name": "blockNumber",
"type": "uint256"   } ],   "name": "Result",   "type": "event" },
{   "inputs": [   {     "internalType": "string",     "name": "document",
"type": "string"   } ],   "name": "storeEduCredentials",
"outputs": [],   "stateMutability": "nonpayable",   "type": "function" } ]
```

Loading the Contract

With the contract deployed, let's create a reference to it using the eth.contract() function by passing it the address and ABI of the contract:

```
address = '0xC1B4338a54bE220672600bbA1e0B6F3d5c1E2E330'

abi = '[ {   "inputs": [],   "name": "cashOut",   "outputs": [],
"stateMutability": "nonpayable",   "type": "function" }, {   "inputs":
[   {     "internalType": "string",     "name": "document",     "type":
"string"   } ],   "name": "checkEduCredentials",   "outputs": [],
"stateMutability": "payable",   "type": "function" }, {   "inputs":
[],   "name": "kill",   "outputs": [],   "stateMutability": "nonpayable",
```

```
"type": "function"  }, {    "anonymous": false,    "inputs": [    {
"indexed": false,    "internalType": "address",    "name": "from",
"type": "address"    }, {    "indexed": false,    "internalType":
"string",    "name": "document",    "type": "string"    },    {
"indexed": false,    "internalType": "uint256",    "name": "blockNumber",
"type": "uint256"    }  ],    "name": "Result",    "type": "event"  }, {
"inputs": [    {    "internalType": "string",    "name": "document",
"type": "string"    }  ],    "name": "storeEduCredentials",    "outputs":
[],    "stateMutability": "nonpayable",    "type": "function"  } ]'

eduCredentialsStore = w3.eth.contract(address = address, abi = abi)
```

The eduCredentialsStore variable now contains a reference to the smart contract.

Base64 Encoding

Remember the educational credentials must be base64-encoded before passing to the smart contract. Here you will define a helper function named base64encode():

```
import base64

def base64encode(message):
    message_bytes = message.encode('ascii')
    base64_bytes = base64.b64encode(message_bytes)
    return base64_bytes.decode('ascii')
```

This function takes in a string and returns its base64-encoded equivalent.

Saving Credentials on the Blockchain

Here is the code snippet to save the educational credential of a student onto the blockchain through your smart contract:

```
# the JSON string containing the exam result
exam_result = '''
{
  "id": "1234567",
  "result": {
```

```
    "math": "A",
    "science": "B",
    "english": "A"
  }
}
'''

exam_result = base64encode(exam_result)

# get the nonce of the account
nonce = w3.eth.get_transaction_count(account1_address)

# estimate the gas fee
estimated_gas = \
    eduCredentialsStore.functions.storeEduCredentials(
        exam_result).estimateGas(
            {'from':account1_address})

# build the transaction
transaction = \
  eduCredentialsStore.functions.storeEduCredentials(
    exam_result).buildTransaction(
    {
        'gas': estimated_gas,
        'gasPrice': w3.eth.gas_price,
        'from': account1_address,
        'nonce': nonce
    })

# sign the transaction
signed_txn = w3.eth.account.sign_transaction(
    transaction, private_key = account1_private_key)

# send the transaction
tx_hash = w3.eth.send_raw_transaction(signed_txn.rawTransaction)
print(w3.toHex(tx_hash))

# wait for the transaction to confirm
receipt = w3.eth.wait_for_transaction_receipt(tx_hash)
```

Let's go through what happens in this code:

- You first base64-encode the exam results stored as a string.

  To call the storeEduCredentials() function in the contract, you use the eduCredentialsStore.functions. storeEduCredentials() function and then use the estimateGas() function to estimate the gas needed to call it. Because this function is only callable from the owner of the contract (which is account1_address), you need to pass account1_address into the function, or you will encounter an error.

```
# estimate the gas fee
estimated_gas = \
    eduCredentialsStore.functions.storeEduCredentials(
        exam_result).estimateGas(
            {'from':account1_address})
```

- You use the buildTransaction() function to build the transaction, passing it the estimated gas required, gas price, account calling the contract, and the nonce:

```
# build the transaction
transaction = \
  eduCredentialsStore.functions.storeEduCredentials(
    exam_result).buildTransaction(
    {
        'gas': estimated_gas,
        'gasPrice': w3.eth.gas_price,
        'from': account1_address,
        'nonce': nonce
    })
```

- You sign the transaction using the sign_transaction() function, using Account 1's private key:

```
# sign the transaction
signed_txn = w3.eth.account.sign_transaction(
    transaction, private_key = account1_private_key)
```

- You send the transaction using the send_raw_transaction() function:

```
# send the transaction
tx_hash = w3.eth.send_raw_transaction(signed_txn.rawTransaction)
print(w3.toHex(tx_hash))
```

- You use the eth.wait_for_transaction_receipt() function to wait for the transaction to confirm. When the transaction is confirmed, the details of the transaction will be stored in the receipt variable.

```
# wait for the transaction to confirm
receipt = w3.eth.wait_for_transaction_receipt(tx_hash)
```

Verifying the Result

With the exam results firmly recorded on the blockchain, let's now verify the result. Here's the code snippet:

```
exam_result = '''
{
  "id": "1234567",
  "result": {
    "math": "A",
    "science": "B",
    "english": "A"
  }
}
'''

exam_result = base64encode(exam_result)

nonce = w3.eth.getTransactionCount(account1_address)
```

```python
# estimate the gas fee
estimated_gas = eduCredentialsStore.functions.checkEduCredentials(
                exam_result).estimateGas(
                    { 'value' : 1000 }
                )  # 1000 is the wei to send

# build the transaction
transaction = eduCredentialsStore.functions.checkEduCredentials(
    exam_result).buildTransaction(
    {
        'gas'      : estimated_gas,
        'gasPrice' : w3.eth.gas_price,
        'from'     : account1_address,
        'nonce'    : nonce,
        'value'    : w3.toWei(1000, 'wei'),   # amount to send to the
    })                                        # function

# sign the transaction
signed_txn = w3.eth.account.sign_transaction(transaction,
                private_key = account1_private_key)

# send the transaction
tx_hash = w3.eth.send_raw_transaction(signed_txn.rawTransaction)
print(w3.toHex(tx_hash))

import time

# create an instance of the event
result_event = eduCredentialsStore.events.Result()

def handle_event(event):
    receipt = \
        w3.eth.wait_for_transaction_receipt(event['transactionHash'])
    result = result_event.processReceipt(receipt)

    # print the content of the Result event
    print(result)
    if result[0]['args']['blockNumber'] != 0:
        print('Result is verified.')
```

```
    else:
        print('Result not found on blockchain.')
    return True

def log_loop(event_filter, poll_interval):
    while True:
        for event in event_filter.get_new_entries():
            result = handle_event(event)
            if result == True:
                return
            time.sleep(poll_interval)

block_filter = w3.eth.filter(
    {
        'fromBlock' : 'latest',
        'address'   : address        # address of contract
    })

log_loop(block_filter, 2)
```

The first part of this code snippet is similar to the previous code snippet. But here's what is happening in this code snippet:

- You estimate how much gas fee is needed when you call the checkEduCredentials () function together with a value of 1000 Wei (the function needs this amount):

```
# estimate the gas fee
estimated_gas = eduCredentialsStore.functions.checkEduCredentials(
                exam_result).estimateGas(
                    { 'value' : 1000 }
                ) # 1000 is the wei to send
```

- You include the amount (1000 Wei) to send to the
  checkEduCredentials() function in the transaction:

```
transaction = eduCredentialsStore.functions.checkEduCredentials(
    exam_result).buildTransaction(
    {
        'gas'      : estimated_gas,
        'gasPrice' : w3.eth.gas_price,
        'from'     : account1_address,
        'nonce'    : nonce,
        'value'    : w3.toWei(1000, 'wei'),   # amount to
                                              # send to the
    })                                        # function
```

- You then create an instance of the Result event so that you can listen
  for this event firing from the smart contract:

```
# create an instance of the event
result_event = eduCredentialsStore.events.Result()
```

- To listen for the Result event, you need to implement your own
  looping mechanism. Here, you first use the w3.eth.filter()
  function to listen for specific events from the contract. You then
  use an infinite loop to keep listening for the events using the get_
  new_entries() function of the event filter. You use the wait_for_
  transaction_receipt() function to listen only for events related
  to this particular transaction. When an event is received, you call
  the processReceipt() function of the event to get the details of the
  event. In this case, as soon as the Result event is fetched, you stop
  listening for future events.

- The event returned by the contract will look something like the following:

```
(AttributeDict({'args': AttributeDict({'from':
'0xAF8b6CA21023A595F0C4919b8B4a9d1F0c1773e7', 'document':
'CnsKICAiaWQiOiAiMTIzNDU2NyIsCiAgInJlc3VsdCI6IHsKICAgI
CJtYXRoIjogIkEiLAogICAgInNjaWVuY2UiOiAiQiIsCiAgICAiZW5nb
GlzaCI6ICJBIgogIHOKfQo=', 'blockNumber': 7973034}),
'event': 'Result', 'logIndex': 301, 'transactionIndex':
177, 'transactionHash': HexBytes('0x85c4ceb53e1f4c3e7844e
ba51f8d33d291a325ac191fa99a0d554ccc1e9f5864'), 'address':
'0xC1B4338a54bE22067260bbA1e0B6F3d5c1E2E330', 'blockHash':
HexBytes('0x752f3634b1970ca613e51c468e28e86186dd3603f215751f
bc727392c9581460'), 'blockNumber': 7973064}),)
```

- The event returned is a tuple. You get the first element in the tuple, then look for the args key, and from there look for the blockNumber key, which will allow you to know if the examination result is authentic:

```
if result[0]['args']['blockNumber'] != 0:
    print('Result is verified.')
else:
    print('Result not found on blockchain.')
```

When you run this code, you will see the output like the following when the Result event is fired:

```
0x85c4ceb53e1f4c3e7844eba51f8d33d291a325ac191fa99a0d554ccc1e9f5864
(AttributeDict({'args': AttributeDict({'from':
'0xAF8b6CA21023A595F0C4919b8B4a9d1F0c1773e7', 'document':
'CnsKICAiaWQiOiAiMTIzNDU2NyIsCiAgInJlc3VsdCI6IHsKICAg
ICJtYXRoIjogIkEiLAogICAgInNjaWVuY2UiOiAiQiIsCiAgICAi
ZW5nbGlzaCI6ICJBIgogIHOKfQo=', 'blockNumber': 7973034}),
'event': 'Result', 'logIndex': 301, 'transactionIndex':
177, 'transactionHash': HexBytes('0x85c4ceb53e1f4c3e7844e
ba51f8d33d291a325ac191fa99a0d554ccc1e9f5864'), 'address':
```

```
'0xC1B4338a54bE22067260bbA1e0B6F3d5c1E2E330', 'blockHash': HexB
ytes('0x752f3634b1970ca613e51c468e28e86186dd3603f215751fbc72739
2c9581460'), 'blockNumber': 7973064}),)
```
Result is verified.

CALLING FUNCTIONS THAT DO NOT REQUIRE TRANSACTIONS

Note that for smart contract functions that do not perform any transaction, you can simply call them using the `call()` function. For example, suppose the `checkEduCredentials()` function does not require any payment and thus it does not perform any transaction. In this case, you can call it like this:

```
eduCredentialsStore.functions.checkEduCredentials(exam_result).call()
```

Summary

Overall, building a Web3 dapp using Python and web3.py is like building one using web3.js. The key difference is that for a Python dapp, you need to get intimate with the transactions yourself: connecting to a full node, signing the transactions, estimating the required gas fee needed, setting the gas price, and then finally waiting for the transactions to confirm and handle the events fired.

## CHAPTER 10

Project: Online Lottery

Now that you have seen how smart contracts work and how to interact with them using the web3.js APIs, it's a good time to explore an application from end to end, from the smart contract to the front end, and perhaps give you some ideas for building your own decentralized applications.

How the Lottery Game Works

For this chapter, you will build a lottery game using a smart contract. In this contract, you will allow players to place a bet on a number. Figure 10-1 shows how the game works.

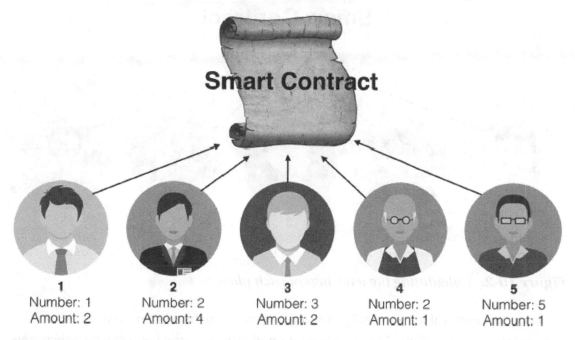

Figure 10-1. *How the online lottery game works*

© Wei-Meng Lee 2023
W.-M. Lee, *Beginning Ethereum Smart Contracts Programming*, https://doi.org/10.1007/978-1-4842-9271-6_10

There are a total of five players. Each player will place a bet on a number. For example, player 1 bets on the number 1 using 2 Ethers, and player 2 bets on the number 2 with 4 Ethers, and so on. The betting will stop when the maximum number of players is reached. Once the betting has stopped, the owner of the contract will set the winning number and the payouts to the winners will be processed.

Suppose the winning number is 2. Based on the example, players 2 and 4 have bet on the winning number. The amount won by each winner is proportional to how much they have bet. The calculation is shown in Figure 10-2.

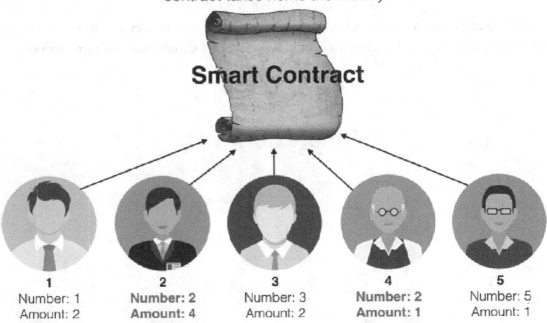

Winning Number: 2
Total Wager: 2+4+2+1+1 = 10 Ethers
Total Winning Wager: 4 + 1 = 5 Ethers
Winnings for *Player 2*: 4/5 * 10 = **8** Ethers
Winnings for *Player 4*: 1/5 * 10 = **2** Ethers

If nobody wins, the owner of the contract takes home the money!

Smart Contract

1	2	3	4	5
Number: 1	**Number: 2**	Number: 3	**Number: 2**	Number: 5
Amount: 2	**Amount: 4**	Amount: 2	**Amount: 1**	Amount: 1

Figure 10-2. *Calculating the winnings of each player*

Your contract will automatically transfer the payout to the winners. If there is no winner for the game, all the Ethers will be retained by the contract and can be transferred to the owner of the contract.

Defining the Smart Contract

In the next few sections, you will walk through the creation of the contract so that you can see how it is built. You will use the Remix IDE to build this contract.

Let's first define some data structures to keep the information of the players within the smart contract.

First, define a structure named Player to keep track of the amount of Ethers the player was wagered and the number that the player has wagered on:

```
// store wager details of each player
struct Player {
    uint amountWagered;    // e.g. 2000 wei
    uint numberWagered;    // e.g. number 5
}
```

Then, define the playerDetailsMapping variable, which is a mapping object:

```
// waging details of all players in a mapping object
mapping(address => Player) playerDetailsMapping;
```

The playerDetailsMapping is a mapping object where the keys are the account addresses of all players. The value for each key is a structure named Player with two members: amountWagered (the amount of Wei bet), and numberWagered (the number that the player is betting on). Figure 10-3 shows the data structure that you will use to store the details of the game.

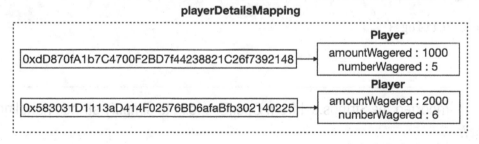

Figure 10-3. *The playerDetailsMapping variable stores the betting details of each player*

In typical dictionary objects in other programming languages, it is easy to iterate through the members of a dictionary and obtain all the keys in it. However, for the mapping object in Solidity, it is not possible to get the keys or iterate through all the members in it. So you must improvise your own solution if you want to do that. The easiest way is to use an array to keep track of all the account addresses (see Figure 10-4):

```
// array of addresses of all players
address payable [MAX_NUMBER_OF_PLAYERS] playerAddressesArray;
```

playerAddressesArray

0xdD870fA1b7C4700F2BD7f44238821C26f7392148

0x583031D1113aD414F02576BD6afaBfb302140225

Figure 10-4. *The playerAddressesArray variable stores all of the players' addresses*

Arrays in Solidity behave more like arrays in traditional programming languages like C and Java: you can iterate through an array, get its length, and so on. Using this array, you can use it to access each of the members in the mapping object and use it to determine the winner of the game.

With the data structure defined, define the contract called Betting:

```
// SPDX-License-Identifier: MIT
pragma solidity ^0.8;
import "@openzeppelin/contracts/utils/Strings.sol";

contract Betting {
}
```

Note   I imported the Strings.sol from OpenZeppelin to simplify strings handling in Solidity.

Let's declare some variables, constants, and events in the contract:

```
contract Betting {
    // record the owner of the contract
    address owner = msg.sender;

    // minimum amount to wage (wei)
    uint constant MIN_WAGER = 1000;

    // maximum number of players allowed for each round
    uint constant MAX_NUMBER_OF_PLAYERS = 3;

    // range of numbers to bet, from 1 to MAX_NUMBER_TO_BET
    uint constant MAX_NUMBER_TO_BET = 10;

    // total amount waged by players so far
    uint totalWager = 0;

    // number of players waged so far
    uint numberOfPlayers = 0;

    // winning number
    uint winningBetNumber = 0;

    // array of addresses of all players
    address payable [MAX_NUMBER_OF_PLAYERS] playerAddressesArray;

    // store wager details of each player
    struct Player {
        uint amountWagered;
        uint numberWagered;
    }

    // waging details of all players in a mapping object
    mapping(address => Player) playerDetailsMapping;

    //---define an event---
    event Winner(
        address winner,
        uint amount
    );
```

```
    // the event to display the status of the game
    event Status (
        uint players,
        uint maxPlayers
    );
}
```

Here are some important points to note:

- `owner` is used to store the address of the account that deployed the contract.

- `MAX_NUMBER_OF_PLAYERS` lets you define the maximum number of players allowed in a game before the winning number is drawn. For ease of testing, it's set to 3. In real life, this could be set to a much larger number.

- `MAX_NUMBER_TO_BET` defines the maximum winning number for the lottery game. The numbers that can be bet on are from 1 to `MAX_NUMBER_TO_BET`.

- `playerAddressesArray` is a fixed size array storing the account address of each player. You prefix the declaration with the `payable` keyword to indicate that each player can send/receive Ethers.

- `Player` is a structure that contains two members: `amountWagered` and `numberWagered`.

- `playerDetailsMapping` is mapping object that stores the details of each player's waging details.

- `Winner` and `Status` are events that are used to notify client applications.

Betting a Number

Next, let's define the `bet()` function within the contract. The `bet()` function allows a player to bet on a number:

```
function bet(uint number) public payable {
    // CHECK #1
```

```
// ensure the max number of players has not been reached
require(numberOfPlayers < MAX_NUMBER_OF_PLAYERS,
    "Maximum number of players reached");

// CHECK #2
// check to ensure caller has never betted
require(playerDetailsMapping[msg.sender].numberWagered == 0,
    "You have already betted");

// CHECK #3
// check the range of numbers allowed for betting
require(number >=1 && number <= MAX_NUMBER_TO_BET,
    string.concat("You need to bet between 1 and ",
        Strings.toString(MAX_NUMBER_TO_BET)));

// CHECK #4
// ensure min. bet (note that msg.value is in wei)
require( msg.value >= MIN_WAGER,
    string.concat("Minimum bet is ",
        Strings.toString(MIN_WAGER), " wei"));

// record the number and amount wagered by the player
playerDetailsMapping[msg.sender].amountWagered = msg.value;
playerDetailsMapping[msg.sender].numberWagered = number;

// add the player address to the array of addresses
playerAddressesArray[numberOfPlayers] = payable(msg.sender);

numberOfPlayers++;
totalWager += msg.value;

//  emit the Status event
emit Status(numberOfPlayers, MAX_NUMBER_OF_PLAYERS);
}
```

Note   Observe that the bet() function has the payable keyword. This means that when a player bets on a number, they must also send in Ethers.

In this function, you need to perform a few checks. First, you need to check if the maximum number of players has been exceeded:

```
// CHECK #1
// ensure the max number of players has not been reached
require(numberOfPlayers < MAX_NUMBER_OF_PLAYERS,
    "Maximum number of players reached");
```

Next, ensure that each player can only bet once by retrieving the `Player` structure in the `playerDetailsMapping` object and checking its `numberWagered` value. If it is zero, it means that the player has not bet previously:

```
// CHECK #2
// check to ensure caller has never betted
require(playerDetailsMapping[msg.sender].numberWagered == 0,
    "You have already betted");
```

Note   If the account address of the player cannot be found in the `playerDetailsMapping` object, the values of the two members in the `Player` structure will be set to their default values, which is 0 for `uint`.

Next, you need to check that the number wagered falls within the range allowed:

```
// CHECK #3
// check the range of numbers allowed for betting
require(number >=1 && number <= MAX_NUMBER_TO_BET,
    string.concat("You need to bet between 1 and ",
        Strings.toString(MAX_NUMBER_TO_BET)));
```

You also need to check that the amount wagered is at least the minimum amount:

```
// CHECK #4
// ensure min. bet (note that msg.value is in wei)
require( msg.value >= MIN_WAGER,
    string.concat("Minimum bet is ",
        Strings.toString(MIN_WAGER), " wei"));
```

Once all these checks are cleared, you need to record the number and amount wagered by the player (msg.sender is the address of the player):

```
// record the number and amount wagered by the player
playerDetailsMapping[msg.sender].amountWagered = msg.value;
playerDetailsMapping[msg.sender].numberWagered = number;
```

You also add the player address to the array of addresses:

```
// add the player address to the array of addresses
playerAddressesArray[numberOfPlayers] = payable(msg.sender);
```

You also increment the number of wagers as well as sum up all the amount wagered so far:

```
numberOfPlayers++;
totalWager += msg.value;
```

Finally, emit the Status event:

```
//  emit the Status event
emit Status(numberOfPlayers, MAX_NUMBER_OF_PLAYERS);
```

Setting the Winning Number and Announcing the Winners

The next function to define is announceWinners(). The announceWinners() function takes in the winning number and calculates the winning for each player and transfers the winnings to them:

```
function announceWinners(uint winningNumber) public {
    require(msg.sender == owner,
        "Only the owner can announce the winner");

    winningBetNumber = winningNumber;

    // use to store winners
    address payable[MAX_NUMBER_OF_PLAYERS] memory winners;
    uint winnerCount = 0;
    uint totalWinningWager = 0;
```

```
// find out the winners
for (uint i=0; i < playerAddressesArray.length; i++) {
    // get the address of each player
    address payable playerAddress = playerAddressesArray[i];

    // if the player betted number is the winning number
    if (playerDetailsMapping[playerAddress].numberWagered ==
        winningNumber) {
        // save the player address into the winners
        // array
        winners[winnerCount] = playerAddress;

        // sum up the total wagered amount for the
        // winning numbers
        totalWinningWager +=
          playerDetailsMapping[playerAddress].amountWagered;
        winnerCount++;
    }
}

// make payments to each winning player
for (uint j=0; j<winnerCount; j++) {

    // calculate thw winnings of each player
    uint amount = (playerDetailsMapping[winners[j]].amountWagered *
        totalWager ) / totalWinningWager;

    // make payment to player
    winners[j].transfer(amount);
    emit Winner(winners[j], amount);
}

// reset the variables
numberOfPlayers = 0;
totalWager = 0;

// clear all arrays and mappings
for (uint i=0; i < playerAddressesArray.length; i++) {
    // get the address of each player
```

```
        address payable playerAddress = playerAddressesArray[i];
        delete playerDetailsMapping[playerAddress];
        delete playerAddressesArray[i];
    }

    // emit the Status event
    emit Status(numberOfPlayers, MAX_NUMBER_OF_PLAYERS);
}
```

Tip   In this implementation, you pass in a winning number to the function. In real life, you may want to connect to a real lottery feed to fetch the winning number. You can do so via *Oracles*. Refer to my article called "*Smart Contracts — Fetching Data From External Sources using Oracles*" (`https://blog.cryptostars.is/ smart-contracts-fetching-data-from-external-sources-using- oracles-bfd73f362375`) for more details.

You first check to ensure that only the owner of this contract can invoke this function:

```
require(msg.sender == owner,
    "Only the owner can announce the winner");
```

You next create an array in memory to store all the winning players, plus two variables for storing the number of winners as well as the total amount of winning wagers:

```
// use to store winners
address payable[MAX_NUMBER_OF_PLAYERS] memory winners;
uint winnerCount = 0;
uint totalWinningWager = 0;
```

You iterate through all the players using the playerAddressesArray array and check if the number they wagered on is the winning number. The winning players are then added to the winners array.

```
// find out the winners
for (uint i=0; i < playerAddressesArray.length; i++) {
    // get the address of each player
    address payable playerAddress = playerAddressesArray[i];
```

```
    // if the player betted number is the winning number
    if (playerDetailsMapping[playerAddress].numberWagered ==
        winningNumber) {
        // save the player address into the winners
        // array
        winners[winnerCount] = playerAddress;

        // sum up the total wagered amount for the
        // winning numbers
        totalWinningWager +=
            playerDetailsMapping[playerAddress].amountWagered;
        winnerCount++;
    }
}
```

You then calculate the winnings for each player and transfer the winnings to them using the `transfer()` function:

```
// make payments to each winning player
for (uint j=0; j<winnerCount; j++) {

    // calculate thw winnings of each player
    uint amount = (playerDetailsMapping[winners[j]].amountWagered *
        totalWager ) / totalWinningWager;

    // make payment to player
    winners[j].transfer(amount);

    // emit the Winner event
    emit Winner(winners[j], amount);
}
```

Finally, reset all the variables so that a new game can start:

```
// reset the variables
numberOfPlayers = 0;
totalWager = 0;
```

```
        // clear all arrays and mappings
        for (uint i=0; i < playerAddressesArray.length; i++) {
            // get the address of each player
            address payable playerAddress = playerAddressesArray[i];
            delete playerDetailsMapping[playerAddress];
            delete playerAddressesArray[i];
        }
```

Getting the Game Status and Winning Number

To allow the outside world to know the winning number as well as get the status of the game, add the following functions to the contract:

```
    function getGameStatus() view public returns (uint, uint) {
        // return the status of the game
        return (numberOfPlayers, MAX_NUMBER_OF_PLAYERS);
    }

    function getWinningNumber() view public returns (uint) {
        // return the winning number
        return winningBetNumber;
    }
```

Cashing Out from the Contract

When there are no winners for the game, the smart contract will hold the Ethers that were sent to it. To send the Ethers back to the account that deploys the contract, you need to add a cash-out function:

```
    function cashOut() public {
        require(msg.sender == owner,
            "Only the owner of contract can cash out!");
        payable(owner).transfer(address(this).balance);
    }
```

Obviously, you need to ensure that only the owner (the one that deploys the contract) of the contract can cash out.

Testing the Contract

With the contract written, it is now time to test it to make sure it works according to plan. The fastest way to test it to test it locally.

In the Remix IDE, make sure that the Remix VM (London) environment is selected (see Figure 10-5). Observe that there are 10 accounts each with 100 Ethers created for your testing.

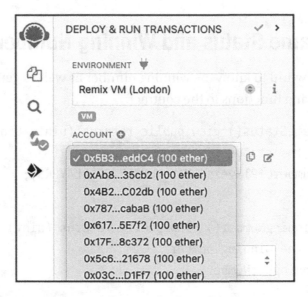

Figure 10-5. *Ten accounts each with 100 Ethers are created for your testing use*

Using the first account, deploy the contract.

Note   The first account is the owner of the smart contract.

When the contract is successfully deployed, you will see the various functions shown in Figure 10-6.

Figure 10-6. *The various functions in the contract*

Using the same first account,

- Bet the number 1 with 2000 Wei (see Figure 10-7).

- Click the **bet** button.

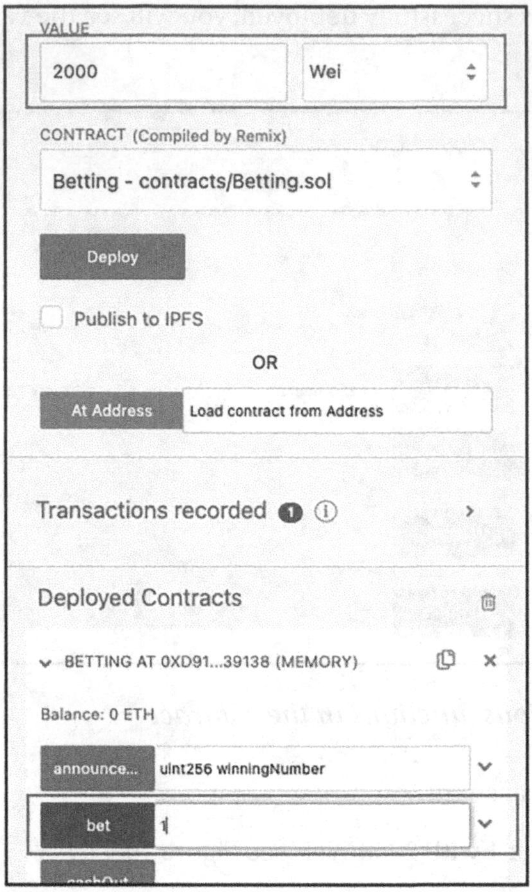

Figure 10-7. *Betting the number 1 with 2000 Wei*

Then, click the **getGameStatus** button and you should see a result of 1 and 3 (see Figure 10-8). The 1 means one player has wagered and 3 means the maximum number of players.

Figure 10-8. *Getting the status of the game*

Using the second account,

- Bet the number 5 with 1000 Wei.

- Click the **bet** button.

Using the third account,

- Bet the number 5 with 2000 Wei.

- Click the **bet** button.

Table 10-1 summarizes the status of the bets.

Table 10-1. *The Numbers Wagered*

Account	numberWagered	amountWagered (Wei)
1 (owner)	1	2000
2	5	1000
3	5	2000

Caution   Remember to switch the accounts under the Account section in the Remix IDE when betting.

Announcing the Winner

Now that all three players have wagered, it is time to announce the winner.

Tip   You don't have to wait for all three players to bet before announcing the winner. Anytime you want to end the game, you can call the **announceWinners** button. You can end the game even if only two players have wagered.

Using the first account,

- Enter the number 5 (see Figure 10-9).

- Click the **announceWinners** button.

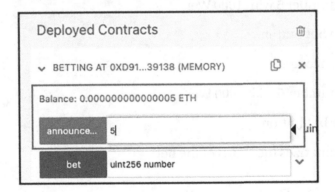

Figure 10-9. *Announcing the winning number*

At the bottom of the Remix IDE, you should see the events fired by the smart contract (see Figure 10-10).

```
logs                    [
                          {
                              "from": "0xd9145CCE52D386f254917e481eB44e9943F39138",
                              "topic": "0x9c2270628a9b29d30ae96b6c4c14ed646ee134febdce38a5b77f2bde9cea2e20",
                              "event": "Winner",
                              "args": {
                                  "0": "0xAb8483F64d9C6d1EcF9b849Ae677dD3315835cb2",
                                  "1": "1666",
                                  "winner": "0xAb8483F64d9C6d1EcF9b849Ae677dD3315835cb2",
                                  "amount": "1666"
                              }
                          },
                          {
                              "from": "0xd9145CCE52D386f254917e481eB44e9943F39138",
                              "topic": "0x9c2270628a9b29d30ae96b6c4c14ed646ee134febdce38a5b77f2bde9cea2e20",
                              "event": "Winner",
                              "args": {
                                  "0": "0x4B20993Bc481177ec7E8f571ceCaE8A9e22C02db",
                                  "1": "3333",
                                  "winner": "0x4B20993Bc481177ec7E8f571ceCaE8A9e22C02db",
                                  "amount": "3333"
                              }
                          }
                        ]  ⬚  ⬚
val                     0 wei  ⬚
```

Figure 10-10. *Events fired by the smart contract containing the winner(s) addresses as well as the amount won*

Since there two players who wagered on 5, there are two winners. The winning amount for the second and third players are 1666 and 3333, respectively. The calculations for the winnings are as follows:

- Total wager amount = 5000 Wei

- Total winning wager = 1000 + 2000 = 3000 Wei

- Winnings for the second account = (1000/3000) * 5000 = 1666 Wei

- Winnings for the third account = (2000/3000)) * 5000 = 2333 Wei

Note that due to rounding, there is a balance of 1 Wei left in the contract (see Figure 10-11).

Figure 10-11. *The balance in the contract*

Click the **getGameStatus** button and you will see that the number of players has been reset to 0.

Saving the ABI of the Contract

To prepare for the creation of the front end for the betting contract, click the **ABI** button located at the bottom of the **SOLIDITY COMPILER** tab (see Figure 10-12).

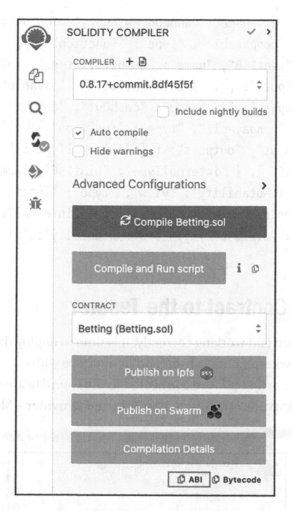

Figure 10-12. *Click the ABI button to get the ABI of the contract*

Paste the ABI onto a text file so that you can refer to it later. Here is the ABI for your convenience:

```
[ { "anonymous": false, "inputs": [ { "indexed": false, "internalType":
"uint256", "name": "players", "type": "uint256" }, { "indexed": false,
"internalType": "uint256", "name": "maxPlayers", "type": "uint256" } ],
"name": "Status", "type": "event" }, { "anonymous": false, "inputs": [ {
"indexed": false, "internalType": "address", "name": "winner", "type":
"address" }, { "indexed": false, "internalType": "uint256", "name":
"amount", "type": "uint256" } ], "name": "Winner", "type": "event" },
{ "inputs": [ { "internalType": "uint256", "name": "winningNumber",
```

"type": "uint256" }], "name": "announceWinners", "outputs": [],
"stateMutability": "nonpayable", "type": "function" }, { "inputs": [
{ "internalType": "uint256", "name": "number", "type": "uint256" }],
"name": "bet", "outputs": [], "stateMutability": "payable", "type":
"function" }, { "inputs": [], "name": "cashOut", "outputs": [],
"stateMutability": "nonpayable", "type": "function" }, { "inputs": [],
"name": "getGameStatus", "outputs": [{ "internalType": "uint256", "name":
"", "type": "uint256" }, { "internalType": "uint256", "name": "", "type":
"uint256" }], "stateMutability": "view", "type": "function" }, { "inputs":
[], "name": "getWinningNumber", "outputs": [{ "internalType": "uint256",
"name": "", "type": "uint256" }], "stateMutability": "view", "type":
"function" }]

Deploying the Contract to the Testnet

With the contract tested and working correctly, it is time to deploy the contract onto the
Goerli testnet so that you can build a front end to interface with it.

In MetaMask, ensure that you are connected to the Goerli testnet. Then, back
in the Remix IDE, change the environment to **Injected Provider – MetaMask** (see
Figure 10-13).

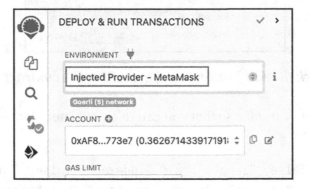

Figure 10-13. *Change the environment to Injected Provider – MetaMask*

Click the **Deploy** button to deploy the contract. For reference, the address of my
deployed contract is 0xA0a4a98562587211CAbdC910721e0020A52AcE11.

Creating the Web Front End

Let's now create the web front end for the lottery game. Create a new text file and name it as OnlineBetting.html. Save it in the web3projects folder (this folder was first created in Chapter 8).

Populate the OnlineBetting.html file as follows:

```html
<!DOCTYPE html>
<html lang="en">
<head>
    <meta charset="UTF-8">
    <title>Document</title>
    <link rel="stylesheet" type="text/css" href="main.css">
    <script src="./node_modules/web3/dist/web3.min.js">
    </script>
</head>
<body>
    <div class="container">
        <h1>Ethereum Lottery</h1>
        <center>
            <label for="numberToWager"
                class="col-lg-2 control-label">
                Number to wager
            </label>
            <input id="numberToWager" type="text">
            <label for="weiToWager"
                class="col-lg-2 control-label">
                Number of wei to wager
            </label>
            <input id="weiToWager" type="text">
            <button id="btnBet">Bet</button>
            <hr/>
            <h2 id="result"></h2>
            <h2 id="status"></h2>
        </center>
    </div>
```

263

```
<script src="https://code.jquery.com/jquery-3.2.1.slim.min.js">
</script>
<script>
    //-----Start of JavaScript functions-----
    async function loadWeb3() {
        //---if MetaMask is available on your web browser---
        if (window.ethereum) {
            web3 = new Web3(window.ethereum);

            //---connect to account---
            const account = await window.ethereum.request(
                {method: 'eth_requestAccounts'});
            console.log(account)
        } else {
            //---set the provider you want from Web3.providers---
            web3 = new Web3(
                new Web3.providers.HttpProvider(
                    "http://localhost:8545"));
            var version = web3.version;
            console.log("Version of web3: ", version);
        }
    }

    async function loadContract() {
        abi = [ { "anonymous": false, "inputs": [ { "indexed":
        false, "internalType": "uint256", "name": "players", "type":
        "uint256" }, { "indexed": false, "internalType": "uint256",
        "name": "maxPlayers", "type": "uint256" } ], "name": "Status",
        "type": "event" }, { "anonymous": false, "inputs": [ {
        "indexed": false, "internalType": "address", "name": "winner",
        "type": "address" }, { "indexed": false, "internalType":
        "uint256", "name": "amount", "type": "uint256" } ], "name":
        "Winner", "type": "event" }, { "inputs": [ { "internalType":
        "uint256", "name": "winningNumber", "type": "uint256" } ],
        "name": "announceWinners", "outputs": [], "stateMutability":
        "nonpayable", "type": "function" }, { "inputs": [ {
```

```
    "internalType": "uint256", "name": "number", "type": "uint256"
    } ], "name": "bet", "outputs": [], "stateMutability":
    "payable", "type": "function" }, { "inputs": [], "name":
    "cashOut", "outputs": [], "stateMutability": "nonpayable",
    "type": "function" }, { "inputs": [], "name": "getGameStatus",
    "outputs": [ { "internalType": "uint256", "name": "", "type":
    "uint256" }, { "internalType": "uint256", "name": "", "type":
    "uint256" } ], "stateMutability": "view", "type": "function"
    }, { "inputs": [], "name": "getWinningNumber", "outputs": [ {
    "internalType": "uint256", "name": "", "type": "uint256" } ],
    "stateMutability": "view", "type": "function" } ]
    //---change the address below to that of your own---
    address = '0x2043C325084A74A3a5105ddC5F999ed24b56D77a'
    return await new web3.eth.Contract(abi,address);
}

async function getCurrentAccount() {
    const accounts = await web3.eth.getAccounts();
    console.log(accounts)
    return accounts[0];
}

async function load() {
    await loadWeb3();
    lottery = await loadContract();

    // handle the Winner event fired by the smart contract
    lottery.events.Winner()
    .on('data', function(event){
        console.log(event.returnValues[0]);  // winner address
        console.log(event.returnValues[1]);  // amount
        $("#result").append("Winner: " + event.returnValues[0] +
                            ", Amount: " + event.returnValues[1] +
                            " wei</br>");
    })
```

```javascript
// handle the Status event fired by the smart contract
lottery.events.Status()
.on('data', function(event){
    console.log(event.returnValues[0]);  // players
    console.log(event.returnValues[1]);   // maxPlayers
    $("#result").append("Status of game: " + event.
    returnValues[0] +
                        " of " + event.returnValues[1] +
                        "</br>");
})
// check the current status of the game
lottery.methods.getGameStatus()
    .call(function(error, result) {
        if(!error) {
            $("#result").append("Status of game: " +
                result[0].toString() + " of " +
                result[1].toString()+ "</br>");
            console.log("Status of game: " + result[0] +
                        " of " + result[1]);
        } else
            console.error(error);
    });
// place bet
$("#btnBet").click(async function() {
    console.log($("#weiToWager").val());
    //---get the account---
    const account = await getCurrentAccount();

    // call the bet() function
    lottery.methods.bet($("#numberToWager").val())
    .send(
        {
            from: account,
            value: $("#weiToWager").val()
        }
    )
```

```
            .on('transactionHash', function(hash){
                $("#result").append("Bet has been submitted</br>");
                console.log("Transaction hash: " + hash);
            })
            .on('receipt', function(receipt){
                $("#result").append("Bet has been accepted</br>");
                console.log("Receipt: " + receipt.toString());
            })
            .on('error', function(error, receipt) {
                $("#result").append("An error has occurred. Betting was
                not successful</br>");
                console.log("Error: " + error + "," + receipt.
                toString());
            });
        });
      }
      load();
      //-----End of JavaScript functions-----
    </script>
</body>
</html>
```

Caution   Remember to change the address of the contract to that of your own.

To test the web front end, type the following commands in terminal:

```
$ cd ~/webprojects
$ serve
```

Using three instances of the Chrome browser, load each browser with the following URL: http://localhost:3000/OnlineBetting.html. You should see all display the same statuses (see Figure 10-14).

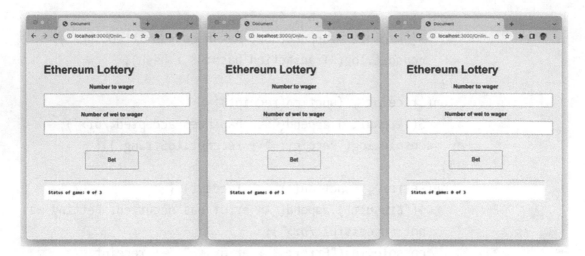

Figure 10-14. *Three instances of Chrome displaying the same page and game status*

Using Account 1 (on the left browser), place a bet on the number 1 using 2 Ethers and click the **Bet** button. Observe that MetaMask will pop up a window showing the amount to be sent to the contract. Click **CONFIRM**. Once you click the **CONFIRM** button, the first browser will show the message "*Bet has been submitted.*" After a while (when the transaction has been confirmed), the app will also display two additional messages (may not be displayed in any specific order; see Figure 10-15):

- Status of game: 1 of 3

- Bet has been accepted

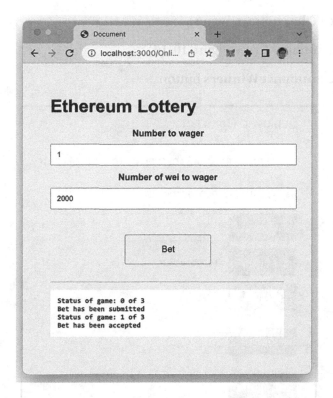

Figure 10-15. *The messages you will see when you have submitted a bet and when the transaction has been confirmed*

On the second browser,

- Using Account 2, place a bet on the number 5 using 1000 Wei.
- Click the **Bet** button.

On the third browser,

- Using Account 3, place a bet on the number 5 using 2000 Wei.
- Click the **Bet** button.

Announcing the Winning Number

Like you did earlier when you tested the contract in the Remix IDE, you announce the winning number using the **announceWinners** button.

Using Account 1 (the contract owner),

- Enter the number 5 (see Figure 10-16).

- Click the **announceWinners** button.

Figure 10-16. *Announcing the winner through the Remix IDE*

When the transaction has been confirmed, the winners will be announced (see Figure 10-17).

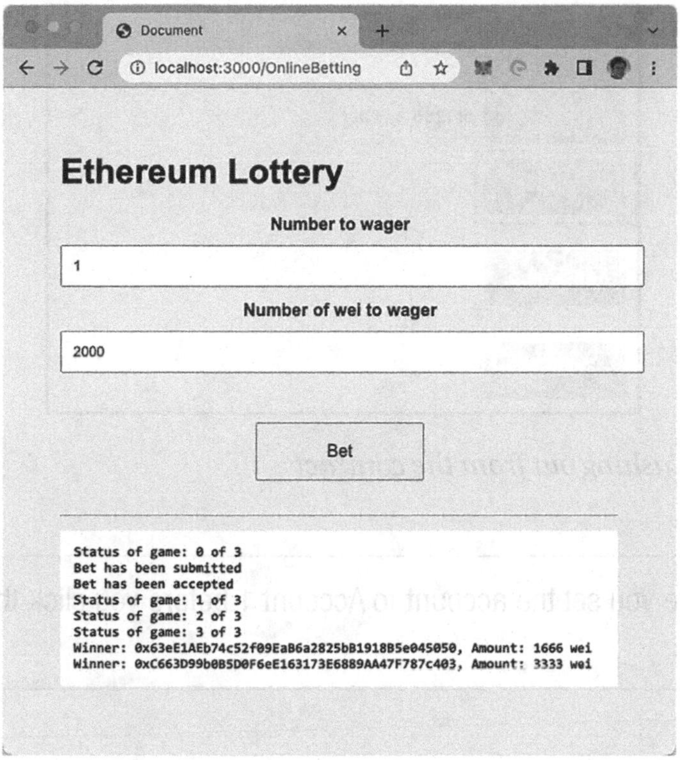

Figure 10-17. *The app displaying the winner(s) and their winnings*

Cashing Out

If there is any balance in the contract, you can cash out (to the owner) by clicking the **cashOut** button in the Remix IDE (see Figure 10-18).

Figure 10-18. *Cashing out from the contract*

Tip   Make sure you set the account to Account 1 before you click the cashOut button.

The Complete Contract

For your convenience, the complete contract is listed here:

```
// SPDX-License-Identifier: MIT
pragma solidity ^0.8;
import "@openzeppelin/contracts/utils/Strings.sol";

contract Betting {
    // record the owner of the contract
    address owner = msg.sender;

    // minimum amount to wage (wei)
    uint constant MIN_WAGER = 1000;

    // maximum number of players allowed for each round
    uint constant MAX_NUMBER_OF_PLAYERS = 3;

    // range of numbers to bet, from 1 to MAX_NUMBER_TO_BET
    uint constant MAX_NUMBER_TO_BET = 10;
```

```solidity
// total amount waged by players so far
uint totalWager = 0;

// number of players waged so far
uint numberOfPlayers = 0;

// winning number
uint winningBetNumber = 0;

// array of addresses of all players
address payable [MAX_NUMBER_OF_PLAYERS] playerAddressesArray;

// store wager details of each player
struct Player {
    uint amountWagered;
    uint numberWagered;
}

// waging details of all players in a mapping object
mapping(address => Player) playerDetailsMapping;

//---define an event---
event Winner(
    address winner,
    uint amount
);

// the event to display the status of the game
event Status (
    uint players,
    uint maxPlayers
);

function getGameStatus() view public returns (uint, uint) {
    // return the status of the game
    return (numberOfPlayers, MAX_NUMBER_OF_PLAYERS);
}
```

```
function getWinningNumber() view public returns (uint) {
    // return the winning number
    return winningBetNumber;
}

function cashOut() public {
    require(msg.sender == owner,
        "Only the owner of contract can cash out!");
    payable(owner).transfer(address(this).balance);
}

function bet(uint number) public payable {
    // CHECK #1
    // ensure the max number of players has not been reached
    require(numberOfPlayers < MAX_NUMBER_OF_PLAYERS,
        "Maximum number of players reached");

    // CHECK #2
    // check to ensure caller has never betted
    require(playerDetailsMapping[msg.sender].numberWagered == 0,
        "You have already betted");

    // CHECK #3
    // check the range of numbers allowed for betting
    require(number >=1 && number <= MAX_NUMBER_TO_BET,
        string.concat("You need to bet between 1 and ",
            Strings.toString(MAX_NUMBER_TO_BET)));

    // CHECK #4
    // ensure min. bet (note that msg.value is in wei)
    require( msg.value >= MIN_WAGER,
        string.concat("Minimum bet is ",
            Strings.toString(MIN_WAGER), " wei"));
```

```
    // record the number and amount wagered by the player
    playerDetailsMapping[msg.sender].amountWagered = msg.value;
    playerDetailsMapping[msg.sender].numberWagered = number;

    // add the player address to the array of addresses
    playerAddressesArray[numberOfPlayers] = payable(msg.sender);

    numberOfPlayers++;
    totalWager += msg.value;

    //  emit the Status event
    emit Status(numberOfPlayers, MAX_NUMBER_OF_PLAYERS);
}

function announceWinners(uint winningNumber) public {

    require(msg.sender == owner,
        "Only the owner can announce the winner");

    winningBetNumber = winningNumber;

    // use to store winners
    address payable[MAX_NUMBER_OF_PLAYERS] memory winners;
    uint winnerCount = 0;
    uint totalWinningWager = 0;

    // find out the winners
    for (uint i=0; i < playerAddressesArray.length; i++) {
        // get the address of each player
        address payable playerAddress = playerAddressesArray[i];

        // if the player betted number is the winning number
        if (playerDetailsMapping[playerAddress].numberWagered ==
            winningNumber) {
            // save the player address into the winners
            // array
            winners[winnerCount] = playerAddress;
```

```
                // sum up the total wagered amount for the
                // winning numbers
                totalWinningWager +=
                    playerDetailsMapping[playerAddress].amountWagered;
                winnerCount++;
            }
        }

        // make payments to each winning player
        for (uint j=0; j<winnerCount; j++) {

            // calculate thw winnings of each player
            uint amount = (playerDetailsMapping[winners[j]].amountWagered *
                totalWager ) / totalWinningWager;

            // make payment to player
            winners[j].transfer(amount);

            // emit the Winner event
            emit Winner(winners[j], amount);
        }

        // reset the variables
        numberOfPlayers = 0;
        totalWager = 0;

        // clear all arrays and mappings
        for (uint i=0; i < playerAddressesArray.length; i++) {
            // get the address of each player
            address payable playerAddress = playerAddressesArray[i];
            delete playerDetailsMapping[playerAddress];
            delete playerAddressesArray[i];
        }

        //   emit the Status event
        emit Status(numberOfPlayers, MAX_NUMBER_OF_PLAYERS);
    }

}
```

Summary

In this chapter, you learned how to build an online lottery game. Apart from using the knowledge that you learned in the previous chapters, you also learned several new things:

- How to transfer Ethers programmatically to another account

- How to use the various data structures in Solidity to store data

In the next chapter, you will learn about tokens and how you can use them in your smart contracts.

CHAPTER 11

Creating Your Tokens

If you have been following the previous chapters, you should have a pretty good understanding of Ethereum smart contracts and how to interact with them through the web3.js APIs.

One exciting feature of Ethereum smart contracts is Ethereum tokens. Tokens are digital assets built on top of the Ethereum blockchain. Developers can use them to pay for services performed by smart contracts and as a means for fund raising. Tokens also drive demand for Ethers, the native cryptocurrency on the Ethereum blockchain.

In this chapter, you will learn what tokens are, how they are created, how to buy them, and how to add them to your MetaMask accounts.

What Are Tokens?

To understand the concept of tokens, let's start off with a real-life analogy. Most people are familiar with a carnival (or fun fair). To play the games at the carnival, the stalls usually do not accept cash payment. Instead, they need you to exchange your cash (or use a credit card) to purchase coins (or tokens) for use at the game stalls (see Figure 11-1).

© Wei-Meng Lee 2023
W.-M. Lee, *Beginning Ethereum Smart Contracts Programming*, https://doi.org/10.1007/978-1-4842-9271-6_11

Figure 11-1. *Tokens used in the real world at carnival games*

The owner of the carnival does this for a variety of reasons:

- The stalls need not deal with cash; this will prevent the workers at the stalls (usually employees of the carnival owner) from pocketing the cash.

- The owner of the carnival receives cash up front before you even play the games, and unused tokens cannot be refunded.

- The owner of the carnival wants to sell you more tokens than you need by giving you incentives to buy more up front.

In the cryptocurrency world, the same concepts apply to tokens. Instead of using fiat currency to buy the tokens directly, you first buy Ethers and then use Ethers to buy the tokens (see Figure 11-2).

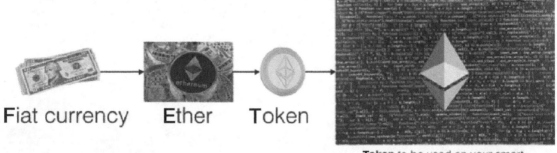

Fiat currency   Ether   Token

Token to be used on your smart contract running on the Ethereum network

Figure 11-2. *Tokens on the Ethereum blockchain*

COINS VS. TOKENS

In the cryptocurrency world, two terms have been used interchangeably: *coins* and *tokens*. So are they the same? First, the definition of a *coin* is that it is an asset that is native to its own blockchain. Examples of coins are Bitcoin, Litecoin, and Ether. Each of these coins exists on their own blockchain. *Tokens*, on the other hand, are created on existing blockchains. The most common token platform is Ethereum, which allows developers to create their own tokens using the ERC-20 standard (more on this in a later section of this chapter). Using Ether (which is the coin native to the Ethereum blockchain), users can exchange them for specific tokens on the Ethereum blockchain. Hence, strictly speaking, coins are not the same as tokens. In fact, tokens are based on coins.

How Tokens Are Implemented?

Now that you have a clear understanding of tokens and how they work, let's see how tokens are implemented in Ethereum.

Tokens are implemented using smart contracts (yes, the same smart contracts you read about in the previous chapters) known as *token contracts*. A token contract is a smart contract that contains a mapping of account addresses and their balances. Figure 11-3 shows an example of the mapping.

Account Addresses	Balance
0x0000...0000	0
0x1234...9a7c	80
0x2a45...9c12	20
0x3d4f...7e2a	100

Total Tokens: **200**

Figure 11-3. *A token contract contains a map of account addresses and their balances*

Conceptually, a token contract is a smart contract that maintains a mapping object containing the balance of accounts onto the blockchain (see Figure 11-4).

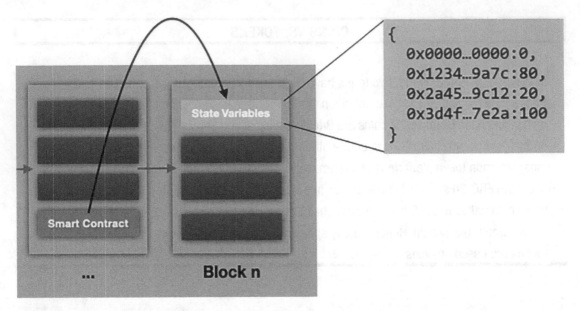

Figure 11-4. *A token contract maintains a mapping object containing account addresses and their balances*

Minting New Tokens

The total supply of tokens can be increased by *minting* new tokens. That is, you (the owner of the token contract) simply increase the balance of an account, as shown in Figure 11-5.

Account Addresses	Balance
0x0000...0000	0
0x1234...9a7c	80
0x2a45...9c12	20
0x3d4f...7e2a	**200**

Total Tokens: **300**

Figure 11-5. *Minting new tokens by increasing the balance of one or more accounts*

Burning Tokens

The total supply of tokens can be decreased by burning tokens. That is, you reduce the balance of an account, as shown in Figure 11-6.

Account Addresses	Balance
0x0000...0000	0
0x1234...9a7c	8̶0̶ **50**
0x2a45...9c12	20
0x3d4f...7e2a	200

Total Tokens: **270**

Figure 11-6. *Burning tokens by decreasing the balance of an account*

Tokens can also be burned by sending them to a dead address, as shown in Figure 11-7. Note that in this case the total supply of tokens does not change.

Account Addresses	Balance
0x0000...0000	**10**
0x1234...9a7c	50
0x2a45...9c12	20
0x3d4f...7e2a	2̶0̶0̶ **190**

Total Tokens: **270**

Figure 11-7. *Burning tokens by sending tokens to a dead address. In this case, the total supply does not change*

Units Used Internally in Token Contracts

In token contracts, *decimal places of precision* represent how divisible a token can be. Consider the example of a fictitious token, **MusicToken**, with each token representing the right to own a song. In this case, the *decimal place of precision* is set to 0. This means that the tokens cannot have a fractional component; you cannot have 1.1 or 1.5 tokens. In other words, the number of MusicToken one can own must be a discrete number (only integer values). Figure 11-8 shows how MusicTokens are represented internally within the token contract.

Internal Representation

Decimals: 0
MusicToken

Account Addresses	Balance
0x0000...0000	0
0x1234...9a7c	8
0x2a45...9c12	2
0x3d4f...7e2a	5

Total Tokens: **15**

Figure 11-8. *Tokens with 0 decimal precision have no fractional component*

Consider another example, the fictitious **GoldToken**, which represents the amount of gold a person owns. In this case, the decimal place of precision could be set to 3, which means that the amount of GoldTokens a person owns can be down to 3 decimal places, such as 2.003. Figure 11-9 shows how the balance of the GoldTokens is represented internally and what the view to the user looks like.

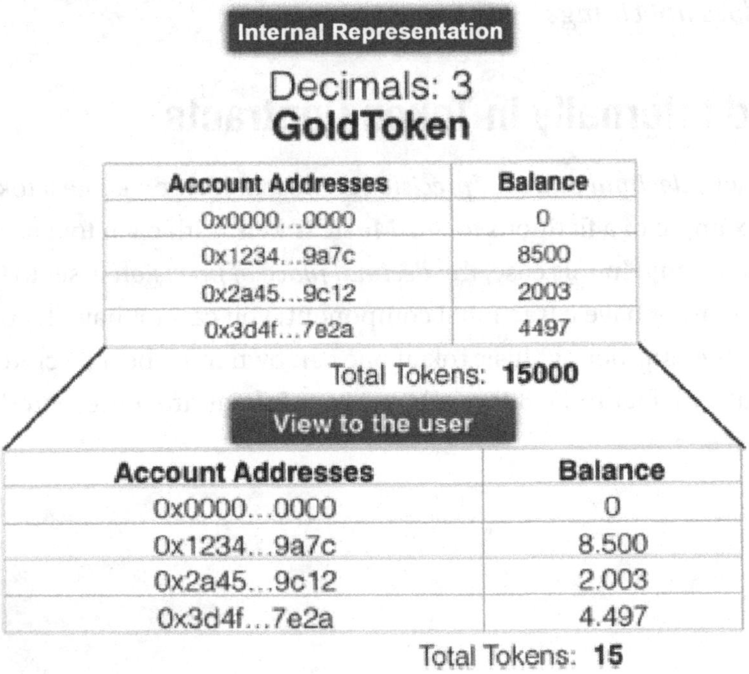

Internal Representation

Decimals: 3
GoldToken

Account Addresses	Balance
0x0000...0000	0
0x1234...9a7c	8500
0x2a45...9c12	2003
0x3d4f...7e2a	4497

Total Tokens: **15000**

View to the user

Account Addresses	Balance
0x0000...0000	0
0x1234...9a7c	8.500
0x2a45...9c12	2.003
0x3d4f...7e2a	4.497

Total Tokens: **15**

Figure 11-9. *Token with three decimal precision, stored internally and viewed from outside*

Internally, for a token with n-decimals of precision, the balance is represented using this formula: ***token_internal = token_external · 10^n***. For example, a user may own 4.497 GoldTokens, but internally, the token contract stores its balance as 4497.

ERC-20 Token Standard

For tokens created on the Ethereum blockchain to be accepted by smart contracts, the tokens must adhere to some particular standards. In the case of Ethereum tokens, that standard is ERC-20. ERC stands for *Ethereum Request for Comments*. In ERC-20, the number 20 refers to the proposal ID number. The proposal ERC-20 defines a set of rules that need to be met for a token to be able to interact with others.

Tip   The ERC-20 standard is a specific set of functions developers must use in their fungible tokens. A fungible token means that the token is divisible and can be broken down into smaller denominations (e.g., 1 token is equivalent to the sum of 0.5 token, 0.3 token, and 0.2 token).

ERC20 tokens must be able to do the following:

- Get the total token supply.

- Get the account balance.

- Transfer the token from one account to another.

- Approve the use of the token as a monetary asset.

Specifically, ERC20 tokens must implement the following interface:

```
contract ERC20Interface {
    function totalSupply() public constant returns (uint);
    function balanceOf(address tokenOwner) public constant
        returns (uint balance);
    function allowance(address tokenOwner, address
        spender) public constant returns (uint remaining);
    function transfer(address to, uint tokens) public
        returns (bool success);
    function approve(address spender, uint tokens) public
        returns (bool success);
```

```
function transferFrom(address from, address to, uint
    tokens) public returns (bool success);
event Transfer(address indexed from, address indexed
    to, uint tokens);
event Approval(address indexed tokenOwner, address
    indexed spender, uint tokens);
}
```

Here are the uses for the various functions and events in the ERC20Interface:

- totalSupply: Returns the total token supply

- balanceOf(address _owner): Returns the account balance of _owner

- transfer(address _to, uint256 _value): Transfers _value to _to and fires the Transfer event. The function should revert if the _from account does not have enough tokens to spend.

- approve(address _spender, uint256 _value): Allows _spender to withdraw from the account several times, up to the _value amount

- transferFrom(address _from, address _to, uint256 _value): Transfers _value from _from to _to and fires the Transfer event. The function should revert unless the _from account has deliberately authorized the sender of the message via some mechanism.

- allowance(address _owner, address _spender): Returns the amount the _spender is still allowed to withdraw from the _owner

- Transfer(address indexed _from, address indexed _to, uint256 _value): Must trigger when tokens are transferred, including zero-value transfers

- Approval(address indexed _owner, address indexed _spender, uint256 _value): Must trigger on any successful call to approve(address _spender, uint256 _value)

Creating Token Contracts

Rather than implement all these functions and events yourself, **OpenZeppelin** provides a base implementation for ERC-20. You can find this implementation at `https://github.com/OpenZeppelin/openzeppelin-contracts/blob/v4.0.0/contracts/token/ERC20/ERC20.sol/`.

Note   OpenZeppelin is an open-source framework for building secure smart contracts. OpenZeppelin provides a complete suite of security products and audit services to build, manage, and inspect all aspects of software development and operations for decentralized applications.

So if you are writing an ERC-20 token contract, you just need to import the base implementation from OpenZeppelin and inherit from it.

For your example, create a new contract in the Remix IDE and name it as `token.sol`. Populate it with the following statements:

```
// SPDX-License-Identifier: MIT
pragma solidity ^0.8;
import "https://github.com/OpenZeppelin/openzeppelin-contracts/blob/v4.0.0/
contracts/token/ERC20/ERC20.sol";

contract MyToken is ERC20 {
  constructor(string memory name, string memory symbol)
  ERC20(name, symbol) {
      // ERC20 tokens by default have 18 decimals
      // number of tokens minted = n * 10^18
      uint256 n = 1000;
      _mint(msg.sender, n * 10**uint(decimals()));
    }
}
```

In this contract, you are creating 1000 tokens (value of n), and each token can go up to 18 decimal places of precision (since the `decimals()` function by default returns 18). Internally within the contract, the number of tokens minted is dependent on n and the precision. In this example, while the total supply is 1000 tokens, the total units of base tokens minted is equal to **1000 x 10^{18}**, or **1,000,000,000,000,000,000,000**.

287

> **Tip** All operations involving tokens are based on the base token units. For example, if I want to send 1 token to another account, I have to transfer 1,000,000,000,000,000,000 base token units of my tokens to the recipient account.

Overriding the Number of Decimal Places of Precision

The decimals() function in the token contract by default returns 18. This means that your tokens created have a denomination as small as 0.000000000000000001 (18 decimal places). However, there are occasions where you don't really need that kind of precision for your tokens. For example, if you do not want your tokens to be fractionized, you can override the decimals() function in the token contract, like this:

```solidity
// SPDX-License-Identifier: MIT
pragma solidity ^0.8;
import "https://github.com/OpenZeppelin/openzeppelin-contracts/blob/v4.0.0/
contracts/token/ERC20/ERC20.sol";
contract MyToken is ERC20 {

    constructor(string memory name, string memory symbol)
    ERC20(name, symbol) {
        // ERC20 tokens have 18 decimals
        // number of tokens minted = n * 10^18
        uint256 n = 1000;
        _mint(msg.sender, n * 10**uint(decimals()));
    }

    function decimals() override public pure returns (uint8) {
        return 0;
    }

}
```

In this example, the decimals() function returns 0, which means that your token does not have any decimal places. If you return 1, the smallest denomination for your token is 0.1.

For simplicity, your token contract will use the default 18 decimal places of precision.

Deploying the Token Contract

To deploy the token contract, you must specify two arguments:

- The name (description) of the token

- The symbol of the token

Tip   Symbols of tokens are not unique, but you should try to keep them to within three to four characters.

Figure 11-10 shows an example name and symbol for a token. Click **Deploy** to deploy the token contract.

Figure 11-10.   *Deploying the token contract with the name and symbol*

Once the contract is deployed, you can expand on the contract name to review the various functions (see Figure 11-11). These are the functions that you need to implement in your ERC-20 token contract (which was implemented by the OpenZeppelin base contract).

Figure 11-11.   *The various functions defined in a ERC-20 token contract*

Copy the address of the deployed token contract (see Figure 11-12).

Figure 11-12.   *The deployed token contract (copy its address to the clipboard)*

Adding the Token to MetaMask

In MetaMask, click the **Assets** tab and click the **Import tokens** link at the bottom of the screen (see Figure 11-13). In the next screen, paste the token contract you copied from the Remix IDE. The token symbol will automatically be displayed. Click the **Add custom token** button. You will see that your account has 1000 WML tokens. Make sure that the account that you are adding the token to is the same account that deployed the token contract.

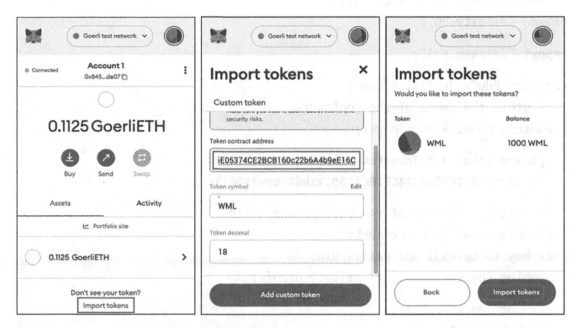

Figure 11-13. *Adding the token to MetaMask*

What Can You Do with the Token?

Now that you have created the token, what can you do with it? It is up to you to create a utility for the token. You can promote your token as a form of investment or a representation of an asset that you are selling (such as properties or securities).

To sell a token, you can ask the recipient to pay you in fiat currency and then transfer them the token. Alternatively, you can also code your token contract to receive Ethers and then programmatically transfer the token to the sender of the Ether.

Using Tokens for Smart Contract Payments

In Chapters 7 and 10 of this book, you wrote a contract that accepts Ethers for a service (the checkEduCredentials() function). What if instead of accepting Ether, you accept tokens for payment? Well, this can be done quite easily. Let's modify the EduCredentialsStore.sol contract from Chapter 10 with the following additional statements in bold:

```solidity
// SPDX-License-Identifier: MIT
pragma solidity ^0.8;

import "./token.sol";

contract EduCredentialsStore {
  // store the owner of the contract
  address owner = msg.sender;

  MyToken token = MyToken(address(
    0xc276658A795E05374CE2BCB160c22b6A4b9eE16C));

  //---store the hash of the strings and their
  // corresponding block number---
  // key is bytes32 and val is uint
  mapping (bytes32 => uint) private proofs;

  //---define an event---
  event Document(
    address from,
    bytes32 hash,
    uint blockNumber
  );
  //=========================================
  // return the token balance in the contract
  //=========================================
  function getBalance() public view returns (uint256) {
    return token.balanceOf(address(this));
  }
  //-------------------------------------------------
  // Store a proof of existence in the contract state
```

```solidity
//------------------------------------------------------
function storeProof(bytes32 proof) private {
  // use the hash as the key
  proofs[proof] = block.number;

  // fire the event
  emit Document(msg.sender, proof, block.number);
}

//------------------------------------------------------
// Calculate and store the proof for a document
//------------------------------------------------------
function storeEduCredentials(string calldata
document) external {
  require(msg.sender == owner,
    "Only the owner of contract can store the
    credentials");
  // call storeProof() with the hash of the string
  storeProof(proofFor(document));
}

//------------------------------------------------------
// Helper function to get a document's sha256
//------------------------------------------------------
// Takes in a string and returns the hash of the
// string
function proofFor(string calldata document) private
pure returns (bytes32) {
  // converts the string into bytes array and then
  // hash it
  return sha256(bytes(document));
}

//------------------------------------------------------
// Check if a document has been saved previously
//------------------------------------------------------
function checkEduCredentials(string calldata
document) public payable returns (uint){
```

```
    // require(msg.value == 1000 wei,
    //    "This call requires 1000 wei");

    // msg.sender is the account that calls the
    // token contract
    // go and check the allowance set by the caller
    uint256 approvedAmt =
      token.allowance(msg.sender, address(this));

    // the amount is based on the base unit in the
    // token
    uint requiredAmt = 1000;

    // ensure the caller has enough tokens approved
    // to pay to the contract
    require(approvedAmt >= requiredAmt,
      "Token allowance approved is less than what you
        need to pay");

    // transfer the tokens from sender to token contract
    token.transferFrom(msg.sender,
        payable(address(this)), requiredAmt);

    // use the hash of the string and check the proofs
    // mapping object
    return proofs[proofFor(document)];
  }

  function cashOut() public {
    require(msg.sender == owner,
      "Only the owner of contract can cash out!");
    payable(owner).transfer(address(this).balance);
  }

}
```

With these additional statements in bold, you make the following changes to the EduCredentialsStore contract:

- Import the token.sol token contract. This is the token contract you deployed earlier in this chapter.

- Create an instance of the MyToken contract. You need to specify the address of the deployed token contract.

- Add a function called getBalance(). This allows you to know the token balance held by the smart contract.

- Modify the checkEduCredentials() function so that now instead of accepting Ethers for payment, you only accept tokens. To do so, you first check how many tokens the caller of the contract has approved for use in this contract. Then you check to make sure that the amount approved to be used is at least 1000 base units (this is the amount that you decide to charge for calling this service). If the amount approved is sufficient, you transfer the tokens to this contract.

Redeploy this EduCredentialsStore contract and take note of its address (see Figure 11-14). For my example, the deployed contract address is 0x913286326233118493F2D5eA62dCA2E90133452B.

Figure 11-14. *Redeploying the modified smart contract to accept tokens for payment*

Before you can call the `checkEduCredentials()` function (which now requires a payment of 1000 base units of the tokens instead of 1000 Wei), the token owner (which is you) needs to approve 1000 base units of the token to be paid to the smart contract. To do that, you need to call the `approve()` function of the token contract with the following values (see also Figure 11-15):

```
0x913286326233118493F2D5eA62dCA2E90133452B,1000
```

This value indicates that you want to approve 1000 base units of the token to be spent on the smart contract whose address is specified (0x913286326233118493F2D5eA62dCA2E90133452B).

Figure 11-15. *Approving the use of the tokens on a smart contract*

Click the **approve** button and MetaMask will show the prompt shown in Figure 11-16. Click **Confirm** to grant the permission for your tokens to be used on the smart contract.

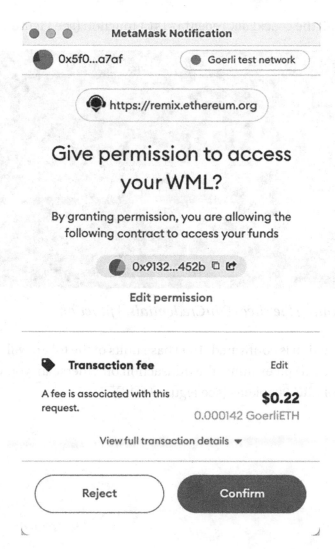

Figure 11-16. *Granting permissions for a token to be spent on a smart contract*

You can now call the checkEduCredentials() function (see Figure 11-17).

Figure 11-17. *Calling the checkEduCredentials() function*

Once the transaction is confirmed, 1000 base units of the token will be transferred to the smart contract. If you examine the transaction on Etherscan, you will observe that there is a transfer of ERC-20 tokens (see Figure 11-18).

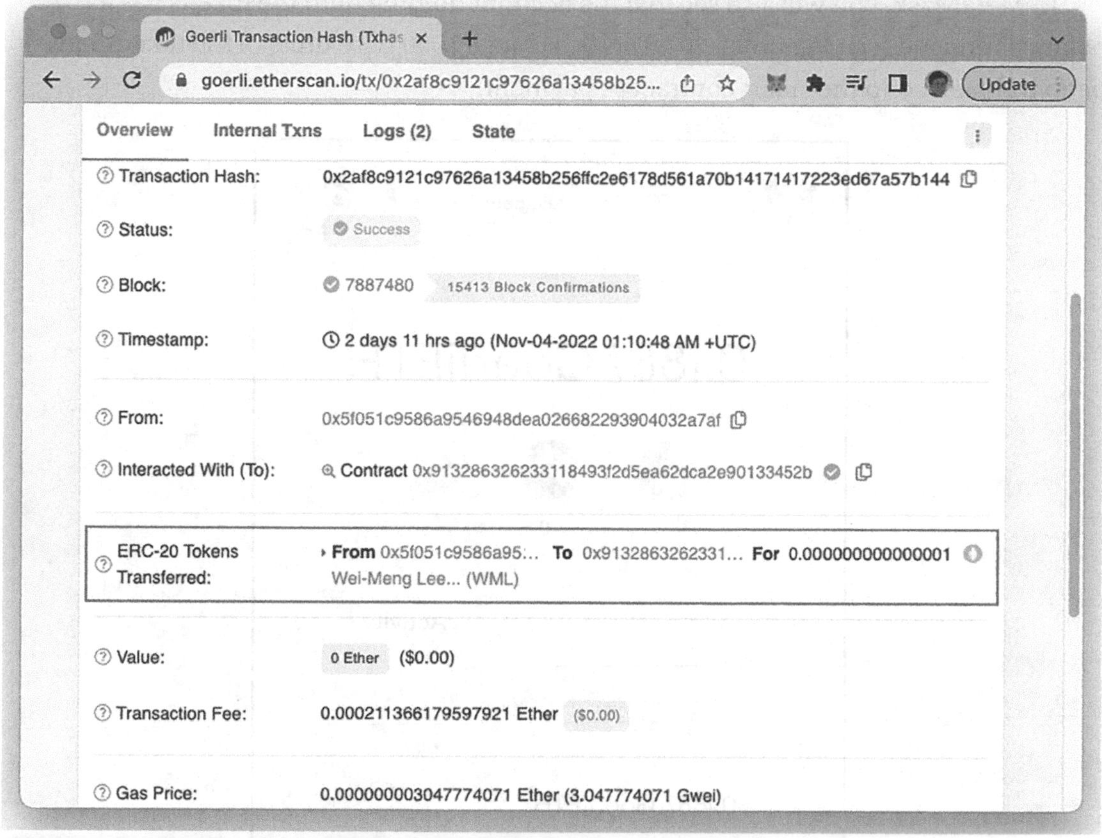

Figure 11-18. *Etherscan records the transfer of tokens from an account to the smart contract*

To verify that the contract did indeed receive the tokens, click the **getBalance** button (see Figure 11-19). You should see a value of 1000.

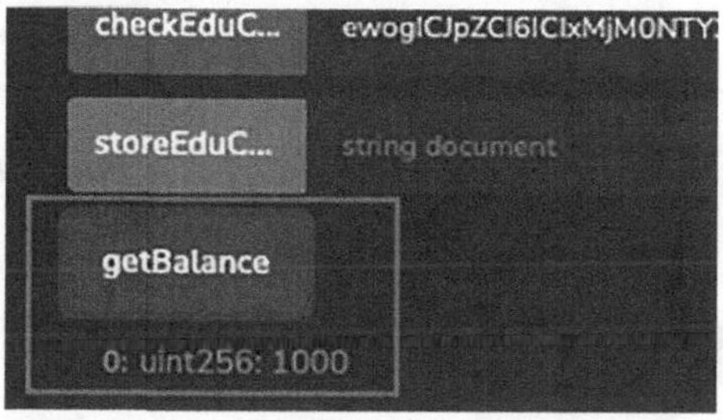

Figure 11-19. *Finding the balance of tokens in a smart contract*

In MetaMask, you will also see that the account holding onto the tokens has its balance reduced (see Figure 11-20). This is because 1000 base units of the tokens have been transferred to the smart contract as payment.

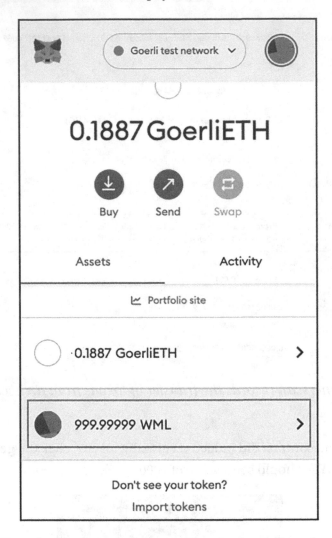

Figure 11-20. *The token balance of the account is also reduced*

Selling Tokens Programmatically

In the previous token contract, you saw how tokens are minted when the contract is deployed to the blockchain and how tokens can be transferred from one account to another. Once an account has the token(s), it can transfer to any account it wish to.

But how do you make money from the tokens? In the real world, you may want to sell the tokens in exchange for Ethers. In fact, you can do this by programming it right onto the token contract.

Here's the improved version of your token contract that allows tokens to be purchased with Ethers:

```
// SPDX-License-Identifier: MIT
pragma solidity ^0.8;
import "https://github.com/OpenZeppelin/openzeppelin-contracts/blob/v4.0.0/
contracts/token/ERC20/ERC20.sol";
contract MyToken is ERC20 {

    // price expressed as how much an ether can buy
    uint256 public unitsOneEthCanBuy  = 10;

    // the owner of the token
    address public tokenOwner;

    constructor(string memory name, string memory symbol)
        ERC20(name, symbol) {

        // address of the token owner
        tokenOwner = msg.sender;

        // ERC20 tokens have 18 decimals
        // number of tokens minted = n * 10^18
        uint256 n = 1000;
        _mint(msg.sender, n * 10**uint(decimals()));
    }

    // this function is called when someone sends ether to the token
       contract
    receive() external payable {
        // msg.value (in Wei) is the ether sent to the token contract
        // msg.sender is the account that sends the ether to the
        // token contract

        // amount is the tokens bought by the sender
        uint256 amount = msg.value * unitsOneEthCanBuy;
```

```
        // ensure you have enough tokens to sell
        require(balanceOf(tokenOwner) >= amount, "Not enough tokens");

        // transfer the token to the buyer
        _transfer(tokenOwner, msg.sender, amount);

        // emit an event to inform of the transfer
        emit Transfer(tokenOwner, msg.sender, amount);

        // send the ether earned to the token owner
        payable(tokenOwner).transfer(msg.value);
    }

}
```

Let's dissect the modified contract above.

- You first define the price of your token using the unitsOneEthCanBuy
  variable (I will discuss this in more detail in the next section).

- You need to save the address of the owner of this token contract, so
  you declare a variable called tokenOwner, which you will initialize in
  the constructor of the token contract.

- You add a new function named received() with the keyword
  payable. The receive() function is called when Ethers are sent
  to the contract. Internally within this function, two variables are
  automatically created for you:

  - msg.value: This is the amount of Wei that is sent to the contract.

  - msg.sender: This is the address of the sender that is invoking the
    contract.

Calculating the Amount of Tokens Bought

In order to sell a token, you need to price it. As you saw earlier, you define the
unitsOneEthCanBuy variable to indirectly indicate the price of a token, expressed as the
number of tokens you can buy with an Ether. Figure 11-21 explains how you can derive
the final formula where 1 Wei can buy 10 tokens (the base token units based on 18
decimal places of precision).

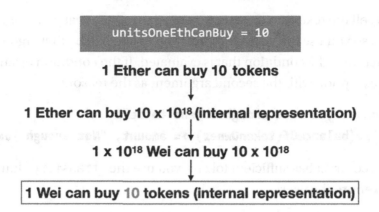

Figure 11-21. *Expressing the price of a token in Ether*

Based on this formula, you can now very easily calculate how many tokens a user can buy when they send Ethers to your token contract. Figure 11-22 shows how many tokens a user will get when they send your token contract 2 Ethers.

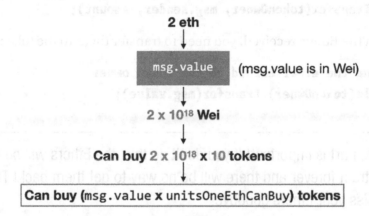

Figure 11-22. *Calculating how many tokens a buyer can buy*

From this explanation, you now know that the amount of tokens a user can purchase is

```
// amount is the tokens bought by the sender
uint256 amount = msg.value * unitsOneEthCanBuy;
```

In order to sell the tokens to the user, you need to ensure that your contract has enough tokens, so you use the `require()` function to check. The first argument in the `require()` function is the condition that is evaluated. If the condition evaluates to `false`, it will raise an exception with the second argument as the reason:

```
// ensure you have enough tokens to sell
require(balanceOf(tokenOwner) >= amount, "Not enough tokens");
```

If the token contract has sufficient tokens, you use the `_transfer()` function to transfer the tokens to the user:

```
// transfer the token to the buyer
_transfer(tokenOwner, msg.sender, amount);
```

When the transfer has been performed, emit the `Transfer()` event:

```
// emit an event to inform of the transfer
emit Transfer(tokenOwner, msg.sender, amount);
```

Finally, with the Ethers received, you need to transfer them to the token owner:

```
// send the ether earned to the token owner
payable(tokenOwner).transfer(msg.value);
```

Caution   This part is important! If you don't do this, the Ethers will be stuck with the token contract forever and there will be no way to get them back! They will be lost forever! Kiss your Ethers goodbye!

Deploying the Contract

Let's deploy the token contract one more time, using the same arguments for the constructor:

"Wei-Meng Lee Token", "WML"

Note   For my token, the deployed contract is 0xbf9e3851D5080457a03FCA00F2f9b92C1dDf7190.

As usual, add the newly created tokens to MetaMask (see Figure 11-23).

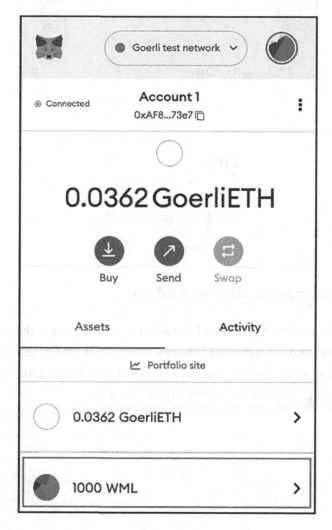

Figure 11-23. *Adding the newly added tokens to MetaMask*

Tip   You can hide previously added tokens in MetaMask by selecting the token, clicking the three vertical dots, and clicking **Hide WML** (see Figure 11-24).

Figure 11-24. *Hiding previously added tokens*

Switch to another account and send the token contract (using the address you got in the previous step) and send it 0.001 Ether (see Figure 11-25). You will see a warning about sending Ethers to a token contract. Click **I understand** and then click **Next** and in the next screen click **Confirm** to pay the transaction fees.

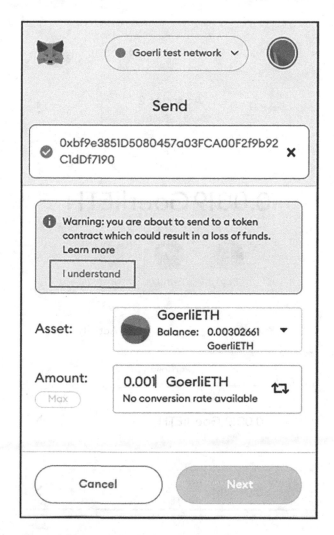

Figure 11-25. Sending Ethers to the token contract

While waiting for the transaction to confirm, add the newly created token to the current account in MetaMask. When the transaction is confirmed, you will see 0.01 WML tokens in MetaMask (see Figure 11-26).

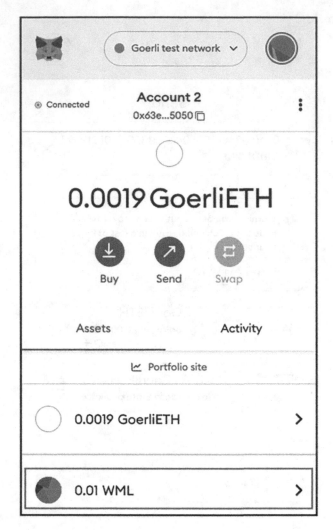

Figure 11-26. *The token created in the buyer's account*

Click the transaction in MetaMask and view the transaction details on the Etherscan blockchain explorer (see Figure 11-27).

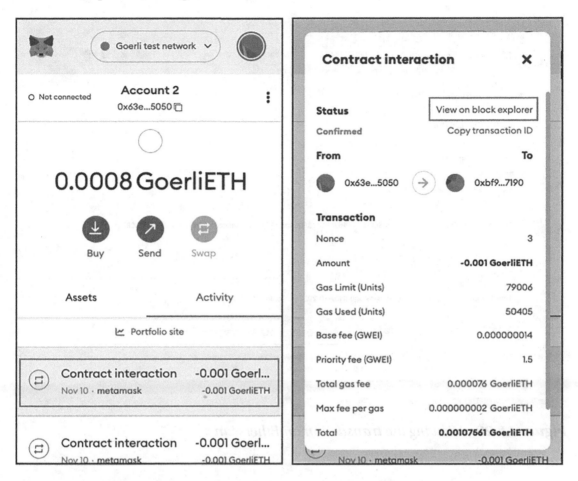

Figure 11-27. *Selecting the transaction to view on Etherscan*

You will see that the contract transfers the received 0.001 Ether to the owner of the contract (see Figure 11-28).

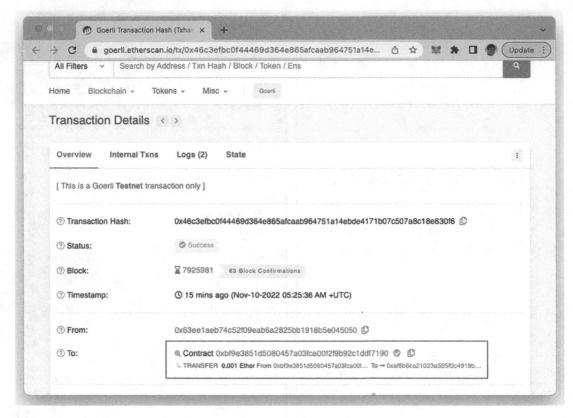

Figure 11-28. *Viewing the transaction on Etherscan*

Summary

In this chapter, you learned how tokens work and you created one yourself using a token contract. You also learned how to add tokens to your MetaMask account and use them to pay for smart contract services. Finally, you learned how you can modify token contract so that one can buy tokens by sending Ethers to it.

CHAPTER 12

Creating Non-Fungible Tokens Using ERC-721

Non-fungible tokens (NFTs) seem to be the latest craze in the world of blockchain lately. Chances are you have heard from friends or the media about some guys getting really rich by selling selfies as NFTs. So, what exactly is an NFT and what do you as a developer need to know about NFTs? This chapter explains what an NFT is and how to mint your own NFTs.

What Is an NFT?

Before you learn what an NFT is and how to mint one, it is important that you understand the meaning of *fungible*. The word *fungible* means "something whose part or quantity may be replaced by another equal part or quantity in paying a debt or settling an account" (source: www.merriam-webster.com/dictionary/fungible).

A good example of a fungible item is the US dollar bill (Figure 12-1).

© Wei-Meng Lee 2023
W.-M. Lee, *Beginning Ethereum Smart Contracts Programming*, https://doi.org/10.1007/978-1-4842-9271-6_12

Figure 12-1. *A US $1 bill (source: https://en.wikipedia.org/wiki/United_ States_one-dollar_bill#/media/File:US_one_dollar_bill,_obverse,_ series_2009.jpg)*

Using the dollar bill as an example, it is fungible because you can use it to pay for any good or service that is equivalent to a dollar. In addition, you can also use it to exchange for 10 dimes. Two people, each holding a dollar note, would be happy to exchange the dollar note with each other because after the exchange they would still have the same buying power.

A baseball card (see Figure 12-2), on the other hand, is *not fungible* because each card has unique qualities and has different values to different people. A baseball card collector may value the card at $1 million, while a storeowner may not see much value in the card and may value the card at $1.

Figure 12-2. *A baseball card (source: https://en.wikipedia.org/wiki/ Baseball_card#/media/File:VernBickford1954Bowman.jpg)*

Now that you know the meaning of fungible, let's discuss what an NFT is. NFT stands for *non-fungible token*. An NFT is basically a record on the blockchain (predominantly on Ethereum but there are alternative blockchains that support NFTs) that records the ownership of a digital art piece (or any item of value, but most NFTs today are digital assets such as images, music, or videos). Buyers of NFTs typically get limited rights to display the digital artwork they represent, but in many ways, they're just buying bragging rights and an asset they may be able to resell later.

Tip   In short, an NFT is nothing more than a unique record on the blockchain with a transactional record and a hyperlink to the digital asset.

Ownership vs. Copyright

A lot of people tend to confuse NFT's ownership property with copyright. Having ownership of an NFT does not imply that you have the copyright of an item. While of course the creator of a digital asset may transfer the intellectual property of the asset to a buyer, this transfer must be made in writing. Merely buying an NFT does not automatically grant you the copyright of that item. A good analogy is this: buying a movie DVD allows you to own that movie, but it does not grant you the rights to replicate the DVD and sell it to your friends.

Where Do You Buy or Sell NFTs?

To buy an NFT or sell your own, you need to go to an NFT marketplace. An NFT marketplace is an online platform that allows you to buy/sell NFTs. Some of the popular NFT marketplaces are

- OpenSea (`https://opensea.io`; see Figure 12-3)

- Rarible (`https://rarible.com`)

- Mintable (`https://mintable.app`)

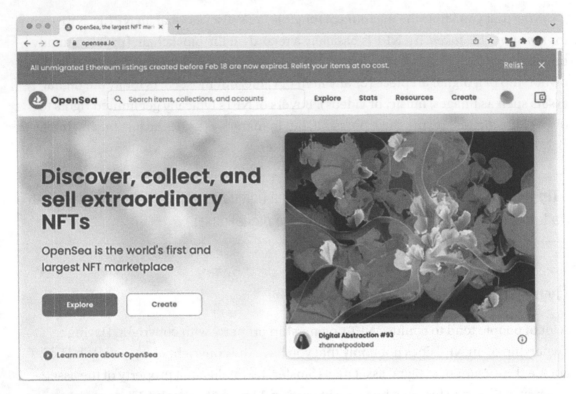

Figure 12-3.   OpenSea is one of the popular NFT marketplaces

Creating NFTs Using Token Contracts

As the name implies, an NFT is a token, and hence it uses a token contract known as an *NFT token contract*.

For NFTs, there are two token contracts that you can use:

- **ERC-721**: Similar to ERC-20 where you can create tokens (which are fungible), ERC-721 is another token standard that allows you to mint NFTs.

- **ERC-1155**: A newer NFT standard than the ERC-20. In ERC-1155, multiple NFTs can be transferred in a single transaction, resulting in lower transaction fees compared to ERC-721.

For this chapter, you will focus on the ERC-721 standard for creating NFTs.

Who Deploys the NFT Token Contract?

If you sell an NFT through a marketplace like OpenSea, OpenSea will automatically mint your NFT using the ERC-721 (or ERC-1155) NFT token contract. However, you can do your minting by writing your own NFT token contract, and you can then list your minted NFT through OpenSea for selling.

Using ERC-721 for Creating NFTs

Let's now see how you can mint an NFT using the ERC-721 NFT token contract. For this, you will use the Remix IDE (https://remix.ethereum.org/).

In the Remix IDE, create a new contract and name it as say MyNFT.sol. Populate it with the following statements:

```
// SPDX-License-Identifier: MIT
pragma solidity ^0.8.0;
import "https://github.com/OpenZeppelin/openzeppelin-contracts/blob/master/
contracts/access/Ownable.sol";
import "https://github.com/OpenZeppelin/openzeppelin-contracts/blob/master/
contracts/token/ERC721/extensions/ERC721URIStorage.sol";
contract MyNFT is Ownable, ERC721URIStorage {
    // name and symbol
    constructor() ERC721("Learn2develop.net NFT", "DLS") {
    }

    function mint(address recipient, uint256 tokenId,
                  string memory tokenURI) public onlyOwner {
        _mint(recipient, tokenId);
        _setTokenURI(tokenId, tokenURI);
    }
}
```

Observe the following points about the NFT token contract:

- You are using the base ERC-721 NFT token contract from OpenZeppelin.

- The arguments passed to the constructor of the contract are the name of the NFT token and its symbol. You can change this to your own desired name and symbol.

- The mint() function takes three arguments: the address of the owner of the NFT, the Token ID, and the TokenURI that points to the details of the NFT.

Deploying the NFT Token Contract

Once you have compiled your contract in the Remix IDE, head over to the **DEPLOY & RUN TRANSACTIONS** section and click **Deploy** (see Figure 12-4).

Figure 12-4. Deploying the NFT contract

Note   For this example, you will be deploying the NFT contract onto the Goerli testnet through MetaMask.

Once the NFT token contract has been deployed, you should be able to expand on the contract address and see the list of functions, as shown in Figure 12-5.

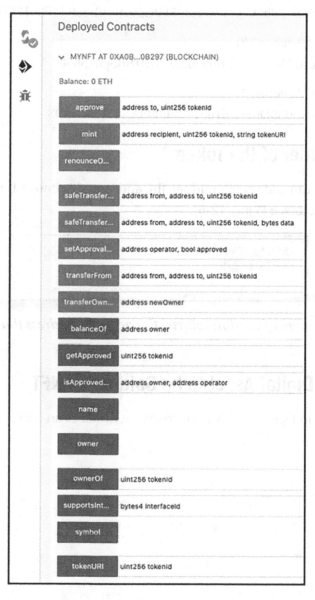

Figure 12-5. *Exploring the various functions in the deployed NFT contract*

Testing the NFT Contract

With the NFT token contract deployed onto the Goerli testnet, you can now test the contract. For the following sections, assume you have the following accounts and their associated addresses:

- Address of **Account 1** (the account that deployed the NFT token contract): 0xAF8b6CA21023A595F0C4919b8B4a9d1F0c1773e7

- Address of **Account 2:** 0x63eE1AEb74c52f09EaB6a2825bB1918B5e045050

- Address of **Account 3:** 0xC663D99b0B5D0F6eE163173E6889AA47F787c403

Getting the Owner of the Token

Click the **owner** button and you should see the address of **Account 1**, the account that deployed the contract (see Figure 12-6).

Figure 12-6. *The owner function returns the account address that deployed the NFT contract*

Preparing the Digital Asset to be Sold as an NFT

Suppose the image in Figure 12-7 is what you want to sell as an NFT.

Figure 12-7. *The image to be sold as an NFT (source: `https://cdn.britannica.com/w:300,h:169,c:crop/24/189624-050-F3C5BAA9/Mona-Lisa-oil-wood-panel-Leonardo-da.jpg`)*

First, you need to upload this digital asset somewhere. One option is to use IPFS. You can use the following page to upload your image using an **IPFS gateway:** `https://ipfs-gateway.cloud` (see Figure 12-8).

Figure 12-8. *You can upload an image to IPFS using an IPFS gateway*

Tip   IPFS is a peer-to-peer network for storing and sharing files. Similar to a blockchain where distributed and decentralized nodes store the ledger (the chain of blocks), nodes in IPFS store files. For more information on IPFS, refer to my article on IPFS at `https://bit.ly/3Gva1Q1`.

Once the file is uploaded to IPFS, you obtain the hash of the image (known as the *Content ID*, or CID) that has been uploaded to IPFS. You can use this hash to fetch the file on IPFS.

You can use an IPFS gateway such as `ipfs.io` (another IPFS gateway) to specify the location of the file using the following format: `https://ipfs.io/ipfs/<hash_of_image>`. For your example, the image can be found using this URL: `https://ipfs.io/ipfs/QmbjYzobwnXvpHbSBjw8aHYuWYitdr33YyoZGeN7q5J4WC`.

IPFS GATEWAY

IPFS gateways are how web users retrieve content on the IPFS network without running their own IPFS node. IPFS gateways allow web users to fetch content that resides on the IPFS network using the file's hash (known as the Content ID, or CID).

The next step is to create the metadata for your NFT. AN NFT metadata file contains details of the NFT. The minimum attributes needed in the metadata are

- name: The name of the NFT

- description: The description of the NFT

- image: The link that points to the digital asset

You can create a JSON file with the following content:

```
{
    "name": "My NFT Artwork",
    "description": "Mona Lisa",
    "image":  "https://ipfs.io/ipfs/QmbjYzobwnXvpHbSBjw8aHYuWYitdr33Yyo
            ZGeN7q5J4WC"
}
```

Save the file and upload the JSON file to IPFS. Then, get the URL that points to the metadata file on IPFS. For this example, the metadata file can be found at https://ipfs.io/ipfs/QmfJahEinm6rYNfsDPynF3vm5x4xQiE9EnKW6TnadKhdky.

Tip   Essentially, the TokenURI in your NFT token contract will point to this NFT metadata file.

Minting the NFT

In the textbox displayed next to the **mint** button, enter the following string:

```
0xAF8b6CA21023A595F0C4919b8B4a9d1F0c1773e7,1,https://ipfs.io/ipfs/
QmfJahEinm6rYNfsDPynF3vm5x4xQiE9EnKW6TnadKhdky
```

Figure 12-9. *Minting an NFT for Account 1*

This string has the following format: `<Owner_of_the NFT>,<TokenID>,<TokenURI>`. In this string, Account 1 is minted with a token with token ID 1, and the link to the NFT metadata is located at `https://ipfs.io/ipfs/QmfJahEinm6rYNfsDPynF3vm5x4xQiE9EnKW6TnadKhdky`. This means Account 1 is now the owner of the NFT.

Note   The TokenID is a number that you can specify to uniquely identify the NFT within the NFT token contract. The TokenURI is usually a URL that points to the location of the NFT metadata. A common storage for the NFT is IPFS. Alternatively, the TokenURI may point to an NFT marketplace such as Opensea.

Click the **mint** button and MetaMask will prompt you to confirm the transaction.

Tip   Note that this mint operation can only be performed by the owner of the NFT token contract, which is the account that deployed it (Account 1 in this case).

Getting the Name and Symbol of the NFT Token Contract

To get the name and the symbol of the NFT token contract, click the **name** and **symbol** buttons (see Figure 12-10).

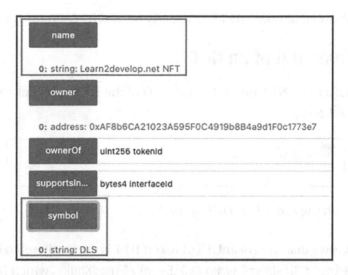

Figure 12-10. *Getting the name and symbol of the NFT contract*

Finding the Balance of NFTs for an Address

To know how many NFTs a particular address has on an NFT token contract, enter the account address and click the **balanceOf** button (see Figure 12-11).

Figure 12-11. *Finding the number of NFTs owned by an account*

In this example, you can see that Account 1 currently has one NFT in the NFT token contract.

Getting the Owner of an NFT

To know who owns a particular NFT (based on the token ID) in the NFT token contract, enter the token ID and click the **ownerOf** button (see Figure 12-12).

Figure 12-12. *Finding out who owns a particular NFT*

This output shows that token ID 1 is currently owned by Account 1.

Getting the TokenURI of an NFT

To get the TokenURI of an NFT, enter the token ID of the NFT and click the **tokenURI** button (see Figure 12-13).

Figure 12-13. *Getting the token URI of an NFT*

This output shows that the TokenURI of token ID 1 is currently set to `https://ipfs.io/ipfs/QmfJahEinm6rYNfsDPynF3vm5x4xQiE9EnKW6TnadKhdky`, which is the path of the NFT metadata file.

Transferring an NFT to Another Account

To transfer an NFT to another account, enter the following string in the textbox next to the **transferFrom** button in the format: `<Account_To_Transfer_From>,<Account_To_Transfer_To>,<TokenID>`.

The following string transfers the NFT from Account 1 to Account 2 (see Figure 12-14):

```
0xAF8b6CA21023A595F0C4919b8B4a9d1F0c1773e7,0x63eE1AEb74c52f09EaB6a2825bB1918B5e045050,1
```

Figure 12-14. *Transferring an NFT from Account 1 to Account 2*

Tip   Note that transferring of NFT tokens can only be performed by the owner of the NFT token, which is Account 1 in this case.

When you click the **transferFrom** button, MetaMask will prompt you to confirm the transaction (see Figure 12-15). Note that the image of the NFT is shown in MetaMask.

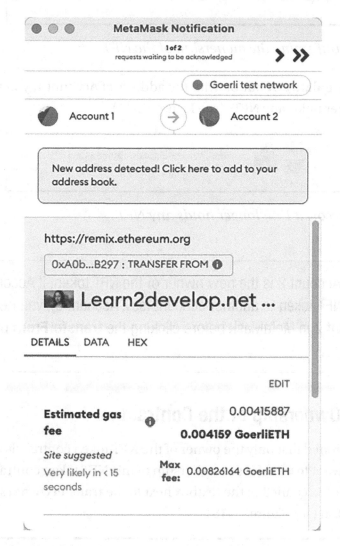

Figure 12-15. MetaMask displays the image of the NFT when you perform a transfer of ownership of the NFT

Once the transaction is confirmed, typing the token ID of 1 and then clicking the **ownerOf** button will confirm that the NFT now belongs to Account 2 (see Figure 12-16).

Figure 12-16. *Confirming the ownership of the NFT*

If you click the **balanceOf** button with the address of Account 1, you will see that Account 1 no longer holds any NFTs (see Figure 12-17).

Figure 12-17. *Account 1 no longer holds any NFT*

Tip   Now that Account 2 is the new owner of the NFT token, if Account 2 wishes to transfer this NFT token to another account (say, Account 3), you need to switch to Account 2 in MetaMask before clicking the **transferFrom** button in the Remix IDE.

Transferring Ownership of the Contract

Recall that I mentioned that only the owner of the NFT token contract is allowed to mint new NFTs. If you want to transfer the ownership of this NFT token contract to Account 3, enter the address of Account 3 in the textbox next to the **transferOwnership** button and then click the button (see Figure 12-18).

Figure 12-18. *Transferring ownership of the NFT contract to Account 3*

Tip   Note that this operation can only be performed by the owner of the NFT token contract, which is the account that deployed it (Account 1 in this case).

You can verify that the NFT token contract belongs to Account 3 by clicking the **owner** button (see Figure 12-19).

Figure 12-19. *Verifying the ownership of the NFT contract*

Summary

In this chapter, you learned what an NFT is and how it works. Using the ERC-721 contract, you learned how to mint an NFT, transfer its ownership, and verify its ownership. I hope this chapter has given you a clearer picture of what an NFT is and how you can create one yourself.

CHAPTER 13

Introduction to Decentralized Finance

The financial system that we are so familiar with today is known as *traditional finance*. It is still largely centralized because it still relies on central authorities, predominantly banks and governments. However, traditional finance has several flaws and I will discuss them in this chapter.

In Chapter 2, you learned about the motivations behind blockchain and how it solves the trust issue that people have with central authorities. Using blockchain, we can build a new financial system known as *decentralized finance* (DeFi).

In this chapter, I will first compare the differences between traditional finance and DeFi, and then introduce you to one key component of DeFi: *stablecoins*. You will also learn how to build a decentralized exchange (DEX) to exchange tokens from one type to another.

Limitations of Traditional Finance

Today, here are some common activities we perform in traditional finance:

- Money transfers
- Loans
- Saving plans
- Insurance
- Stock markets

© Wei-Meng Lee 2023
W.-M. Lee, *Beginning Ethereum Smart Contracts Programming*, https://doi.org/10.1007/978-1-4842-9271-6_13

However, there are some problems/limitations with traditional finance:

- Some people are not able to create bank accounts and access financial services. For example, due to sanctions, certain political figures may not have access to financial services. A good example is Carrie Lam (former leader of Hong Kong). She has no access to banking services after the United States imposed sanctions on her in response to a draconian security law China imposed on the city.

- A hidden charge of financial services is your personal data. Your financial information is not a secret; people in the banks know how many assets you have and constantly monitor you to sell you financial products.

- Governments and centralized institutions can close down markets at will. A good example of this happened in 2022 when the Canadian government warned of freezing the bank accounts of those who were linked to the ongoing anti-vaccine mandate protests in Ottawa.

- Money transfers take a long time and cost too much. It typically takes a few working days to remit money from one country to another and banks typically charge a significant amount of transaction fees.

Decentralized Finance

With blockchains, we can now have an open and global financial system built for the Internet age, known as decentralized finance (DeFi). DeFi is an alternative to the traditional finance system that is opaque, tightly controlled, and built using decades-old technologies and systems.

With DeFi, we can now

- Eliminate (or reduce) fees imposed by banks and other financial companies for using their services

- Have more options to borrow from anyone in the world, not only banks

- Hold our money in a secure digital wallet instead of keeping it in a bank

- Use our funds without needing approval from anyone

- Transfer funds in seconds and minutes

Components in DeFi

To make DeFi possible, you need the following key components:

- **Decentralized infrastructure**: A blockchain implementation such as Ethereum

- **Ethereum with smart contracts**: A good example is the ERC-20 token specification, which allows you to build *fungible* tokens.

- **Stablecoins**: Stablecoins are fungible tokens that are usually pegged to an asset (such as USD, cryptos, gold, etc.). Stablecoins can also be unpegged and the price adjusted algorithmically through smart contracts.

  Stablecoins play a very important role in DeFi as they not only replace fiat currencies; they are an increasingly important asset in the DeFi lending market, where users can lock their stablecoins in platforms such as *Compound* and *Aave* and earn lending interest rates from 0.15% to 12% APY.

Tip   Both **Compound** and **Aave** are decentralized cryptocurrency protocols that allow users to borrow and lend cryptos.

In the next section, you will learn more about stablecoins and the different types that exist today.

Stablecoins

In Chapter 11, you learned about the ERC-20 specification that allows you to create your own tokens. You also learned that tokens can be used as a form of investment and used for paying smart contract services. In this section, you will learn about a specific implementation of tokens in the real world, commonly known as *stablecoins*.

So, what exactly are stablecoins? Stablecoins are cryptocurrencies where the price is pegged to a reference asset, such as fiat currency, other cryptocurrencies, or gold. As the name implies, stablecoins are built to withstand volatility that other cryptocurrencies can't tolerate.

Note   The whole purpose of stablecoins is to minimize volatility by maintaining stability.

MOTIVATION BEHIND STABLECOINS

To really understand the motivation behind stablecoin, you just need to look at Bitcoin. In 2011, one BTC (bitcoin) was worth approximately US$1. However, at its peak in 2021, one BTC was worth more than US$65,000. Imagine paying for two cups of Starbucks coffee with four BTC in 2011. The same four BTC could buy you a Ferrari in 2021!

Apparently, the aim of using Bitcoin as a fiat replacement is not feasible due to its wild fluctuations in prices!

There are three main types of stablecoins:

- **Fiat-backed stablecoins**: Stablecoins that are backed by currencies such as USD, EUR, GBP, or other fiat currencies

- **Crypto-backed stablecoins**: Stablecoins that are backed by other cryptocurrencies such as Ether and Bitcoin

- **Non-collateralized stablecoins**: Also known as algorithmic stablecoins, these types of stablecoins do not hold any kind of collateral. To keep the value stable, they depend on smart contracts, which alter the supply of stablecoins depending on market demand.

- **Commodity-backed stablecoins**: Stablecoins that are backed by commodities such as gold. One coin is equally worth one unit of the pegged commodity (such as one ounce of gold).

The following sections will discuss the first three types of stablecoins in more detail.

Fiat-Backed Stablecoins

A fiat-backed stablecoin is a stablecoin backed by fiat-currency, such as the US Dollar, Euro, or Pound. A good example of a fiat-backed stablecoin is the **USD Coin** (**USDC**).

Note   USD Coin is managed by a consortium called Centre, which was founded by Circle and includes members from the cryptocurrency exchange Coinbase and Bitcoin mining company Bitmain, an investor in Circle.

Figure 13-1 shows how USDC works.

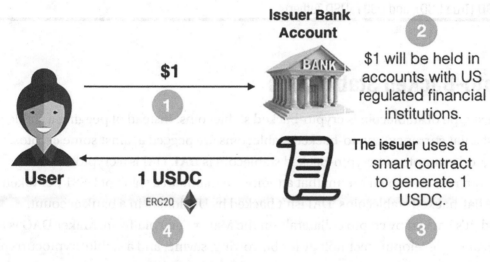

Figure 13-1. *What happens when you buy an USDC*

To buy a USDC,

1. The user sends $1 to the issuer's bank account.

2. The $1 will be held in a US regulated issuer's bank account.

3. The issuer uses a smart contract to generate a USDC ERC-20 token.

4. The USDC token is then transferred to the user's wallet.

So why do you want to buy USDC? Well, using USDC you can send money cheaply and near-instantly anywhere in the world without a traditional bank account (a huge improvement over wire transfers, which can be expensive and take days). You can also earn rewards on USDCs held in a Coinbase account. In addition, you can earn even higher yields by lending your USDC via a variety of decentralized finance (DeFi) applications.

EXAMPLES OF FIAT-BACKED STABLECOINS

Besides USDC, some other examples of fiat-backed stablecoins include **BUSD** (Binance USD), **TUSD** (True USD), and **USDT** (USD Tether).

Crypto-Backed Stablecoins

The next type of stablecoin is crypto-backed stablecoins. Instead of pegging a stablecoin against a fiat currency, crypto-backed stablecoins are pegged against some cryptos.

A good example of a crypto-backed stablecoin is **DAI**. DAI is a crypto-backed stablecoin running on Ethereum that attempts to maintain a value of US$1 per token. Unlike fiat-backed stablecoins, DAI isn't backed by US dollars in a bank account. Instead, it's backed by crypto collaterals on the Maker DAO platform. Maker DAO is an organization developing technology for borrowing, saving, and a stable cryptocurrency on the Ethereum blockchain.

Tip   DAO stands for Decentralized Autonomous Organization.

What Is a DAO Exactly?

The key idea of DAO is that it is an organization designed to be automated and run by code (which is essentially smart contracts in the world of Ethereum). The idea of DAO seems strange, at first glance. But let's look at how organizations function today (Figure 13-2).

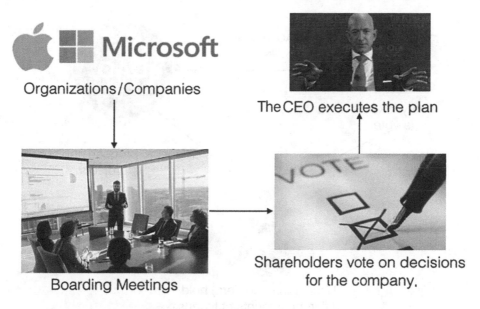

Figure 13-2. *How organizations work today*

A typical organization has board members, and they hold board meetings to discuss and plan strategic directions for the company. Major decisions made by the board must be approved by the shareholders, who vote on decisions for the company. Once the votes have been tallied, the CEO of the company executes the plan.

A DAO, on the other hand, does not have board members. Instead, a DAO is created using a smart contract. Central to the DAO is the DAO's token, which is used to manage membership in the organization and structure within the DAO (Figure 13-3).

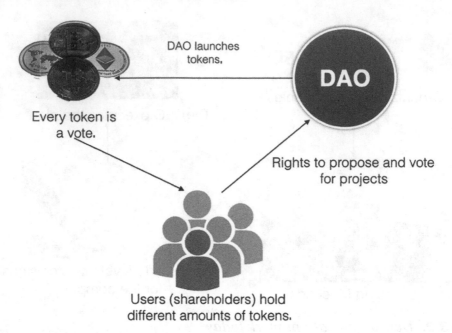

Figure 13-3. *How a DAO works*

Each member in the DAO can hold a different amount of tokens, which gives them voting rights to propose and vote for projects.

Tip   To learn more about DAO, check out my article at `https://bit.ly/3iviryS`.

How DAI Works

Figure 13-4 shows how a user can buy DAI.

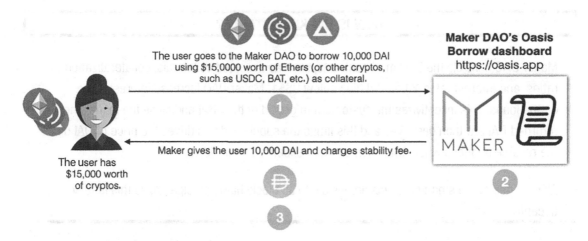

Figure 13-4. *What happens when you buy a DAI*

1. The user goes to the Maker DAO and borrows 10,000 DAI using
    $15,000 worth of cryptos (such as Ether, BAT, etc.). These cryptos
    will be used as the collateral for the 10,000 DAI borrowed.

2. Maker DAO generates 10,000 DAI for the user.

3. Maker DAO sends the 10,000 DAI to the user and charges the user
    a stability fee.

Tip   According to the creator of Maker DAO, Rune Christensen, DAI is based on
the Chinese character 貸, which means "to lend or loan."

In this example, the **collateral ratio** for Ether is 150% (this varies for other cryptos).
This overcollateralization accounts for the volatility of cryptocurrency.

The price of DAI is kept in check through a system of smart contracts automatically
executing themselves. If the price of DAI fluctuates too far from one dollar, Maker DAO
will adjust the interest fees to stabilize the price of DAI.

Tip   You can also buy DAI from all major exchanges like Kraken and Coinbase.
You can use fiat currency to exchange for DAI or sell some of your crypto assets
for DAI.

HOW IS DAI KEPT STABLE?

Maker DAO controls the DAI smart contracts, such as accepted collaterals, collateralization ratios, and interest rates. When DAI dips below US$1, Maker DAO increase interest rates on the loans. This incentivizes the customers to get rid of their DAI and close the loans. The returned DAI are then destroyed and this limits the supply and this drives the price of DAI up; the reverse happens when DAI becomes more expensive than US$1.

All changes to the smart contracts are visible to all blockchain participants, so this is fully decentralized.

DAI can be used as payment for smart contracts as well as for passive income. You can put your DAI into a **DAI Saving Rate** (DSR) program to earn interest.

EXAMPLES OF CRYPTO-BACKED STABLECOINS

Besides DAI, some other examples of crypto-backed stablecoins include **WBTC** (Wrapped Bitcoin) and **MIM** (Magic Internet Money).

DAI Liquidation

Since DAI uses cryptos for collateral, and crypto prices fluctuate wildly, what happens if the price of Ether drops? In this case, Maker DAO will perform a process known as **liquidation**. Figure 13-5 shows the formula for liquidation.

Liquidation Ratio is 1.5

$$\text{Liquidation Price} = \frac{\text{Generated DAI} * \text{Liquidation Ratio}}{\text{Amount of Collateral}}$$

Figure 13-5. *The formula for calculating liquidation price*

Here is the meaning of the various variables in the formula:

- The **liquidation ratio** is the ratio of the equivalent worth of cryptos used against DAI for collateralization. If $1.5 worth of crypto exchanges for 1 DAI, then the liquidation ratio is 1.5.

- The **liquidation price** is the price in which the collateral would be auctioned off and the balance returned to the buyer of DAI.

- **Generated DAI** is the amount of DAI generated for the user.

- **Amount of collateral** is the units of cryptos used for collateral (such as 1 or 2 Ethers, etc.)

Let's work out an example to understand how liquidation works. At the time of writing, the **liquidation ratio** is **1.5**, which means than if 1 Ether is worth $150 today, it can be exchanged for 100 DAI. With this, **liquidation price** would now be (100 DAI * 1.5) / 1 Ether = $150.

Tip   The liquidation price means that if one Ether falls below $150, the vault would be closed and collaterals auctioned. The Maker Protocol generates new DAI through smart contracts known as Maker **Vaults**.

If 1 Ether falls to, say, $140 (<$150), the vault would be liquidated! It is therefore advisable not to withdraw all the generated DAI. Assuming that only 90 DAI is withdrawn, then the **liquidation price** becomes (90 * 1.5) / 1 = $135. Hence even if Ether falls to $140, liquidation will not occur.

To prevent liquidation, you can

- **Add more collateral**: Assuming you add more collateral (e.g., add an addition 0.5 Ether), the liquidation price would now be (100 * 1.5) / 1.5 = $100. This significantly reduces the liquidation price.

- **Repay DAI**: Assuming that you now repay 20 DAI (from a loan of 100 DAIs), the liquidation price would now be (80 * 1.5) / 1 = $120. Again, this significantly reduces the liquidation price.

If a vault is liquidated, a liquidation penalty of 13% is charged to the vault owner (the buyer of the DAI). This fee is added to the vault's total outstanding DAI loaned and this will result in more of the collateral sold on auction. Owners will receive the leftover collateral after the auction.

SIMILARITY TO HOW A PAWN SHOP WORKS

The whole liquidation process is very similar to how a pawn shop works in real life. It goes like this:

- You bring something valuable (such as gold) to the pawnshop and use it as collateral.

- The pawn shop loans you money against the collateral. If the gold is worth $15,000, the pawn shop will give you something like $10,000. This overcollateralization offers protection to the pawn shop in case the price of gold falls.

- When you repay the loan plus the interest, you get back your collateral.

- If you don't pay back the loan, the pawn shop keeps the collateral.

Non-Collateralized Stablecoins

Non-collateralized stablecoins, also known as *algorithmic stable coins*, do not make use of any reserve asset. Instead, they make use of smart contracts to regulate their prices. For example, if a coin is trading at too high a value from its intended price, the supply is increased through minting and then sold on the open market. This supply is increased until the price returns to $1. Likewise, if the coin is traded too low, the smart contracts will buy up more coins in the market to reduce the supply.

EXAMPLES OF NON-COLLATERALIZED STABLECOINS

Some examples of algorithmic stablecoins include **Ampleforth**, **Carbon**, and **Basis**.

Crypto Exchanges

With all the discussions about cryptos (coins) and tokens, an important question remains: how do you buy them? The answer is, through *exchanges*. A crypto exchange is a platform on which you can buy and sell cryptocurrencies. There are two types of crypto exchanges:

- **Centralized exchanges** (CEX): A CEX typically allows you to buy cryptocurrencies using fiat currency. Examples of CEX are Coinbase (www.coinbase.com), Binance (www.binance.com), and Kraken (www.kraken.com). Most CEXs also allow you to swap tokens from one token to another.

- **Decentralized exchanges** (DEX): A DEX is a peer-to-peer marketplace where transactions occur directly between crypto traders. DEXs allow you to swap tokens without going through an intermediary (like a CEX). DEX is implemented using smart contracts.

For most crypto beginners, a CEX provides a user-friendly platform for getting into the crypto world. Without knowing too much on how cryptos works, a user can buy cryptos using their credit card for a fixed price (typically). However, CEX has several risks involved that you should know. First, there is always the risk of credit default (think of FTX, CoinBene, and Celsius).

Tip Visit www.cryptowisser.com/exchange-graveyard/ to see a list of exchanges that have failed.

Second, CEXs need to comply to KYC (Know Your Customer) and AML (Anti Money Laundering) regulations, which defeats the idea of using cryptos in the first place (anonymity). CEXs, as its name implies, are centralized as they are usually regulated by the governments of countries that they operate it. Finally, CEXs are susceptible to cyber-attacks and security breaches. As shown in Figure 13-6, when you buy cryptos from CEXs, your cryptos are stored in wallets maintained by the CEXs. Unless you transfer the cryptos to your own wallet (such as MetaMask or a hardware wallet), a security breach at the CEX puts your cryptos at risk as hackers may illegally transfer your cryptos to other wallets.

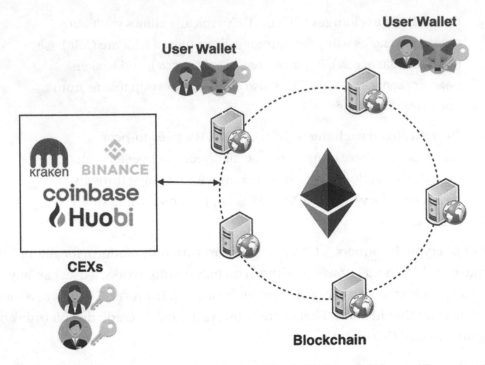

Figure 13-6. *A CEX stores your cryptos, which are subsceptible to cyber attacks*

A DEX, on the other hand, does not have the limitations of a CEX. Using smart contracts, DEXs allow you to exchange tokens easily and quickly from one type to another. This allows users full flexibility and control over their own funds.

Tip   Some popular DEXs are **Uniswap**, **Sushiswap**, and **Pancakeswap**.

Creating a Decentralized Exchange

Since DEXs are implemented using smart contracts, it makes perfect sense for you to understand how they work by applying all that you have learned in the previous 12 chapters in this book. For this section, you will create a DEX contract to allow users to swap two different ERC-20 tokens.

Creating the Token Contract

Let's create a new token contract in the Remix IDE and name it as token.sol. Populate it with the following statements:

```solidity
// SPDX-License-Identifier: MIT
pragma solidity ^0.8;
import "https://github.com/OpenZeppelin/openzeppelin-contracts/blob/v4.0.0/
contracts/token/ERC20/ERC20.sol";
contract MyToken is ERC20 {

    // price expressed as how much an ether can buy
    uint256 public unitsOneEthCanBuy  = 10;

    // the owner of the token
    address public tokenOwner;

    constructor(string memory name, string memory symbol)
        ERC20(name, symbol) {

        // address of the token owner
        tokenOwner = msg.sender;

        // ERC20 tokens have 18 decimals
        // number of tokens minted = n * 10^18
        uint256 n = 1000;
        _mint(msg.sender, n * 10**uint(decimals()));
    }
}
```

This contract is the same basic ERC-20 token contract you saw in Chapter 11.

Deploying the Token Contract

For this example, you will need two accounts with some test Ethers, Account 1 and Account 2. You will use these two accounts to create two tokens, **WML** and **LWM** tokens.

Using Account 1, deploy the **MyToken** contract using the following arguments for the constructor (see also Figure 13-7):

```
"WML token","WML"
```

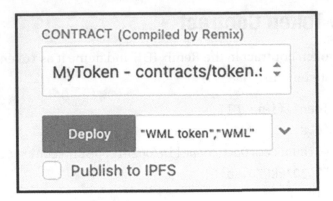

Figure 13-7. *Deploying the first token, WML*

This creates the **WML** token. Next, use Account 2 and deploy the same token contract, this time with the following constructor argument:

`"LWM token","LWM"`

This creates the **LWM** token. At this moment, the Remix IDE should have the token contracts deployed as shown in Figure 13-8.

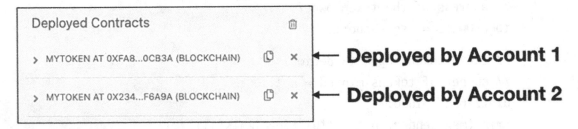

Figure 13-8. *The two tokens created and their addresses*

Record the addresses of the tokens:

- WML token: **0xfa8b8F0fd75ABf2aF088bf2D1115E6F97ED0cB3a**

- LWM token: **0x234273bD4D1aa3D233135dD49A26675dA7eF6A9a**

Tip Replace the above contract addresses with that of your own

---

Add both tokens to Account 1 and Account 2 in MetaMask. At this moment, both Account 1 and Account 2 should have the token balances shown in Figure 13-9.

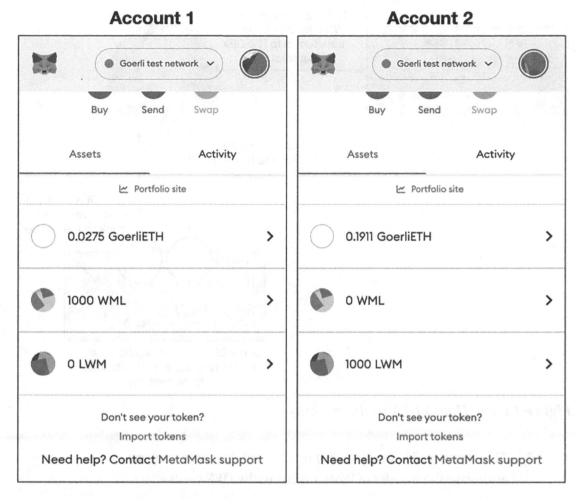

Figure 13-9. *The balance of tokens in both accounts*

Creating the DEX Contract

With the two tokens created, let's create the DEX contract. Before you create the contract, you need to first understand how a user can use a DEX contract to swap tokens.

Figure 13-10 summarizes the flow of events when a user swaps **WML** tokens for **LWM** tokens.

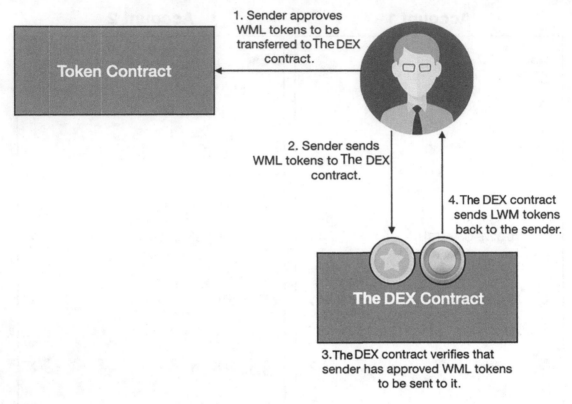

Figure 13-10. *How a DEX contract works*

1. The sender calls the approve() function of the token contract to authorize the transfer of WML tokens to the DEX contract.

2. The sender sends the WML token to the DEX contract.

3. The DEX contract needs to verify that the sender has authorized the transfer of WML tokens to it. If this is true, the WML tokens are transferred from the sender to the DEX contract.

4. The DEX contract calculates the amount of LWM tokens to be transferred and sends it to the sender.

Tip   All transfers of tokens involve the token contract updating the amount of tokens held by users and the DEX contract.

In the Remix IDE, create a new contract named DEX.sol and populate it with the following statements:

```solidity
// SPDX-License-Identifier: MIT
pragma solidity ^0.8;
import "https://github.com/OpenZeppelin/openzeppelin-contracts/blob/v4.0.0/
contracts/token/ERC20/ERC20.sol";

contract DEX {
    ERC20 WML_token;
    ERC20 LWM_token;

    //======================
    // constructor of the DEX
    //======================
    constructor() payable{
        //---be sure to replace the following addresses with your own---
        WML_token = ERC20(address(
            0xfa8b8F0fd75ABf2aF088bf2D1115E6F97ED0cB3a));
        LWM_token = ERC20(address(
            0x234273bD4D1aa3D233135dD49A26675dA7eF6A9a));
    }

    //===================================
    // find the tokens balance in the DEX
    //===================================
    function getBalance() public view returns (uint256,uint256) {
        return (WML_token.balanceOf(address(this)),
                LWM_token.balanceOf(address(this)));
    }

    function compareStrings(string memory a, string memory b)
    private pure returns (bool) {
        return (keccak256(abi.encodePacked((a))) ==
                keccak256(abi.encodePacked((b))));
    }

    //=================
```

```
// exchange tokens
//==================
function exchange(string calldata from_token,
                  string calldata to_token,
                  uint256 amount) public {
    // Remember that all transactions are based on the smallest units
    in the token

    //=========
    // CHECK #1
    //=========
    // ensure the amount to convert is > 0
    require(amount > 0, "You need to convert at least some tokens");

    // record the token contracts to convert from and to
    ERC20 from;  // the tokens to convert from
    ERC20 to;    // the tokens to convert to

    if (compareStrings(from_token, "WML")) {
        from = WML_token;
    } else {
        from = LWM_token;
    }

    if (compareStrings(to_token, "WML")) {
        to = WML_token;
    } else {
        to = LWM_token;
    }

    // obtain the allowance set by the sender to send to this DEX
    uint256 approvedAmt;
    approvedAmt = from.allowance(msg.sender, address(this));

    //=========
    // CHECK #2
    //=========
    // ensure the sender has enough tokens approved to convert
```

```
    require(approvedAmt >= amount,
        "Token allowance is less than what you want to convert");

    //=========
    // CHECK #3
    //=========
    // get the balance of tokens (that the sender wants to convert to)
    in the pool
    uint256 dexBalance = to.balanceOf(address(this));

    // need to check that DEX has enough "to" token to send to sender
    require(amount <= dexBalance,
        "Sorry, not enough tokens in the DEX");

    // transfer the tokens from sender to DEX
    from.transferFrom(msg.sender, address(this), amount);

    // transfer the exchanged tokens to the sender
    to.transfer(msg.sender, amount);
    }
}
```

Here are the details of the DEX contract:

- You need to import the base definition of the ERC-20 token contract written by OpenZeppelin.

- In the constructor, you create instances of the two tokens you are swapping (both instances of ERC20 tokens). If you are trying this out, remember to replace the contract addresses for the WML and LWM tokens with your own.

- You have a function named getBalance(). It returns the balances of the WML and LWM tokens held by the DEX contract.

- In Solidity, you cannot compare strings using the == operator. To compare strings, you need to compare their hashes instead. The compareStrings() helper function compares two strings to check if they are identical.

- The exchange() function allows two tokens to be swapped. For simplicity, assume that one unit of a WML token is equivalent to one unit of a LWM token.

- There are a number of checks you need to perform before you can exchange the tokens. First, ensure that the amount to swap is more than 0. Second, ensure that the account performing the swap has approved the tokens (that they are converting from) to be sent to the DEX. The final check is to ensure that the DEX has sufficient tokens for swapping.

- Once all the checks have passed, the DEX can transfer the tokens from the caller to the DEX, followed by transferring the token (that the caller wants to swap into) to the caller.

You can now deploy the DEX contract (using Account 1 or Account 2 does not matter).

Note   For my example, the address of my deployed DEX contract is 0xF4d9A3b468FBc0b256Da59B5B40CB20e5eD137c6.

At this point, the Remix IDE should have two token contracts and one DEX contract deployed, as shown in Figure 13-11.

Figure 13-11.   *The three contracts in the Remix IDE*

Expand the DEX contract and click the **getBalance** button (see Figure 13-12). You should see two 0s returned. This is because at this moment the DEX contract has 0 WML and 0 LWM tokens.

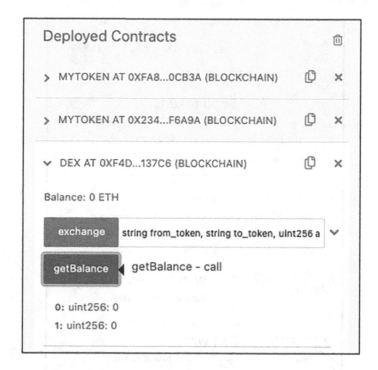

Figure 13-12. *Examining the token balances in the DEX contract*

Funding the DEX

For a DEX to function properly, it needs some tokens so that users can use them to swap tokens. So, let's fund the DEX contract with some WML and LWM tokens.

In MetaMask, use Account 1 and send the DEX contract 500 **WML** tokens (see Figure 13-13).

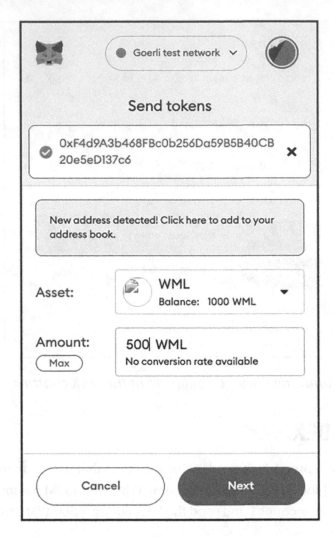

Figure 13-13. *Funding the DEX contract with 500 WML tokens*

Next, use Account 2 and send the DEX contract 500 **LWM** tokens (see Figure 13-14).

Figure 13-14. *Funding the DEX contract with 500 LWM tokens*

Once the transactions are confirmed, the DEX contract has 500 WML tokens and 500 LWM tokens. Table 13-1 shows the current token balances for Account 1, Account 2, and the DEX contract.

Table 13-1. *The Balances for the Two Accounts and the DEX Contract*

Balance	Account 1	Account 2	DEX
WML Token	500	0	500
LWM Token	0	500	500

Swapping WML Tokens for LWM Tokens

You are now ready to use the DEX contract to swap tokens. Suppose Account 1 wants to exchange 100 WML tokens for 100 LWM tokens.

Tip   Switch to Account 1 in MetaMask now.

The first step that Account 1 needs to do is to go to the first deployed token contract (WML token) and fill in the following (see Figure 13-15) and click the **approve** button:

0xF4d9A3b468FBc0b256Da59B5B40CB20e5eD137c6,100000000000000000000

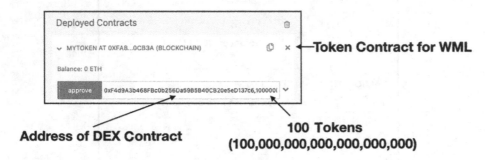

Figure 13-15. *Approving the transfer of tokens to the DEX contract*

This statement grants the DEX contract permission to transfer up to 100 WML tokens from Account 1 to the DEX contract.

MetaMask will display a popup asking you to confirm (see Figure 13-16). Click **Confirm**.

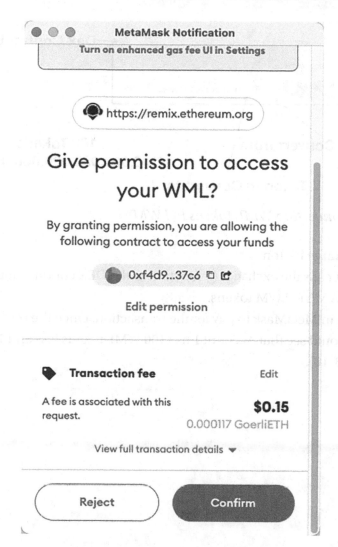

Figure 13-16. *Confirming permission to let the DEX contract access the WML tokens*

Once the transaction is confirmed, Account 1 is ready to send 100 WML tokens to the DEX contract. Fill in the following statement next to the **exchange** button for the DEX contract (see Figure 13-17): "WML", "LWM", 100000000000000000000.

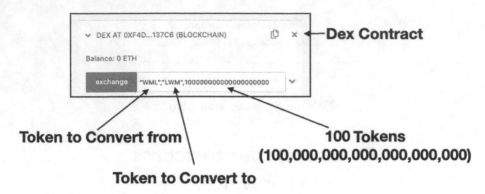

Figure 13-17. *Converting WML tokens to LWM*

Click the **exchange** button.

This statement calls the exchange( ) function in the DEX contract and indicates you want to swap 100 WML to LWM tokens.

Click **Confirm** in MetaMask to pay for the transaction. Once the transaction is confirmed, you should see that Account 1 has 100 WML tokens less and 100 LWM tokens now (see Figure 13-18).

Figure 13-18. *Account 1 now has 100 LWM tokens*

If you go to the DEX contract and click the **getBalance** button, you will that it has 600 WML tokens and 400 LWM tokens.

Figure 13-19. *The DEX contract now has 100 more WML tokens and 100 fewer LWM tokens*

Table 13-2 shows the updated current token balances for Account 1, Account 2, and the DEX contract.

Table 13-2. *The Balances for the Two Accounts and the DEX Contract*

Balance	Account 1	Account 2	DEX
WML Token	400	0	600
LWM Token	100	500	400

Likewise, if Account 2 wants to exchange 100 LWM tokens for 100 WML, they need to do the following:

- Go to the token contract for LWM and approve 100 tokens (100,000,000,000,000,000,000) to be transferred to the DEX contract

- Go to the DEX contract and convert 100 tokens of LWM to WML: `"LWM","WML",100000000000000000000`.

Summary

In this chapter, you explored a few important topics:

- You learned what DeFi is and the use of it

- You learned what stablecoins are, the different types, and how they work to maintain price stability

- You learned how to buy cryptos through the different types of crypto exchanges.

- More importantly, you learn how to implement a DEX using a smart contract.

Index

A

add_node() member, 69
add_transaction() method, 59
admin.addPeer() function, 99, 100
admin.peers property, 100, 102
Algorithmic stable coins, 340
announceWinners() function, 249, 250
Anti Money Laundering (AML), 341
append_block() method, 58
Application binary interface (ABI), 148, 158–162, 175–177, 194, 230, 260–262
Application-specific integrated circuits (ASICs), 41
--authrpc.port option, 97
Auto compile option, 152
Avalanche effect, 4

B

base64-encoded JSON string, 173, 177, 179, 185, 188
base64-encoded string, 173, 177, 179, 185, 188
base64 encoding, 17, 168, 172, 178, 231
Baseball card, 312
bet() function, 246, 247
Binance USD (BUSD), 334
BIP 39 (Bitcoin Improvement Proposals) seed phrase, 117
Bitcoin, 23, 40, 41, 332

Bitcoin's implementation, 37
32-bit instructions, 41
Blockchain, 1
  block, 43
  block header, 43
  blocks confirmations, 35
  centralized databases and institutions, 30
  chaining, 31–34
  components, 52
  consensus protocols, 35–37
  decentralized database, 30
  distributed ledger, 29
  genesis block, 31
  immutability, 34, 35
  merkle root, 47, 48
  merkle tree, 47
  PoS, 41–43
  PoW, 37–41
  testing, 62–66
  transactions and timestamp, 30
  types of nodes, 44–46
Blockchain class, 59, 60, 68–71
Blockchain network, 20, 44, 45, 67, 68, 76, 87
blockchain.py, 56, 60, 62, 72
Brew, 88, 89
Broadcasting, 37, 40
buildTransaction() function, 233
Bytecode, 148, 158–162, 175
bytes() function, 6

© Wei-Meng Lee 2023
W.-M. Lee, *Beginning Ethereum Smart Contracts Programming*, https://doi.org/10.1007/978-1-4842-9271-6

C

Caesar Cipher, 2
Calculator, 150, 151, 156
calculator.sol, 149
calldata keyword, 171, 172
call() function, 213, 214, 239
cashOut() function, 192
Centralized exchanges (CEX), 341
checkEduCredentials button, 179,
        185, 186
checkEduCredentials() function, 171, 173,
        182, 188, 190, 213, 214, 292
Chrome Web Store, 113
Ciphertext, 2, 7, 9, 11, 12, 14
compareStrings() function, 349
Conceptual blockchain
        implementation, Python
    adding transactions, 59, 61, 62
    appending block, 58, 59
    exposing Blockchain class,
        REST API, 60
    class declaration, 56, 57
    code, 78
    finding nonce, 57, 58
    importing modules and libraries, 56
    installing flask, 55
    obtaining full blockchain, 60
    obtaining nonce, 53, 54
    performing mining, 60, 61
Consensus protocols, 35–37, 41
contract keyword, 151
Crypto beginners, 341
Cryptocurrencies, 23, 24, 26, 34, 41, 45, 62,
        117, 279–281, 331–334, 337,
        340, 341
Crypto exchanges
    CEXs, 341, 342

DEXs
    address, 350
    approve() function, 346
    creation, 342
    details, 349, 350
    DEX.sol, 347–349
    events, 345, 346
    exchange tokens, 342
    LWM tokens, 352, 353
    Remix IDE, 350
    token balances, 350, 351, 353
    WML tokens, 351, 352
swapping
    approve button, 354
    conversion, 355, 356
    exchange() function, 356
    LWM tokens, 356–358
    permission, 354, 355
    token balances, 358
    WML tokens, 356–358
token contracts
    creation, 343
    deployment, 343–345
    types, 340, 341
Cryptographic algorithms, 1, 2, 19, 21
Cryptographic hash, 34, 47
Cryptography module, 8, 12
Cryptography
    asymmetric (see Asymmetric
        cryptography)
    Caesar Cipher, 2
    ciphertext, 2
    definition, 1
    hashing, 3–6
    symmetric cryptography, 7–9
    types, 2
Cryptography in blockchain
    cryptographic algorithms, 19

digital signature, 20, 21
    hashing, 19
    symmetric and asymmetric
        cryptography, 19, 20
Currencies, 25

D

DAI Saving Rate (DSR), 338
Data encryption, 11, 12
Decentralization, 26–29
Decentralized Autonomous
        Organization (DAO), 334–336
Decentralized exchange (DEX), 112, 329,
    341, 342
Decentralized finance (DeFi),
    329–331, 334
decrypt() function, 9
Developers, 279, 281, 285
difficulty_target, 57, 65
Digital signature, 10, 15–21
Distributed ledger, 23, 29–30

E

Educational credentials, 167, 173,
    180–182, 231
eduCredentialsStore contract, 295
eduCredentialsStore.functions.
    storeEduCredentials()
    function, 233
eduCredentialsStore.sol, 169
eduCredentialsStore variable, 231
Elliptic Curve Digital Signature Algorithm
    (ECDSA), 20
encrypt() function, 9, 17
Energy-efficient consensus protocol, 37
Enode key, 100

Enode value, 100
.env file, 223, 224
eth.blockNumber property, 103
eth.coinbase property, 109
eth.contract() function, 230
Ethereum, 19, 23, 34, 37, 41
Ethereum blockchain, 23, 87, 88, 90, 95,
    112, 125, 148, 188, 195, 215, 216,
    279, 281, 285
Ethereum client
    definition, 87
    installing Geth, Linux, 89
    installing Geth, macOS, 88, 89
    installing Geth, Windows, 89
    types, 88
Ethereum crypto-wallet
    MetaMask (*see* MetaMask)
Ethereum networks, 111–113, 121, 122,
    126, 141
Ethereum protocol, 91
Ethereum Request for
    Comments (ERC), 285
Ethereum test networks, 90–91, 111, 148
Ethereum transactions, 111
Ethereum virtual machines (EVMs), 147
Ethers, 20, 23, 42, 106, 107, 110, 129, 131,
    134, 182, 188, 279, 280, 292, 295,
    301, 303, 304
    denominations, 183, 184
Etherscan, 112, 124, 125, 187, 188, 192,
    298, 299, 308–310
eth.gas_price attribute, 226
eth.getBalance() function, 96
eth.getBlock() function, 104, 105
eth.getBlock(eth.blockNumber).
    miner, 105
eth.get_transaction_count() function, 225
eth.send_raw_transaction() function, 226

eth.sendTransaction() function, 106
EVM compatibility, 147
exchange() function, 350, 356

F

Fernet class, 8, 9
Finney, 184
Flask microframework, 55
Full nodes, 34, 45–47, 215, 221
Fungible, 311, 312, 331

G

Gas, 134
Gas fee, 133, 134, 172
generate_key() function, 8
Genesis block, 31, 57, 63, 91, 93, 103
getCurrentAccount() functions, 202
Geth directory, 94
Geth client, 88, 90
Geth JavaScript Console, 95, 102
Geth source, 88
Goerli testnet, 145, 162–166, 168, 176, 221,
    230, 262, 318
Goerli Test Network, 113, 121, 122,
    221, 225
GPU excels, 41

H

hash_block() method, 57
Hash function
    blockchain, 5
    data mapping, 32
    definition, 3
    features, 4, 32
    fixed-length output, 3

hashlib module, 6
    immutable, 33
    multiple computers, 33
    next block, 32
    roles, 5
    sha256() function, 6
    transactions, 33
Hashing, 3, 4, 19, 23, 31, 33, 38, 41, 168
Hash of the previous block, 5, 19, 33, 43,
    52, 53, 57, 61
Hash of transaction A (H$_A$), 47
Hash of transaction B (H$_B$), 47
HTTP, 195
Hyperinflation, 25

I

Identical blockchain, 67
Index, 52, 53, 59
index.html, 203
Infura, 112, 113, 215–223, 226
INFURA nodes, 112, 113
__init__() function, 57
IPC, 195
IPFS, 319–321

J

JSON string, 158, 167, 168, 172, 177, 178
Jupyter Notebook, 220, 223

K

Keccak256 hashing algorithm, 20, 108
Keccak256 hash, 108
keystore directory, 94
kill() function, 193
Know Your Customer (KYC), 341

L

last_block, 59
License, 151
Light node, 46–48
Liquidation process, 340
loadContract() function, 210, 211
load() function, 202, 211
loadWeb3() functions, 200, 202

M

main.css, 202
Main Ethereum Network, 113, 121, 141
Managing accounts
    coinbase setting, 109, 110
    private key, 108
    public key, 108
    removing account, 109
    UTC file, 107
mapping object, 171, 173, 243, 244, 281
memory keyword, 171
Merkle root, 43, 44, 46–49
Merkle tree, 47–49
MetaMask, 162, 215–217, 223, 262, 268
    creating additional accounts, 126–128
    creating new wallet, 115
    entering password, 116
    Ethereum crypto-wallet, 111
    exporting accounts, 138, 140, 141
    extension icon on Chrome, 119
    importing accounts, 142, 143
    INFURA nodes, 112, 113
    install, MetaMask extension, 113, 114
    pinning to Chrome, 119
    recovering accounts, 135–138
    role, 111
    Secret Recovery Phrase, 116–118

    switching between accounts, 129
    transferring Ethers, 129, 131
    viewing wallet, 120
MetaMask Chrome extension, 111, 144, 145
MetaMask extension, 113, 114, 119–120, 201
Miner hashes, 39
miner.setEtherbase() function, 110
Miners join, 39
miner.start() function, 103, 105
miner.stop() function, 104
Miners/validators, 21
Mining nodes, 37, 38, 46
Mining process, 38–41
MIT License, 151
MyTestNet, 91
MyTestNet directory, 92, 94
MyTestNet folder, 92
~/MyTestNet/data/node1/keystore directory, 96, 107, 109

N

Network broadcasting, 37
Network difficulty level, 53
Network difficulty target, 38, 39, 43
--networkid option, 97, 98
Network latency, 37
node2 directory, 94
Node.js project, 196
Nodes, 45
Node's blockchain, 78
--nodiscover option, 97
nodes member, 68, 69
Nonce, 39, 41, 43, 52–54, 57–59, 225, 233
Non-fungible tokens (NFTs), 313
    buyers, 313

Non-fungible tokens (NFTs) (*cont.*)
    buying/selling, 313, 314
    deployment, 316, 317
    ERC-721, 315, 316
    OpenSea, 315
    ownership *vs.* copyright, 313
    testing
        account, 318
        balance, address, 323
        digital asset, 318–321
        minting, 321
        name/symbol, 322
        owner, 318, 323
        ownership, 326, 327
        TokenURI, 324
        transaction, 324–326
    token contracts, 314
Number used once, 39

O

Online lottery game, 241
    betting, 246–248
        players, 248
    calculation, 242
    cash-out function, 253
    complete contract, 272–276
    payout, 242
    players, 242
    smart contract
        Betting, 244
        declaration, 245
        key points, 246
        mapping object, 244
        playerAddressesArray, 244
        playerDetailsMapping, 243
        Solidity, 244
        structure, 243

status/winning number, 253
web front end (*see* Web front end)
winning number/winners
    announceWinners() function,
        249, 250
    create array, 251
    owner, 251
    playerAddressesArray, 251
    transfer() function, 252
    variables, resetting, 252
OpenZeppelin, 244, 287, 289, 315, 349

P, Q

package.json, 196
Parity, 88
Pawn shop, 340
Peer-to-peer fashion, 34
personal.newAccount() function, 95, 105,
    106, 109
personal.unlockAccount()
    function, 106
--port option, 97
Pragma solidity statement, 151
private keyword, 171
Private Ethereum test network creation
    blockchain node initiation, 93, 94
    folder creation, storing node data, 92
    genesis block, 91
    nodes, 90, 91
    node start up (*see* Starting up nodes)
    peers and transactions, 90
Private functions, 171
Private key, 10–17, 19, 20, 108, 109, 111,
    112, 117, 138, 141–144, 223, 224,
    226, 227, 234
Programming languages, 1, 88, 244
proofFor(), 171

Proof of Stake (PoS)
Ethereum, 41
vs. PoW, 42, 43
transaction fees, 42
transactions, 42
validators, 42
proof_of_work() function, 40, 41, 57, 58
Proofs, 171
Public blockchains, 19, 23, 168
Public key, 10–16, 18, 20, 108, 117
pure keyword, 151, 171
Python-based dapp, 217, 239
python-dotenv module, 223
Python program, 1, 223

R

Remix IDE, 148–150, 152, 154–156,
161–164, 166, 169, 174, 176–178,
181, 182, 186, 191, 192, 195, 243,
254, 262, 269, 287, 315, 343, 347, 350
Remix VM, 154, 155, 162, 254
require() function, 181, 183
Resultant hash, 3, 6, 32, 39, 47, 53
Root key, 117
Ropsten test network, 113

S

Secret Recovery Phrase, 116–118
selfdestruct() function, 193, 194
send() function, 212, 213
Sepolia Test Network, 113, 121, 126
sha256() function, 6
SHA256 hash function, 3, 4, 6
Shared key, 7–10
sign_transaction() function, 234
Simplified payment verifications
(SPV), 46, 47

Smart contracts, 23
ABI, 158
Bytecode, 158, 160
compiling contract, 174–176
creating, 169–174
definition, 145
deploy, 176, 177
educational credentials, 180
Ethers, 188
functions, 146, 147
funds, 146
Ganache Provider, 154
Injected Provider-Metamask, 154, 162
interacts with the user, 172
Remix IDE, 148
compiling contract, 152
creating new contract, 149, 150
Remix VM, 154, 155, 162
selfdestruct() function, 193
state variables, 146, 173
as a store of proofs, 167, 168
testing the first function, 157
testing the second function, 157
use of blockchain, 145
using Goerli testnet, 162–165
Visual Studio Code, 148
Stablecoins
Bitcoin, 332
crypto-backed
DAI, 334
DAO, 334–336
DAI
buying, 336, 337
collateral ratio, 337
DAO, 337, 338
liquidation, 338, 339
price, 337
smart contracts, 338

Stablecoins (*cont.*)

    uses, 338

  definition, 332

  fiat-backed, 333, 334

  non-collateralized, 340

  types, 332

start() function, 103

Starting up nodes

  account balance check, 96

  account creation, 95, 96

  block examination, 104, 105

  getting information, 98, 100

  mining, 105

  pairing, 100–102

  performing mining, 103, 104

  starting another node, 97, 98

  stopping the node, 97

  transferring ethers, 106, 107

State variables, 151, 171, 173, 182

storeEduCredentials() function, 171, 173,
       177, 178, 181, 185, 194, 212, 233

storeEduCredentials button,
       177, 178, 185

storeProof(), 171

Symmetric cryptography, 7

  approaches, 11

  decryption using private key, 14

  definition, 7

  encryption using public key, 14

  public key algorithm, 10

  public/private key pair
      generation, 12, 13

  shared key, 7, 10

  shared key generation, 8

  symmetric decryption, 9

  symmetric encryption, 9

  uses and applications, 7

  verifying digital signature, 18

Synchronizing blockchain

  blockchain.py application, 67

  multiple nodes, 72–78

  /nodes/add_nodes, 71

  nodes member, 68, 69

  update_blockchain() method, 70, 71

  valid_chain(), 69, 70

Szabo, 184

T

Testing, contract

  ABI, 260–262

  accounts, 254

  betting number, 255–257

  betting status, 257

  deployment, 262

  functions, 255

  getGameStatus, 256, 257

  Remix IDE, 254

  winner announcement

    balance, 259, 260

    calculations, 259

    events, 258, 259

    winning number, 258

TestWeb3.html, 197

Timestamp, 43, 52, 54, 55, 59

Token contracts

  creation, 287

  decimals() function, 288

  deployment, 289, 290

    arguments, 304

    buyers account, 307, 308

    Ethers, 306, 307

    Hide WML, 305, 306

    MetaMask, 305

    transaction,

      Etherscan, 309, 310

Ethers, 301, 302
MetaMask, 291
modification, 302
NFTs (*see* Non-fungible
   tokens (NFTs))
selling
   buyer, 303
   require() function, 304
   token owner, 304
   token price, 302, 303
   tokens, 303
   _transfer() function, 304
   transfer() event, 304
   unitsOneEthCanBuy, 302
selling token, 291
smart contract payments
   approve() function, 296
   balance reduction, 300
   checkEduCredentials() function,
     296, 298
   eduCredentialsStore, 295
   EduCredentialsStore.sol, 292–294
   Etherscan, 298, 299
   getBalance, 299
   MetaMask, 300
   permissions, 296, 297
   redeployment, 295
  token.sol, 287, 295, 343
  token units, 288
  utility, 291
Tokens, 279
  burning, 282, 283
  carnival games, 279, 280
  carnival owner, 280
  vs. coins, 281
  ERC-20, 285
   definition, 285
   functions/events, 286

interface, 285
  Ethereum blockchain, 280
  Ethers, 301
  implementation, 281
  minting, new tokens, 282
  platform, 281
  units, 283, 285
Traditional finance, 329
  activities, 329
  problems/limitations, 330
Transaction fee, 38, 41, 42, 133, 134, 185,
   306, 330
Transactions, 35, 37, 53, 66
True USD (TUSD), 334
Trust
  decentralization, 26–29
  goods/services, 24
  institutions, 24, 25
  issues, 25, 26
  placement, 24
12-word pass phrase, 136
12-word secret phrase, 117, 136, 143

U

Unconfirmed transactions, 38
update_blockchain() method, 70, 71
USD Coin (USDC), 333, 334
USD Tether (USDT), 334

V

Validators, 42, 43, 45
valid_chain() method, 69, 70
valid_proof() method, 58
verify() function, 18
view keyword, 171, 182
Visual Studio Code, 148

W, X, Y, Z

web3-bzz, 195

Web3 decentralized applications (dapps),
215, 216

  dapp creation using Python, 227

    base64 encoding, 231

    educational credential, 231–234

    loading contract, 230

    verifying result, 234–238

  Ethereum interaction using Python

    checking, balance of Account 1, 225

    connecting to Infura, 220, 221

    fetching a block, 221

    registering with Infura, 218–220

    setting up, Ethereum
accounts, 223–225

    transferring Ethers between
accounts, 225–227

web3-eth, 195

web3.fromWei() function, 96

web3.js, 112

  definition, 195

installing web3.js, 196

interacting with smart
contract, 202–214

modules, 195

using MetaMask, 200–205

web3projects folder, 196

web3projects folder, 196–198, 203,
207, 263

web3.py library, 216, 220, 221, 225, 227

web3-shh, 195

web3-utils, 195

Web front end

  accounts, 268, 269

  cashing out, 271, 272

  Chrome, instances, 267, 268

  messages, 268, 269

  OnlineBetting.html file, 263–265, 267

  testing, 267

  winning number, 269, 271

WebSocket, 195

Wei, 184, 188

window.ethereum, 200, 201

Printed in the United States
by Baker & Taylor Publisher Services